STRANGE ENCOUNTERS

THE UnXPLAINED

STRANGE ENCOUNTERS

UFO Phenomenon •

Mysterious Creatures •

Mysterious Lands and People •

Alien Encounters •

Time and Space •

Hauntings •

Phantom Encounters •

p

For Bridget and Laison Richards

First published in 2000 by Parragon

Parragon
Queen Street House
4 Queen Street
Bath BA1 1HE, UK

Produced by Magpie Books, an imprint of
Constable Robinson Ltd, London

ISBN 0-75253-597-8

Illustrations courtesy of Fortean Picture Library

Page design by Sandie Boccacci

A copy of the British Library Cataloguing-in-Publication Data
is available from the British Library

Printed and bound in the EC

Contents

PART THREE: Mysterious Lands and People

PART FOUR: Time and Space

PART FIVE: Hauntings

PART SIX: Phantom Encounters

Introduction

• •

In 1875 the Director of the American Patent Office sent his resignation to the Secretary of the Board of Trade. His reason for resigning was simple; he said he was quitting because there was "nothing left to invent".

Before we laugh at this parable of technological short-sightedness, we should first remove the log from our own eye.

It is amusing how so-called modern man is so smug and complacent about "his" planet. This false sense of security is fostered by the notion that we are living in an age of technological marvels. We have, after all, split the atom, made vital human organ transplants commonplace, read the genetic code, walked on the surface of the Moon, travelled 32 times the speed of sound, and created complex computers that can easily carry out 250 million floating point operations per second.

But, despite these breakthroughs, we are still underachievers in many other areas. We still bury and burn refuse instead of recycling it, and no one has yet found an environment-friendly way to safely neutralize lethal toxic and nuclear waste. Because of the industrial nations' neglectful attitude to nature, we have now inherited acid rain, extensive ozone depletion, global warming, polluted rivers, levelled rainforests, and many more ecological problems. Disregard about nutritional needs of the animals slaughtered for our plates has created another problem of a particularly chilling and insidious nature: bovine spongiform encephalopathy – BSE – better known as "Mad Cow Disease". This incurable viral brain condition came about because farmers fed cattle meal containing cattle-meat. This enforced cannibalism upon ruminants, who only eat grass and leaves, resulted in the slow agonizing deaths of many cows. But by the time the agricultural scientists knew what BSE was, it was already killing humans who had eaten beef from the BSE-stricken cows. Many scientists think that Mad Cow Disease is still entering the food chain, and they are warning farmers not to feed meat to chickens and sheep.

On the exploration front, man has made six brief visits to the Moon, but there are still many unexplored regions on this planet. The Amazon Basin, the Poles, Alaska, Greenland, the Himalayas, the impenetrable jungles of New Guinea, Micronesia (which is comprised of 2000 islands east of the Philippines), and the highlands of Guiana are still largely unexplored. The same goes for the oceans that cover 70 per cent of our planet's surface.

When we take these facts into consideration, it becomes clear that man still inhabits a world where the maps and the scientific theories are still incomplete; a world in which people and their ships and planes can still disappear without a trace. There is so much on this earth – and off it – that is unknown to man, and only a fool or a devout sceptic can fail to realize this.

So, we have established that the unknown is all around us. Many brave freethinkers throughout the ages have dared to confront the unknown head-on, even in the face of ridicule. In the long history of human stupidity there have been many who have steered us from ignorance and superstition. Here are just a few of these pioneering torchbearers.

Nicolas Copernicus (1473–1543), the Polish astronomer, dared not publish his theory that planets orbited the Sun before he died, because he feared the wrath of the Church (the Establishment of its day).

The Italian astronomer Galileo Galilei (1564–1642) was almost burned at the stake because he said he saw craters on the Moon and spots on the Sun through his newly invented telescope. Pope Urban VIII declared this heresy, because the Sun and Moon were perfect and unchanging. Today we know that the Sun is a below-average middle-aged star.

Charles Darwin (1809–82) was laughed at in his day because of his theory of natural selection. As late as 1928 Darwin's theory was still being fought in the law courts of Tennessee.

Sigmund Freud (1856–1939), the founder of psycho-analysis, was labelled a charlatan because he believed the mind had a dark unknown region called the subconscious.

When the French chemist Louis Pasteur (1822–95) told the scientific community that diseases were transmitted by "little beasties" (bacteria), everybody said he was an idiot.

The list goes on: Hertz's radio waves, Bell's telephone, Edison's electric light, the Wright Brothers' aeroplane. All of these people and their inventions were hooted and howled at in their day. Entrenched authority (from the Church or scientists) has always opposed new concepts without fail, so the subjects of this book – UFOs and aliens, time-travel, lost lands, ghosts and the supernatural – will most definitely be dismissed and mocked by those with closed minds, but, as we can see from the aforementioned cases, the sceptics have an abysmal track record.

Many people who have experienced something which defies explanation often decide to remain silent, because they fear they'll lose their job, or because their friends will think they're crazy.

Society's attitude to the paranormal has always been largely hypocritical. There are many people who scoff at the super-natural and flying saucers but believe their "lucky" numbers will come up in the lottery one day. There are also sceptics of the paranormal who nevertheless check the horoscope column of the daily newspaper to see what the stars have in store.

In the meantime, reports of paranormal phenomena refuse to go away, and hardly a month goes by without news of a haunting or a UFO encounter. Many serious Fortean research groups are now combating society's ignorance of the psychic sphere by approaching the universities, where they hope the paranormal and Forteana will one day be recognized as legit-imate branches of science. Already, in the University of Edinburgh, a Chair of Parapsychology has been created, while in London, the Koestler Foundation – set up by the late Arthur Koestler – is an open-minded institution dedicated to the promotion of interest and research into areas just beyond the border of what can be explained by our present science. Also, in March 1999, Liverpool's John Moores University opened a

Psi Lab to investigate practical ways of making telepathy a reliable form of communication. So far, results of experiments at the lab have been nothing short of sensational, and there is mounting evidence that anyone can utilize telepathy after basic training.

Even the law is beginning to recognize the world of the paranormal. In a landmark ruling in July 1991 the New York Supreme Court officially acknowledged the existence of ghosts when it legally opened the way for a husband and wife to sue the former owner of the house they bought for the return of their $32,000 deposit. Jeffrey and Patrice Stambovsky were allegedly driven from their luxurious 18-room riverfront house in Nyack, New York, by two spectres which evidently dated from the days of the American Revolution. The five appeal court judges voted by three to two to declare that "as a matter of law, the Stambovsky's house is haunted", overturning a ruling by the trial judge. In time to come, the Stambovsky case will no doubt be regarded as an important milestone in the annals of the paranormal.

Some think that the widespread interest in the paranormal is due to the fact that we are currently entering the long-awaited Age of Aquarius, which will herald an epoch of peace and understanding, when the inner nature of the bellicose and the bigoted will change for the better. Whether this mystical age will arrive, one cannot say, but in recent years there has been nothing short of an explosive increase in the number of worldwide reports of unexplained phenomena such as crop circles, encounters with UFOs, ghosts and poltergeists, and so on.

We have already seen that even the lawcourts of America are now acknowledging the existence of ghosts, so why do scientists have a problem accepting apparitions?

Well, it seem that most scientists think phantoms run right against the grain of good old common sense. When a person dies, that's the end of the story. No one has ever returned from beyond the grave to take part in a repeatable, controlled scientific experiment to prove survival of death, therefore, ghosts don't exist, and anyone who claims they have seen an apparition of a deceased individual is either mistaken or simply a liar. That's how most scientists view the subject of the paranormal. But then, scientists are a prejudiced lot, and have only recently admitted in a roundabout way that good old common sense just cannot be trusted when dealing with the real, topsy-turvy world of modern physics. We don't even have to go into the origins of the universe or the nature of time to illustrate the point. Here's a much more basic example.

In 1830 a scientist named Thomas Young carried out an experiment that showed without a doubt that light is a wave of energy. But then, over a century later, scientists made the disturbing discovery that light also behaves as if it were a particle; but how can a beam of light be a wave *and* a particle? Surely that goes right against common sense! The wave/particle problem is still unsolved and is so baffling that it even had Einstein stumped for an answer. Stephen Hawking is no wiser either. When Einstein died in 1955, he was attempting to solve a host of similar problems by trying to formulate a Grand Theory that could explain how gravity and light were connected and how the forces of the atom interacted. Einstein's ambitious theory to explain how everything in the universe functioned was called the "Unified Field Theory", but it was a dismal failure. It seems that even Einstein was confounded by the metaphysical working of the cosmos. If the greatest minds of science are at a loss to explain the fundamental nature of light and gravity, how can they possibly dismiss paranormal phenomena?

Until 21st-century science can unravel the laws of what we collectively call "the Occult", we will have to form our own opinions about the strange encounters that are catalogued on the following pages.

PART ONE

The UFO Phenomenon

• •

UFOs throughout History

In 1320 an English scribe records that:

> The Abbot of Durham Abbey died on the feast of St
> Gregory and was buried in the choir of St Leonard
> before the great altar, and after his death there
> appeared in the sky a light like the rays of the sun. It
> seemed to shine over the burial place. Anon, it
> descended and moved from that place to another . . .
> Many saw this, and it was harmless, but they fell on the
> ground in terror.

To the fourteenth-century monks the nocturnal light was
probably interpreted as some type of religious omen, but to
modern minds the incident could equally be viewed as a UFO
sighting. Even further back in history, in Saxon times, come
more reports of strange lights in the sky. The English scholar,
historian and theologian the Venerable Bede recorded an
intriguing incident which took place in AD 664 in Book IV of
his *Ecclesiastical History*:

> In a monastery at Barking near the Thames in the burial
> ground at night as the nuns were singing at the graves,
> they beheld suddenly a light sent from Heaven like a great
> sheet which came upon them, and the light lifted up,
> moved to the other side of the monastery, then withdrew
> to the heights of Heaven. The selfsame brightness of the
> light made the sun at midday seem dark; in the morning
> young men in the Church reported that the beams of light
> entering the chinks of the door and windows did seem to
> pass all brightness of the day before.

There is no meteorological phenomenon to account for the "light sent from heaven" and there is certainly no mundane explanation which can account for the next excerpt from a later entry in the same book:

> *Tortygyth, a sister at Barking monastery, on a certain night when the daylight began to appear, as she went out of her chamber that she abode in, saw plainly as it were a corpse brighter than the sun wound up in muslin and being carried upwards, being taken indeed from the house in which the sisters were wont to rest. And as she diligently marked what it should be that drew the corpse upwards, this vision of the glorious body which she beheld, she saw that it was lifted up on high as if by cords brighter than gold, until it was taken into the open heavens and could be seen by her no longer.*

Bede seems to be describing a sinister body-snatching incident by something or someone from above. A similar incident was chronicled over 40 years earlier in AD 600: "Peter, Abbot of St Augustine Monastery near Canterbury, was sent as legate to God and was drowned near Ambleteuse. For several nights, a light from heaven played over his body."

Amazingly, similar sinister celestial goings-on have been recorded in ancient hieroglyphics. Egyptologists remain baffled by the annals of Pharaoh Thutmose III – who reigned circa 1504 to 1450 BC – because they contain references to strange aerial craft. One report, inscribed on papyrus, mentions a fleet of flying objects described as "circles of fire that were coming in the sky. It had no head, the breath of its mouth had a foul odour. Its body one rod long and one rod wide." Another report on the time-worn parchment tells of "flying discs" traversing the skies which were brighter than the sun.

Another historical personage who encountered the flying discs wasn't a man who was prone to flights of fancy. He was Alexander III, King of Macedon – better known to us as Alexander the Great – the supreme military conqueror of the civilized world and a former pupil of the Greek philosopher and scientist Aristotle. In fact, Alexander was more than a conqueror; he diffused the language and civilization of

Greece, and to him the ancient world owed an enormous proliferation of its knowledge in geography and natural history. In the year 329 BC, Alexander and his immense army were attempting to cross the Jaxartes river to battle the Scythians when they were suddenly attacked by two strange craft which came diving out of the sky. They were described as silvery circular flying shields which spat fire around their rims as they swooped down from the heavens. The gleaming saucers sent thunder rumbling across the sky – just as modern jet fighters do when they create a sonic boom – and the terrific noise together with the flashing discharge from the discs caused the horses, elephants and soldiers of Alexander's army to panic and scatter in disarray. This recorded historical fact cannot be explained by any known meteorological or astronomical phenomena, nor was the account a one-off. There is a record by the Italian historian Alberto Fenoglio which states that the flying shields were also encountered by Alexander and his army during the siege of Tyre in 332 BC. Fenoglio writes:

> The fortress would not yield, its walls were 50 feet high and constructed so solidly that no siege engine was able to damage it. The Tyrians disposed of the greatest technicians and builders of war-machines of the time and they intercepted in the air the incendiary-arrows and projectiles hurled by the catapults on the city.
>
> One day suddenly there appeared over the Macedonian camp these flying shields, as they had been called, which flew in triangular formation led by an exceedingly large one, the others smaller by almost a half. In all there were five, and they circled slowly over Tyre while thousands of warriors on both sides stood and watched them in astonishment. Suddenly from the largest shield came a lightning flash that struck the walls, and they crumbled, and other flashes followed. The walls and towers dissolved as if they had been built of mud, leaving the way open for the besiegers, who poured like an avalanche through the breaches. The flying shields hovered over the city until it was completely stormed when they very quickly disappeared aloft, soon melting into the blue sky.

Similar "flying shields" also intervened in later historical battles. In AD 776 two of them descended and unleashed a barrage of laserlike beams of flame on the Saxons, who were battling with the Franks at Sigilburg on the River Lippy. The Saxons were stricken with terror and fled the scene of the battle.

In the fourth century AD a Roman writer named Julius Obsequens compiled a book of strange historical incidents which he entitled *Prodigonium Liber*. The work is riddled with numerous reports of UFO sightings. Here are just a few of them. In 216 BC "things like ships were seen in the sky over Italy. At Arpi, a round shield was seen in the sky." In 99 BC "When C. Murius and L. Valerius were consuls in Tarquinia, a round object like a globe or a round circular shield took its path in the sky from west to east." In 90 BC "At Aernarie, while Livius Troso was promulgating the laws at the beginning of the Italian war, at sunrise, there came a terrific noise in the sky, and a globe of fire appeared burning in the north. In the territory of Spoletum, a globe of fire, of golden colour, fell to the earth gyrating. It then seemed to increase in size, rose from the earth and ascended into the sky, where it obscured the sun with its brilliance. It revolved toward the eastern quadrant of the sky."

In 42 BC Julius Obsequens of Rome gives us a tantalizing reference to another anachronistic event – the launch of a rocket: "Something like a sort of weapon, or missile, rose with great noise from the earth and soared into the sky."

Who had flying discs and rockets in the days before Christ? The first crude solid-fuel rockets were made in China and India over a thousand years ago. The Chinese had certainly perfected gunpowder made up of charcoal, sulphur and potassium nitrate by AD 1000, and this explosive was soon utilized as a simple rocket propellant. According to a Chinese tale of the time, a mandarin once made an attempt at powered flight by hanging from two paper kites driven by a battery of rockets. The outcome of this pioneering and dangerous experiment, however, is not recorded.

Although rocket-propelled missiles as instruments of war were being deployed by the Tartars in AD 1241 at the Battle of Legnica (in Lower Silesia, which is now in Poland), these crude rockets were largely ineffective as missiles, and could not be guided to change course once launched. The modern liquid-fuelled rocket can be traced back to the work of Peruvian engineer Pedro Poulet, who built and patented a rocket engine in 1895. Poulet's engine was injected with a mixture of nitrogen peroxide and petroleum, and ignited by a candle! But, as unbelievable as it may seem, someone in the Middle Ages actually constructed a three-tiered, solid-fuelled space rocket more advanced than Wernher Von Braun's V2 rockets of World War II. In 1961 Doru Todericiu, the Professor of Science and Technology at the University of Bucharest, discovered an old manuscript in the archives of the Sibiu Library. It was a volume containing three essays and reports on artillery, aeronautics and rocketry. The first section, written in AD 1417, was penned by one Hans Haasenwein, the second part was written by an anonymous author in 1460, and the third section was authored by Conrad Haas, the head of the Sibiu artillery depot. This latter segment of the book is the most astounding, because it not only refers to an account of an experimental launch of a multiple-stage rocket in 1529, but also contains detailed diagrams of two such rockets. Haas states that the solid fuel used in both types of rocket was produced by mixing various powders with ethyl acetate ammoniac. Amazingly, the futuristic-looking rockets in the diagrams have delta wings for stability. Conrad Haas does not divulge where he got his rocket designs from, and it seems highly unlikely that he alone invented them.

Nonetheless, explaining away the flying discs of the type which Alexander the Great encountered as ahead-of-their-time inventions is preposterous. Whoever built those discs knew not only about antigravity, but also how to destroy fortresses with high-powered beams of energy, described by terrestrials of the time as "spitting fire". Without a doubt there are geniuses in every age who are centuries ahead of their time; Leonardo Da Vinci was a prime example with his quaint but unworkable helicopter and flying machine designs. But what genius in the early seventeenth century could have been responsible for the following incident?

At 8 p.m. on 5 August 1608, hundreds of citizens of Nizza (now the French town of Nice) were alarmed to see three enormous discs in the sky approaching the citadel which overlooked the harbour. The silent discs were travelling at a low altitude and descended until they were just 1 metre from the waters. At that point the waters below the circular ships began to hiss and bubble, and gave off a dense yellow vapour. The populace wondered if the discs were an omen of some sort. A circular door slid open in one of the hovering ships, and a humanoid being emerged, followed by another. They had large globular heads and wore strange silvery-red suits. One observer got a better look at the strange visitors through his telescope. He saw that the occupants of the unearthly ships were wearing helmets with two circular holes at the front which served as some sort of eyepieces. Two tubes ran from a black cylinder on the front area of the helmet to some sort of apparatus on the back of the visitor.

The inhabitants of the town thought an invasion was imminent when more figures left the ships and made their way inland on vehicles resembling modern water skis. The invaders from the sky never came ashore, but patrolled the waters for two hours and acted as if they were looking for something. At 10 p.m. they returned to their craft, which were still suspended a few feet above the waters, and minutes later the three ships made a rumbling sound and took off at a phenomenal speed towards the east.

The people of Nizza were sure that the eerie visitation had been a warning from God, and the Church held processions and marches through the streets carrying crucifixes and statues of the Virgin Mary. Priests tried to quell the hysterical mobs by openly praying to the Lord for forgiveness. The religious hysteria gradually died down after a couple of weeks, and the Church solemnly announced that God had granted the people of Nizza a spiritual reprieve, and that the "demons from the sky" would never return. That, however, is not the end of the story, because just a few days after the religious authorities of Nizza's announcement, the discs returned to the Italian coast, this time in Genoa. On 22 August the three discs hovered on the coastal waters, as they did previously, but the Genovese authorities (who had heard about the "demons from above" who had terrorized Nizza) quickly drafted in an artillery unit. Over 800 cannon balls were blasted at the hovering craft, but failed to inflict the slightest scratch on them. The salvos of cannon fire did discourage the helmeted humanoids from venturing outside their ships, but at a cost. One of the saucers climbed steadily into the air, then drifted inland until it was positioned over the centre of the town. As its gigantic disc-shaped shadow crawled across the streets, the people sensed something terrible was about to happen, and they stampeded for the outskirts.

Twelve people were trampled to death in the exodus, and more deaths took place which are harder to explain. People directly beneath the levitating craft screamed in agony as they felt their insides burn. Their skins turned red and blistered. Others became blind. After an unspecified period the menacing machine hanging overhead moved away from the city and rejoined the other craft, before all three of them took off, again towards the east, at an incredible velocity. There was one further sighting of just one of the malign saucers on 25 August above Martigues, a fishing village near Nizza. On that last occasion two figures, seemingly identical to those seen at Nizza, emerged from their craft and flew around the sky. Minutes later the humanoids flew back into their ship and it raced skywards, leaving a low rumbling sound in its wake.

The three UFO encounters were witnessed by hundreds of people, but the incidents were left in the local archives and forgotten until the 1950s.

From the depths of time – 12,000 years ago, in fact – there comes another intriguing record of extra-terrestrials coming to Earth. It all began in 1938, high in the mountains of Bayan-Kara-Ula, which lie on the borders of Tibet and China. A team of Chinese archaeologists led by Professor Chi Pu Tei were conducting a detailed survey of mountain caves in the region which were interlinked by passages. In these caves, strange-looking skeletons were found; they were the bones of an unidentified humanoid species which had spindly bodies and huge, over-developed skulls. They were initially presumed to be the skeletal remains of an extinct race of apes, but Professor Chi Pu Tei noted that most of the skeletons had been interred in the ground or entombed in a blocked-up cave, and he knew apes did not bury their dead.

Stranger still, on the walls of the caves there were elaborate drawings of the Sun, Moon and the constellations, as well as elliptical lines. These drawings and the skeletons were subsequently dated – they were 12,000 years old.

While the professor and his team were carrying out further excavations in the caves to get to the bottom of the mysterious cave-dwellers, they unearthed something which caused shockwaves in the archaeological, scientific and theological world. Buried under the dust of thousands of years, the archaeologists uncovered a large heavy disc. The disc was dusted down and scrutinized. There was a hole at its centre, and radiating from this hole in a close spiral there ran a groove to the outer edges of the disc, just like the groove in the old gramophone records. Upon even closer inspection with a powerful magnifier, Professor Chi Pu Tei saw that the groove was not just a continuous etched line, but a trail of engraved unfamiliar characters. A further 716 discs were uncovered in the caves, and they all bore the same tight spiral of tiny hieroglyphics. Scores of experts attempted to decipher the glyphs on the discs without success – until 1963. That year, Dr Tsum Um Nui – a wizard at code-breaking and encryption – finally deciphered the code on the discs, but when he translated the information from the discs into Chinese, his colleagues thought the doctor had taken leave of his senses. Dr Tsum Um Nui read his translations to his peers and they reacted by smiling nervously, uttering sighs of amazement and shaking their heads. The master code-breaker said: "The Dropas came down from the clouds in their aircraft. Our men, women and children hid in the caves ten times before sunrise. When at last they understood the sign language of the Dropas, they realized that the newcomers had peaceful intentions." There were howls of laughter from the academics, but Dr Tsum Um Nui persevered, and he told a fascinating story related in the translated text by a tribe called the "Ham". This tribe said they felt pity for the Dropas because their ship had crash-landed in such a remote and inaccessible range of mountains. The Dropas tried unsuccessfully to repair their ship and often made drawings on the cave walls of their world in the sky.

Dr Tsum Um Nui's translated text was later corroborated when anthropologists learned more about the sequestrated peoples of the Bayan-Kara-Ula region. The legends of these isolated societies – which had been passed down for count-less generations – tell of the small, gaunt, yellow-faced men who came down from the clouds long ago. These men had large bulging heads and puny bodies, and they were so ugly that many of them were hunted down and killed by the local tribesmen on horseback. The physical descriptions of the invaders tallied well with the skeletons discovered by Professor Chi Pu Tei in the system of interconnected caves.

Scientists in the Soviet Union showed great interest in the 12,000-year-old discs and made repeated requests to inspect them. The Chinese authorities finally acquiesced and sent three to Moscow. The Soviet scientists subjected the discs to a rigorous examination. Chemical analysis revealed that the discs contained large amounts of cobalt and various alloys of remarkable uniformity for an era when iron ore had not even been smelted. Further tests uncovered an unusual property of the discs: when an electrical current was passed through them, they resonated to produce a low humming sound.

What are we to make of the discs? Do they contain records of an aborted space mission by aliens 12,000 years ago? Alas, China later requested the return of its discs from the Soviet Union. In 1964 China exploded its first atom bomb to emphasize its independent status as a "superpower" and secluded itself from the West. The Chinese also regarded the Soviet Union with a paranoid eye, and challenged its role as the principal patron of international Marxism. Western scientists and archaeologists asked to see the discs of Bayan-Kara-Ula, but their requests were not even acknowledged. If the present political climate is anything to go by, it might be some time before China lets Westerners examine them.

What are we to make of the aforementioned accounts of the sightings and visitations of spacecraft and beings from another world? There have been too many reports of UFOs and visiting aliens throughout recorded history to be explained away as myths and hallucinations. UFOs have been recorded in tapestries, frescos, paintings and petroglyphs, and in all probability the gods of our ancestors were simply visitors from other worlds. While some sceptics have difficulty in accepting the concept of extra-terrestrials dropping in on the planet Earth, most scientists now believe that the universe is teeming with life. All those stars we see at night are suns, and each star is now known to have a planetary system. When we consider that there are over 100,000 million stars in our galaxy alone, we realize that the chances of an Earth-type planet orbiting one of those stars is very likely indeed. Our galaxy is just one of billions in the universe, so to say that we are the only intelligent life in existence is illogical and nonsensical.

There are hundreds of historical reports of UFO sightings and encounters hidden from the light of day in archives and ancient texts all over the world. Some ufologists even claim that there are numerous references to UFOs and extra-terrestrials in the best-selling book of all time: the Bible. These astounding claims are our next subject.

UFOs in the Old Testament

Within the unimaginable depths of the universe there is a small family of worlds circling about a star we call the Sun; it is just a single star among the billions upon billions which are shining in the cosmos. Against the awesome backdrop of the infinite blackness of space, our world is just another planet; nothing more than an insignificant speck on the cosmological scale of things, but it is our home, and as yet we have found no other planets which are remotely like Earth. The history of our world is a story which is still largely incomplete. Just a few centuries ago the most learned historians knew virtually nothing about events beyond 3000 years ago. These students of the past had a surplus of legends about the origin of Man and his world, but the fables and myths were seemingly at variance with the fossilized bones of dinosaurs and ape-like beings. These archaeological finds clashed severely with the beliefs and religions of people who took the Hebrew Bible's account of Genesis as a literal authentic history of the world. If prehistoric monsters roamed the Earth in the past, why were they not mentioned in the Book of Genesis? The halcyon tales of the Garden of Eden only mention Adam and Eve; there is no reference to the now-extinct races of ape-men and men-apes such as the Neanderthals, the Cro-Magnon people, and other sub-human anthropoids.

Despite the conflicting evidence of the fossil records, the Church attempted to circumvent the problem by seriously asserting that the Devil had maliciously fabricated the fossils of ancient plants and animals and had planted them in rocks to disprove the biblical scriptures. In fact, by meticulous analysis of the Book of Genesis, the Archbishop of Armagh (1581–1656) even came to the conclusion that God had created the world at 9 a.m. on 23 October 4004 BC!

Some writers and thinkers have conjectured that there is a theological no-man's land where the biblical view and scientific version of man's history can co-exist. One of the earliest attempts to reinterpret the books of the Old Testament as a terrestrial account of alien visitations can be found in *Yezad*, a 1922 science fiction novel by George Babcock. Babcock's sci-fi treatment of the Old Testament was branded by many as sacrilegious, while others thought his concept was preposterous.

In the early 1950s the Old Testament was once again interpreted from a scientific angle by the distinguished academic and Freudian psychiatrist Immanuel Velikovsky. After his extensive researches into Israelite history, Velikovsky proposed that certain parts of the Bible's Old Testament were factual, and he offered many outrageous theories to describe biblical events as misinterpretations of cosmic incidents. Velikovsky argued that Earth had been involved in a near-collision with Venus. The effects of this hypothetical planetary near-miss on the Earth's axis and rotational speed would have been responsible for the account in the Book of Joshua 10:12–13: "The Sun stood still in the midst of Heaven and did not go down about a whole day."

Why did Velikovsky think Venus was the culprit? Well, until the second millenium BC, that planet was not grouped by astronomers with the rest of the planets; it was in fact always described as a menacing comet-like body which was said to have rained fire down on the Earth in the past. The Aztecs called Venus "the star that smoked" and claimed that it once passed by the world blazing, and killed many people in its wake. The Peruvians called Venus "Chaska" – which means wavy-haired. Strangely enough, the Greek myths tell how a blazing star named Phaeton almost destroyed the world with fire before being transformed into the planet Venus. The Jews also regarded Venus in a similar manner for some reason, and a passage in the Talmud states: "Fire is hanging down from the planet Venus." Venus – the nearest planet to ours – was also classed as a dangerous fire-spitting planet by the Egyptians, Assyrians, Babylonians, Arabs, Hindus, Chinese and even the Samoans. Velikovsky strongly backed up his "wandering planet" hypothesis with more historical references to our nearest planetary neighbour in his controversial book *Worlds In Collision* (1950), but, predictably, the historians and astrophysicists ridiculed the work. The biblical fundamentalists also attacked the book for equating the works of God as mere cosmic cataclysms. But other writers came along with even more controversial interpretations of the historical events which have allegedly inspired the world's religions and cultures.

In 1967 a book called *Chariot of the Gods?* was published, and within the space of five years it had become a best-seller in 38 countries and was translated into 26 languages. The author of the book was Erich von Daniken, the managing director of a Swiss 5-star hotel. The claims made by von Daniken in his work were bold and blasphemous. Von Daniken had been educated at the College of St-Michel in Fribourg, where even as a student he had occupied all of his spare time studying ancient holy writings. His lengthy research led him to the following conclusions – humanoid aliens from a remote galaxy had visited the Earth around 10,000 years ago, apparently after an intergalactic war. These "sons of the stars" created the human race in their own image by tinkering with the genes of the primates. The alien visitors so overawed their creations with their far superior technology that they were worshipped as gods. Evidence, such as artefacts and relics of the visiting ancient astronauts, have been uncovered by archaeologists but unrecognized. Many of the fabulous stories in the Bible and other sacred books are actually accounts of the ancient spacemen intervening in human affairs.

Von Daniken was heavily criticized by theologians, archaeologists, social anthropologists, cultural historians, astronomers and astrophysicists, but his first book sold $5\frac{1}{2}$ million copies and captured the imaginations of people the world over. *Chariots of the Gods?* spawned a deluge of books with the same theme of ancient astronauts, many of which became best-sellers. Today, Erich von Daniken still holds dearly to his beliefs, although he admits there were some errors in his books. In 1985 he wrote a book about the errata in his works, entitled *Did I Get It Wrong?*, and he even asked his readers to consider if he had misconceived the whole "ancient astronauts" theory in the first place.

Could there be at least a grain of truth in the claims of von Daniken and the other writers who say God was an astronaut? Let us analyze the Bible in our quest for ancient spacemen. The Christian sacred book is actually a collection of books, divided into two parts: the Old Testament and the New Testament. The former contains 39 books (according to the Protestants), plus a supplement of 14 books known as the Apocrypha. These are books of doubtful authority, included in the Greek (Septuagint) and Latin (Vulgate) versions of the Old Testament, but usually viewed as non- canonical or of little value by most Christians and Jews. The Old Testament was compiled during a period ranging from the thirteenth century to the first century BC. No original manuscripts have actually survived, and the present versions are based on two main sources: the Septuagint (a Greek translation made from the Hebrew in Alexandria in about 250 BC) and the Massoretic Text, which resulted from the collaborations of a group of Jewish scholars, beginning in the sixth century after Christ. This group of scholars assigned themselves to the task of preserving the Hebrew versions then available, and the Massoretic Text was finally finished at the end of the tenth century.

The Septuagint became the accepted Old Testament of the Christians, and the Massoretic Text became the Hebrew canon. There were, however, even more versions of the Old Testament; they were the Samaritan Pentateuch (a fourth century BC text preserved by the Samaritan community) and a Latin translation by St Jerome (begun in AD 382) called the Vulgate, which is the authorized Roman Catholic version.

The New Testament of the Bible was most probably written in Greek during the first century. Without a doubt, the New Testament is riddled with mistakes, but none of them is significant enough to affect the essential doctrine of the texts. These errors occurred through numerous textual changes which were accidentally introduced through poor copying, misinterpretations that were added, and accidental – and deliberate – omissions. Some of these alterations were made for political and religious reasons. The great British scientist Isaac Newton became an atheist after learning Hebrew. After retranslating the Bible from the original Hebrew texts, he discovered that in the fourth century, during a bloody power struggle within the Christian Church, key passages in the Bible were altered by the Christian leader Athanasius. Newton was devastated to learn that the text was falsified by Athanasius to elevate Christ on a level with God and the Holy Spirit in the doctrine of the Holy Trinity. Newton decided that Jesus, then, was just another prophet like Moses, and thought the worshipping of Christ as God's equal was nothing short of idolatry. This illustrates the problem of authenticity faced by modern theologians. If we take the Bible literally, as it is intended to be taken, according to Christians, then its scriptures are open to some intriguing interpretations. In Genesis, we are told that:

> In the beginning God created the heaven and the Earth. And the Earth was without form and void; and darkness was upon the face of the deep. And the Spirit of God moved upon the face of the waters . . .

Further on, another passage reads:

> And God said, Let the Earth bring forth grass, the herb yielding seed, and the fruit tree yielding fruit after his kind, whose seed is in itself, upon the Earth: and it was so. And the Earth brought forth grass, and herb yielding

seed after his kind, and the tree yielding fruit, whose seed
was in itself, after his kind: and God saw that it was good.

If we are to interpret the aforementioned passages not as some sacred account of Creation, but as a primitive allegorical interpretation of a real higher intelligence transforming a cratered, barren planet into an oasis, we would see striking parallels with the far-sighted plans the scientists of today have for "terraforming" planets in our solar system which are at present too hostile for human colonization. The late astronomer and astrophysicist Carl Sagan once put forward an ingenious plan for terraforming (making a planet hospitable) the currently infernal world of Venus. Sagan calculated that if we bombarded Venus with 1000 rocket-loads of blue-green algae, some of the hardy one-celled organisms would reproduce in the upper atmosphere before crashing down to the surface, which has a temperature of 900 degrees Fahrenheit. This incredibly hot temperature is nothing to some algae that thrive in boiling hot springs on Earth. Rocket-loads of the tough algae cells released into the thick cloud cover continually over a period of years would ultimately allow a flourishing colony of cells that would convert the carbon dioxide in the Venusian atmosphere into oxygen. After several hundred years, enough oxygen would be formed on Venus to cool down the planet and vastly reduce the Venusian greenhouse effect. This in turn would allow the significant amounts of water vapour which is known to exist in the atmosphere of Venus to fall as rain. The end product would be a cycle of rainfall and the formation of rivers and lakes on the planet. Sagan's plans are not pipe dreams; computer simulations have determined that a terraforming programme for Venus is entirely feasible if enough time, money and technology is provided for the project, which would reap literally astronomical profits.

A transformed Venus would not only become a second Earth for humanity to colonize, it would present unprecedented territorial ownership disputes among the nations of Earth. As Venus has no tectonic plate system like Earth; it would be earthquake free. Secondly, the Venusian day lasts 243 Earth days; that would be 243 days of continual sunshine in the planet's tropical belt, which entails obvious advantages over Earth's tourist industry. Venus would become the ultimate retreat for this planet's millionaires, and the ultra-novel extra-terrestrial holiday location would require a sizeable workforce from Earth. The prolonged period of sunshine on Venus would probably necessitate subterranean or air-conditioned dwellings where artificial night could be simulated. Another possibility at simulating a localized form of night could work by orbiting inflatable reflective myelin mirrors around the planet. The shadows of these mirrors falling on the surface of Venus would create an oasis of darkness which the inhabitants would experience as a solar eclipse effect. Alternatively, perhaps anyone tiring of the eight-month day could even journey to the dark side of Venus, where the stars would be on view for as long as there were clear skies. Of course, no one is entirely sure what resources lie beneath the Venusian crust, but as the planet is almost a twin of the Earth in size and gravity, we must surmise that there will be radioactive ores, gold, silver and many other precious metals and minerals present. This brings us back to the problem of who would own these resources.

When NASA landed its first astronauts on the Moon, the Soviet Union, China and many other nations frowned at America planting the tinfoil flag of the Stars and Stripes in the lunar soil. The other nations of the world argued that a united banner of humanity should have been planted there instead. This suggestion outraged NASA and the American government, which had spent billions of dollars and lost a number of astronauts in order to reach the Moon. If an American company as successful as Microsoft financed the Venus terraforming venture, there would be similar squabbles amongst the Terran leaders of our much-hyped "global village". In fact, it is highly likely that wars would rage over the possession of the new world, perhaps even a war of independence for the new Venusians who wish to become autonomous and free from the Earth governments.

Going back to the biblical texts of Genesis, is it possible that a similar war over planetary possession was fought when the gods transformed the Earth from a lifeless sphere "without form and void" into the Garden of Eden? Curiously, American Charles Fort (1874–1932), the great student of the unexplained and collector extraordinaire of bizarre newspaper clippings and reports, once made a profound statement in 1919 in his *Book of the Damned*, an incredible examination of the holes and contradictions in our scientific understanding of the universe. Fort wrote:

> *I think we are property.*
> *I should say we belong to something.*
> *That once upon a time, this earth was No-Man's land, that other worlds explored and colonized here, and fought among themselves for possession, but that now it is owned by something.*
> *That something owns this earth – all others warned off.*

Did Fort hit on a truth? It would explain all the tales in Apocrypha and other religious works about the ancient conflict called the "War in Heaven" which was fought by dissenting factions of angels, led by rogue Archangel Lucifer against his master, Yahweh, the God who made a lifeless world fertile and created homo sapiens to tend to his Garden of Eden. In the Book of Isaiah 14:12, it says of Lucifer: "O Shining star, son of morning, how you have fallen from the heavens . . ." For you said in your heart, I will go up to the heavens; I will raise my throne above the stars of God."

Most people equate the name "Lucifer" with Satan. However, the Bible implies that this is not the case, and the name Lucifer is only mentioned in one passage of the Old Testament. According to the Book of Job 26:11–13, when Lucifer, "the Boastful Angel", and his followers rebelled, Yahweh destroyed their dwelling places (a place in the heavens called "Rahab"), which was reduced by God to "stones of fire". The Book of Enoch hints that Rahab was an actual world in the sky which God obliterated. In some accounts Rahab is curiously connected with the mythical planet Phaeton, which was said to have been destroyed by a catastrophe millions of years ago. Is there any physical evidence that Rahab once existed?

Each planet in our solar system is somewhere between 1.3 and 2.0 times distant from the Sun's nearest neighbouring

Lucifer is cast out of Heaven   *Gustav Doré*

planet. The one exception in this numeric relationship is the fifth planet Jupiter; it is 3.4 times as far from the Sun as Mars. This inconsistent gap puzzled astronomers for years, especially after Uranus was discovered in 1781. It was quite obvious that a planet was missing which should have been orbiting between Mars and Jupiter. Astronomers scanned this gap in the orbits for years, hoping to discover the absent planet, but only in 1801 was the first fragment of the missing planet discovered by stargazers. It was a carbonaceous chunk of rock, 620 miles in diameter, and it was named Ceres. By 1807 more enormous fragments were spotted and, as the century progressed, it became clear that there were thousands of chunks of something spread in a belt around the sun between the orbits of Mars and Jupiter.

Today, it is known that there are at least 100,000 asteroids in the belt, and the debate still rages over just what the asteroids are the remnants of. Some astronomers think they are left-over material from the birth of the solar system which never formed into a planet, while others think the asteroids are the remains of a world that exploded in the distant past. What force could destroy an entire planet? Cometary collisions, even geological catastrophes, could have been responsible. Water from the planet's oceans seeping down through faults in the crust to the core would be sufficient to generate a super-heated blast of steam that would blow a planet into oblivion. This scenario was witnessed on a small scale here on Earth in 1883 when sea water seeped into the active volcano on the East Indian island Krakatoa. The ensuing blast destroyed the island, killed 36,000 people, and hurled fragments over an area of 300,000 square miles.

The evidence for the demolished world of Rahab could, then, be the hundreds of thousands of rocks floating about between Mars and Jupiter, but in the search for an extra-terrestrial angle on the Bible, we must now turn our attention to the chronicled events which allegedly happened here on Earth.

One thing which does seem absolutely certain in the Old and New Testaments is that something unearthly caused a stir in the Middle East in the time of Moses and in the period Jesus was on Earth. Let us begin with the Old Testament. Whatever way we look at it, something that was literally not of this world commanded Moses to lead the Israelites out of the bondage of the Pharaoh and through the wilderness to the Promised Land. It all began when Moses was 18 years old, according to the Talmud. The sight of the wickedness being inflicted upon his people by the Egyptians moved Moses to tears, and it culminated in his killing an overseer who was beating a Hebrew labourer. Moses was saved from execution by an angel and transported instantly to Ethiopia where he fought as a general. Soon after the death of Kikanus, Moses was crowned king and Queen Adonith became his wife. However, Moses abdicated and journeyed to Midian, where he married Zipporah, the daughter of Jethro, and for 40 years lived as a shepherd. Scriptures then give a strange account about Moses' encounter with an unearthly entity:

> *Moses was minding the flock of his father-in-law, Jethro, Priest of Midian. He left the flock along the side of the wilderness and came to Horeb, the mountain of God. There the angel of the Lord appeared to him in the flame of the burning bush. Moses noticed that although the bush was on fire, it was not itself being burned up; so he said to himself "I must go across to see this wonderful sight. Why does not the bush burn away?"*
>
> *When the Lord saw that Moses had turned aside to look, he called out to him out of the bushes, "Moses, Moses". And Moses answered, "Yes, I am here."*
>
> *God said "Come no nearer; take off your sandals; the place where you are standing is holy ground."*

This passage has been interpreted by researchers looking for scriptural spaceships as perhaps some account of a bush silhouetted against an illuminated spacecraft which had landed on the secluded mountain. The "Lord" warning Moses to keep his distance has also been construed as the amplified intercom voice of the captain or pilot of the landed ship advising Moses to keep out of range of harmful radiation emanating from the craft.

The Lord told Moses to deliver the Israelites out of bondage and lead them to the Promised Land "flowing with milk and honey". Aided by his elder brother, Aaron, Moses finally led the 600,000 Israelites out of thraldom and embarked on the epic 40 years of wandering to Canaan. In the Book of Exodus 13:21 it is written: "And Yahveh went before them by day in a pillar of cloud, to lead them the way; and by night in a pillar of fire, to give them light; to go by day and night. He took not away the pillar of the cloud by day, nor the pillar of fire by night, from before the people."

The pillar has been the subject of much speculation to scholars, critics and theologians over the centuries. One biblical scholar, M. Daniel-Rops, asserts that the pillar of cloud – the visible sign of Divine Presence in the eyes of the Hebrews – was nothing more than a side-effect of the

"Qadim", a sirocco-like wind of Arabia, which raised opaque clouds of spiralling dust. But Mr Daniel-Rops neglects to explain how this whirlwind of sand kept going for 40 years, and how it became highly luminous and fiery upon nightfall. What we can assume, without the risk of being sacrilegious, is that the pillar of cloud and light was not of this Earth, and definitely not a product of weather conditions. Something from above was intervening in the affairs of the Hebrews, and it was not some mass hallucination affecting the thousands of Israelites and the Egyptian nation; something real and tangible was taking place.

The Pharaoh was well aware of the reality of the Hebrew Lord when he decided to send his cavalry and chariots after the fleeing Israelites. Faced with the obstacle of the Red Sea, Moses could lead his persecuted people no further, but at the Lord's behest, Moses suddenly stretched out his hand towards the river, and the waters parted. A tremendous wall of sea water moved off to the right, and another water-wall roared off to the left, exposing a vast tract of dried sea-bed stretching from one shore to the next. Moses and his people fled across the dry land to the safety of the other side, but when the Egyptian army tried to follow them the water came thundering back down on top of them and they were drowned.

No natural phenomenon can account for the parting of the Red Sea, but if we are open-minded enough to entertain the hypothesis that extraterrestrials were responsible, we could imagine some potent antigravity forces pushing back the waters. We can already manipulate liquids at a distance with electrostatic forces. Many computer printers utilize this effect by using electrical fields to manoeuvre jets of charged ink around paper. If you let a thin stream of water run from a tap, then comb your hair and place the comb inches from this stream, the static electricity in the comb will actually bend the flow. If the static charge was greater, the water would flow at right angles, and if the electricity was charged further by a Van de Graaf generator, you would be able to draw up gallons of water from a swimming pool. To part the Red Sea would take millions of watts of power, but that would easily be expendable to a space-faring race.

Two more incidents mentioned in Exodus give the impression that something akin to a spaceship landed on Mount Sinai: "And the Lord came down upon Mount Sinai, on the top of the Mount; and the Lord called Moses up to the Mount; and Moses went up." Also, we read:

> And it came to pass on the third day in the morning that there were thunders and lightnings, and a thick cloud upon the Mount, and the voice of the trumpet exceeding loud; so that all the people that was in the camp trembled. And Moses brought forth people out of the camp to meet with God, and they stood at the nether part of the Mount. And Mount Sinai was altogether on a smoke because Yahveh descended upon it in fire; and the smoke thereof ascended as the smoke of a furnace, and the whole Mount quaked greatly.

Scripture then records that Moses advances towards the landing of Yahveh, but is given a stern warning by the Lord not to let anyone near the landing site. Only Moses is allowed to proceed. Yahveh says to the leader and prophet: "And thou shall set bounds unto the people round about, saying, Take heed to yourselves that ye go not up into the Mount, nor touch the border of it: whosoever toucheth the Mount shall be surely put to death: there shall not an hand touch it, but he shall surely be stoned, or shot through; whether it be beast or man it shall not live."

Intriguingly, after an undefined period of time has elapsed, Yahveh lifts his exclusion zone from around the mountain, and Moses is allowed to take Aaron and 70 elders with him as he goes up to get a closer look at the mysterious cloud-pillar, although they all maintain a respectful distance from the supernatural sight. But then they see the awe-inspiring figure of Yahveh: "And they saw the God of Israel and there was under his feet as it were a paved work of sapphire stone."

Standing on a blue scintillating platform, they actually see the elusive but powerful God who coordinated the Exodus of the Jews after sending ten plagues against Egypt, the last of which resulted in the death of the Egyptian first-born (and may have affected only the Pharaoh's family). The celestial deity instructs Moses to construct a large tent of specific dimensions with the aid of the craftsmen in the encampment. The Hebrew lawgiver was told that the tent would be a "Dwelling Place" for Yahveh and would also serve as a rendezvous where Moses and Aaron could meet with the extra-terrestrial host. The specialized enclosure, also known as the Tent of Reunion, later served as the shelter of one of the most enigmatic objects in history: the Ark of the Covenant.

The Ark of the Covenant was an ornate chest of acacia wood that accompanied the Israelites throughout their nomadic wanderings. The Ark contained Aaron's rod, a pot of manna, and the broken stone tablets of the Decalogue – or Ten Commandments. It was 2.5 cubits (3 ft 9 in) in length and 1.5 cubits (2 ft 3 in) in height, and was carried by poles at the long sides. Bezaleel, a Judahite artisan who was highly skilled at working in metal, wood and stone, was the principal architect of the Ark, but it was built to plans revealed to him by God, not to his own designs. The instructions imparted from Yahveh were very intriguing indeed. The poles used to carry

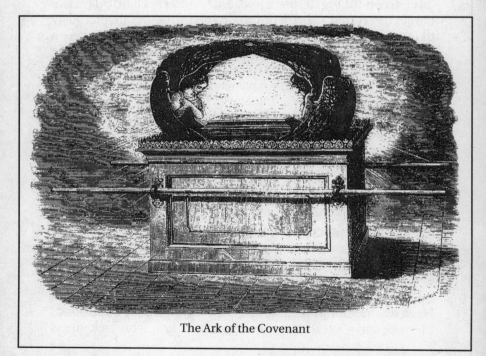

The Ark of the Covenant

the Ark were to be made of acacia and overlaid with gold leaf. In order to transport the Ark, these poles were to be carefully inserted into specially made receiving rings mounted on the sides of the chest. The poles were to remain in the rings at the sides of the Ark and never to be removed. The instructions for transporting the Ark of the Covenant were equally specific. Only the Kohathites – a clan of Levi – were allowed to carry the Ark and the holy things associated with the tabernacle. God warned that anyone else who touched those things would meet a swift death. What potent power did this Ark contain to be so jealously guarded? It was soon discovered why there were so many precautions regarding the handling of the Ark: as it was being transported by oxen, the beasts of burden stumbled, and a man named Uzzah (who was not a Kohathite or of the clan Levi) instinctively reached out to steady the Ark in case it toppled off the cart – and he was struck down dead by a tremendous bolt of energy (2 Samuel 6:7). The religious interpretation of this tragic event is that God smote Uzzah for being disobedient to his conditions, but one freethinking French writer, Robert Charroux, has conjectured that the Ark of the Covenant seems suspiciously like some high-voltage condenser which may have been a part of an apparatus for communicating with the heavenly Yahveh. Erich von Daniken has also opted for this startling possibility, and the idea was also alluded to in the 1981 Spielberg film, *Raiders of the Lost Ark*.

The fate of the Ark is not known. Some scholars have concluded that it was captured by the Babylonians in 587 BC, when the destruction of Jerusalem and the Temple was completed by Nebuchadnezzar. Yet for some unknown reason the Ark was not recorded in the list of the Babylonians' stolen booty. The current theory is that the Ark is in Ethiopia, because of an old legend which goes as follows. The Queen of Sheba once visited King Solomon and was highly impressed by his wisdom (as is mentioned in the Book of Kings). She had an affair with him and when she returned to her nation, the queen discovered she was having Solomon's child. The queen subsequently gave birth to a son, who was called Menelik, meaning "Son of the Wise One". Upon adulthood, Menelik travelled to Israel to seek his father, who welcomed him with honour. Solomon gave so much attention to his illegitimate son, the elders complained and demanded that Menelik should return to Ethiopia. Solomon agreed, but only on the condition that all of the elders' eldest sons would accompany Menelik. The elders had to agree with the king, and Azarius, the eldest son of Zadok, the high priest of Israel, went to Ethiopia with Menelik – after stealing the sacred Ark of the Covenant. When Menelik reached Ethiopia, Azarius revealed the Ark, but Menelik believed that the theft would not have been successful without God's consent. And so, it is said that to this day the Ark of the Covenant is under lock and key in the Church of St Mary of Zion in Axum. Should a thorough investigation ever get under way and successfully trace the Ark, it will be interesting to see if it is just an acacia chest – or something more hi-tech.

In other sections of the Bible there are other fascinating descriptions of fantastic events which have parallels with the modern UFO era. One apparent close encounter with a craft from the sky takes place in the Book of Ezekiel. Ezekiel was one of the Jews deported to Babylon during the first exile of 597 BC. His call to be a prophet came in Babylon and his entire prophetic ministry was carried out there. By the River of Babylon – the Khobar – Ezekiel was sitting, in a sad mood, on the "fifth day of the fourth month of the fifth year since the captivity" (the year 593 BC) when he suddenly saw what he assumed to be a "chariot of Yahveh" coming towards him through the sky. In a state of shock the prophet stood transfixed, looking skywards at the strange craft:

> And I looked, and behold, a whirlwind came out of the north, a great cloud, and a fire unfolding itself, and a brightness was about it, and out the midsts thereof as the colour of amber, out of the midsts of the fire. Now as I beheld the living creatures, behold, one wheel upon the earth by the living creatures, with four faces. The appearance of the wheels and their work was like unto the colour of beryl [a greenish sheen] and they four had one likeness: and their appearance and their work was as it were a wheel in the middle of a wheel. When they went, they went upon their four sides, and they turned not

when they went. As for their rings, they were so high they were dreadful, and their rings were full of eyes [portholes?]. And when the living creatures went, the wheels went by them: and when the living creatures were lifted up from the earth, the wheels were lifted up. Whithersoever the spirit was to go, they went, thither was their spirit to go; and the wheels were lifted up over against them: for the spirit of the living creature was in the wheels.

Ezekiel goes on further, to say that above the discs there was another amazing object which he enigmatically alludes to as "something that had the appearance of the likeness of the glory of Yahveh". In earlier books of the Old Testament the glory of Yahveh is always referred to as pillars of gold or fire. Perhaps that was what Ezekiel was seeing above the landed object he could hardly describe in his limited language.

There are other accounts of possible UFOs in the Old Testament: The outstanding narrative concerning the adventure of Elijah when he is taken up by a "whirlwind" – the same description Ezekiel uses for his UFO. Then there is the incredible tale related in a fourth-century apocryphal work known as the Vision of Isaiah: "After taking Isaiah to Heaven, the angel was requested to return the prophet to earth. Isaiah said: 'Why so soon? I have only been here two hours.'

The angel said: 'Not two hours, but thirty-two years . . . do not be sad, you will not be an old man.' "

This seems like the well-documented effects of time-dilation. If Isaiah had been on board a spacecraft capable of travelling near to the speed of light, time for him would move slowly compared with someone back on Earth. Einstein was one of the first scientists to predict this curious effect, and in the 1970s an experiment was carried out to prove the time-dilation theory. Two highly accurate atomic clocks were synchronized so they both had the same read-out, right down to the last decimal place. One clock was put on the supersonic airliner Concord, and flown from London to New York and back, while the other clock remained on the ground.

When the read-outs from the clock on the ground and the travelled clock were compared, it was seen that the clock from Concord had somehow lost microseconds. In short, with a risk of oversimplification, the faster an object moves through space, the slower it moves through time compared to a stationary object. Simple extrapolation and a modicum of mathematics will tell us that if you were to embark on a two-hour trip into outer space at a speed close to the velocity of light, you would return to find your friends and family decades older than when you left, while you would only be two hours older. This complicated effect was only predicted by the Theory of Relativity in the twentieth century, so how did the author of the Vision of Isaiah know about it?

As we have seen from our brief tour of the Old Testament, there is more to the biblical tales of pillars of clouds and whirlwinds. If they were contemporary accounts of visitations from extra-terrestrials, are there any similar accounts of this superior race's activity in the New Testament? That question is the subject of the next chapter.

UFOs in the New Testament

The gospel of St Matthew opens the New Testament with a frightening visit from a sky-borne being who descends from the starry heavens to proclaim a sensational message to terrified shepherds attending their flocks: "Behold, a virgin shall be with child and shall bring forth a son, and they shall call his name Emmanuel, which being interpreted is, God is with us." This event (if it happened at all) would have occurred between four and eight years before the era which came to bear Christ's name: Anno Domini – which is Latin for "in the year of our Lord".

Like his death and alleged resurrection, the birth of Jesus of Nazareth is cloaked in mystery. Just as the pillar of light led the Israelites through the wilderness to the Promised Land in the Old Testament, another enigmatic object served to guide those with wisdom to the birthplace of a carpenter's son in the New Testament. The ufological angle certainly seems to fit the account of this guiding light in the sky which is depicted on millions of Christmas cards all over the world. It is sung about in carols, it shines down from the tops of Christmas trees, and foil imitations of it twinkle over Nativity scenes. But just what was the Star of Bethlehem? Is it just a myth or did the starry messenger really exist in the skies of Judaea? For centuries, theologians and scientists have argued over their interpretations of the celestial event, which was recorded only by the apostle Matthew. In the second chapter of his gospel, Matthew tells us: "When Jesus was born in Bethlehem of Judaea in the days of Herod the King, behold, there came wise men from the East to Jerusalem, saying, 'Where is he who is born King of the Jews? For we have seen his star in the East and have come to worship him.'"

According to Matthew, Herod summons the mysterious Wise Men and tells them that if they should find the new-born king, they must divulge the child's whereabouts to him. Later, the Wise Men see the guiding star in the East and it leads them to the stable where the babe Jesus is sleeping.

In the seventeenth century the great German astronomer Kepler sent shockwaves through the Christian world when he suggested that the star the Wise Men had followed might have been nothing more than a conjunction of the planets Saturn and Jupiter. However, it is now known that no such conjunctions were visible in the Holy Land during the period St Matthew mentions, which historical scholars estimate to be 4 or 5 BC. After Kepler's heretical attempts to explain away the Star of Bethlehem as a natural phenomenon, many other scientists also tried to formulate theories to rationalize the stellar oddity. Halley's Comet was blamed but astronomers have calculated that the comet had already visited and left the heavens before Christ's birth. Another theory proposed that the star that hovered over the stable was actually a distant star which had exploded – or gone supernova, to use astronomers' jargon. Such explosions do occur from time to time and can remain visible in the sky for weeks, even during the daytime.

Now, it is recorded in ancient Chinese texts that such a supernova explosion did occur . . . around 4 BC. Chinese astronomers of the time recorded that a star flared up in the constellation of Aquila the Eagle, just below the bright star

Altair. What's more, it has been computed that to anyone standing at the South Gate of Jerusalem the brilliant star would appear to be over Bethlehem.

The American scientist A. J. Morehouse, who discovered the Chinese record, therefore believes that the Star of Bethlehem is still in the sky, but it is very faint.

Opponents of Morehouse's theory have pointed out that the exploding star of 4 BC occurred too late to be associated with the birth of Christ. Also, such a bright spectacle in the night sky would hardly have gone unnoticed by Herod and the other inhabitants of Judaea. Moreover, a supernova cannot hover in the sky as the Star of Bethlehem did over the manger.

Just as enigmatic as the Star are the Wise Men who followed it. Matthew simply states that they were from the East without specifying what countries they came from, and, contrary to popular belief, St Matthew does not actually say there were three of them. In fact, according to the early versions of the Nativity in medieval times, there were 12 Wise Men!

Whatever their number, most biblical scholars agree that the Wise Men were students of astrology, which was very popular among the Jewish community at the time. This theory was strengthened by the discovery of the Dead Sea Scrolls in 1947. Among the time-worn Hebrew and Aramaic texts – some of which date back to the birth of Christ – there are astrological charts depicting signs of the Zodiac, and mystical texts referring to the influence of the stars and the planets on the newly born. The scrolls also mention an unnamed individual who lived at the time of the Jesus who was known as the Teacher of Righteousness.

In the end, despite all the conjecture and historical research, we are still no nearer to uncovering the truth about the most mysterious herald in history – the Star of Bethlehem. If it wasn't a comet, nor a planetary conjunction, then surely there is only one logical hypothesis which can explain a light in the sky that behaves as if it is controlled by an intelligence: the Star of Bethlehem was a spacecraft; and if we can accept this explanation, we must ask – What was it doing hovering over the stable where Jesus was born?

The Christians have longed claimed that the arrival of Christ at Bethlehem had been predicted centuries before. In the Book of Micah 5:2 (written in the eighth century BC), it states that the Messiah (Hebrew for "the anointed one") would be born in Bethlehem, and in the Book of Isaiah 7:14 (also written in the eighth century BC) scripture specifically asserts that the person who will come as God's representative in the flesh would be born of a virgin. In the Book of Malachi 3:1 it is foretold that someone would go ahead of the Messiah to prepare the way. Most Christians have interpreted this as being John the Baptist. In Isaiah 9:1–2 it predicts that the Messiah would live and work around Galilee in a northern province remote from the centres of power, and that he would heal people. The Book of Zechariah foretells that the long-awaited Messiah, who would restore his people to a position of power and prosperity which they enjoyed under David and Solomon, would ride into Jerusalem humbly, on a donkey, and not on the war-horse of a military conqueror. In that same book a passage eerily maintains that the Messiah will be betrayed to his enemies for 30 pieces of silver. This prophecy seems to have been fulfilled by one Judas Iscariot.

There are more amazingly accurate predictions in Psalms, the nineteenth book of the Old Testament. Crucifixion – execution by nailing the condemned to a cross – was unknown to the Hebrews until the Romans came to power; yet in Psalm 22 there is a graphic description of the way the Messiah will be put to death, hundreds of years before Jesus of Nazareth was crucified. The passages say his hands and feet will be pierced, and that his executioners would mock him and gamble for his clothes. All of the incidents foretold by the Jewish scriptures, if applied to the life of Jesus, are astoundingly more accurate than the prophecies of Nostradamus.

Little is known about the early days of Jesus, especially the circumstances of his conception and birth. Traditionally, 25 March is held as the Day of the Annunciation, when the angel Gabriel announced to Mary that she would give birth to the Messiah. Curiously, in May 1999 Israeli historians researching ancient copies of the Apocrypha told the newspaper *National Midnight Star* that one translation of the

Virgin Mary's conception after a visitation from God described a chilling tale which sounded very similar to the accounts of people who had undergone gynaecological examinations in UFO abduction experiences. Reporters pressed the codex researchers to comment further on their intriguing claims, but the historians were evidently advised by the religious authorities to withhold further interpretations of the time-worn texts.

Even the hardened scientific sceptic, philosopher and historian H. G. Wells – who was not at all impressed by Christianity – once wrote of Jesus: "Christ is the most unique person in history. No one can write a history of the human race without giving first and foremost place to the penniless teacher from Nazareth."

In this age of scientific and medical marvels, it is possible through the techniques of artificial insemination to produce a child in the womb of a woman who is a virgin. In Japan and America scientists are making rapid progress with the development of artificial wombs which will allow the development of a fertilized ovum into an embryo and finally a nine-month-old baby. These "baby hatcheries" were described in 1932 within the pages of Aldous Huxley's far-sighted novel *Brave New World*, although Huxley confidently assured his shocked readers that cloning and mechanical wombs were three centuries away. In 1962, the year before Huxley died, the English physicist Francis Crick and American biochemist James Watson shared the Nobel Prize in medicine and physiology for discovering the double-helix structure of DNA – the genetic code of the human body. Five years later the British biologist John B. Gurdon cloned a South African clawed frog. Eleven years after that, British doctor Patrick Steptoe and his colleagues overcame the problem of sterility in women by producing the first test-tube baby outside the womb in July 1978. Twenty years after that, scientists had cloned sheep and higher mammals, and it was recently claimed that cloned humans in America and Korea had been allowed to develop to an embryonic stage before being destroyed.

Envisage, then, a superior race from another world steering the affairs of mankind. This higher race implants the embryo of Jesus into a peasant woman's womb so she becomes a surrogate mother. Jesus is born in an obscure village, and as he grows he probably becomes aware of the psychic superhuman talents he possesses. He works in a carpenter's shop in Nazareth until he is 30, then embarks on a three-year mission which will sow the seeds for the most momentous sociological and philosophical revolution in world history. Immediately the authorities realize that he is not an average prophet, for he raises three dead people: a young girl (Matthew 9:18–19), a young man (Luke 7: 11–15), and a man named Lazarus (John 11:1–44). The Jews believed that only God could control the weather to induce storms and stop them, so they were amazed when Jesus stopped a storm (Matthew 8:23–7). There are also accounts of Jesus (or Yeshua, as he was known) walking on water, exorcising evil spirits from possessed people, healing the sick and crippled, restoring the sight of blind people, turning water into wine, and feeding the multitudes (on two different occasions).

All of these supernatural acts proved Jesus was no ordinary human being, and he himself said the kingdom or realm he came from was "not of this world". He also maintained that his father was in the heavens, and he spent many lengthy periods in the vast isolation of the Sinai Desert, where he may have received the instructions for his revolutionary programme to change civilization. Perhaps this was the rendezvous point for meeting his extra-terrestrial kin. There are many instances of luminous objects descending above Jesus and shining rays towards him. All of these incidents are interpreted as religious omens among the primitive people of the time, but what can we make of them? For example, in Luke 3: 21–2, it is recorded: "Now, when all the people were baptized, it came to pass, that Jesus was also being baptized and praying, the heaven was opened. And the Holy Ghost descended in a bodily shape like a dove upon him."
What was this thing which resembled a luminous dove? We are none the wiser now. Nor can we explain the significance of the following episode, mentioned in detail in Matthew 17: 6–9:

> Jesus too, Peter and John and James went up into a
> mountain to pray. And as he prayed, the fashion of his

countenance was altered, and his rainment was white and glistening. And behold, there talked with him two men, which were Moses and Elias; who appeared in glory, and spake of his decease which he should accomplish at Jerusalem. But Peter and they that were with him were heavy with sleep: and when they were awake, they saw his glory, and the two men that stood with him. And it came to pass as they departed from him, Peter said unto Jesus, Master, it is good for us to be here; and let us make three tabernacles; one for thee, and one for Moses, and one for Elias: not knowing what he said. While thus he spake, there came a cloud, and overshadowed them: and they feared as they entered into the cloud. And there came a voice out of the cloud, saying, This is my beloved Son: hear him. And when the disciples heard it, they fell on their faces and were sore afraid. And Jesus came and touched them and said Arise and be not afraid. And when they had lifted up their eyes, they saw no man, save Jesus only. And as they came down from the mountain, Jesus charged them, saying, Tell the vision to no man until the Son of Man be risen again from the dead. And they kept it close, and told no man in those days of the things which they had seen.

Why did Jesus ask the disciples to keep quiet about the incident? How did Peter, John and James know the figures with Jesus were Moses and Elias, who had lived a thousand years before they were born? And what mysterious process was going on during the miraculous transformation of Jesus, which made his face and clothes "brighter than the sun"? What mysterious forces were at work on the summit of that mountain? Was Jesus being "recharged" by some energy source hidden in the cloud which hovered overhead? So many intriguing but, alas, unanswered questions.

Of course, the ultimate proof that Jesus was no ordinary Earthman came with his physical resurrection, which was mentioned in all four gospels and referred to in Corinthians 15:3–7. Mark relates that Jesus of Nazareth was scourged and treated brutally by the Roman guards, who crowned him with thorns, mocked him, then crucified him at the ninth hour

(3 p.m.) of the day. Jesus had to be buried before the sabbath began at 6 p.m., so that his corpse should not profane the holy day. A secret disciple of Jesus, named Joseph of Arimathea, bravely asked the Roman governor Pontius Pilate if he could bury Christ. Pilate was surprised that Jesus had died so quickly, and after checking with his centurion to see if Christ had indeed passed away, he allowed Joseph to take charge of the preacher's body.

Joseph wrapped the corpse of Christ in a fine linen; this cloth was afterwards rumoured to feature a miraculous imprint of the body of Christ, and some think the burial cloth is still extant as the famous Turin Shroud. The shrouded body of Jesus was hurriedly laid in a sepulchre hewn out of a rock, and the entrance to this tomb was sealed with an enormous stone. There can be no doubt that at this point Jesus was not faking death, although some researchers have claimed that he had not died on the cross, but had only swooned. But the facts say this was not possible, for a Roman scourging was so terrible and traumatic that many victims died before being crucified. Then there is the graphic account of John, who says a soldier named Longinius thrust a spear into Jesus' side while he was on the cross and that "blood and water" came out. This is a medically accurate description of what happens when the pericardium is pierced, and such a wound is always fatal.

Shortly before dawn on the Sunday morning following the Jewish sabbath (which is a Saturday), Mary Magdalene went to visit the tomb where Jesus was laid to rest, and noticed that the heavy stone had been rolled back. In John 20: 1–9 it states:

> The first day of the week cometh Mary Magdalene early, when it was yet dark, unto the sepulchre, and seeth the stone taken away from the sepulchre. Then she runneth, and cometh to Simon Peter, and to the other disciple, whom Jesus loved, and saith unto them, They have taken away the Lord out of the sepulchre, and we know not where they have laid him. Peter therefore went forth, and that other disciple, and came to the sepulchre. So they ran both together: and the other disciple did outrun Peter, and came first to the sepulchre. And he, stooping down,

*and looking in, saw the linen clothes lying, yet went he
not in. Then cometh Simon Peter, following him, and
went into the sepulchre, and seeth the linen clothes lie,
And the napkin that was about his head, not lying with
the linen clothes, but wrapped together in a place by
itself. Then went in also that other disciple, which first
came unto the sepulchre, and he saw, and believed. For
as yet they knew not the scripture that he must rise again
from the dead.*

The events of that first Easter morning soon came together
like a mystical jigsaw puzzle. The Jewish council, the
Sanhedrin, trembled when they heard the news of the empty
tomb. They heard strange accounts of how in the early hours
of that Sunday morning a being in "snow-white clothes" with
a light on its head as bright as lightning had descended from
the low oppressive clouds and terrified the Roman soldiers
guarding the tomb of Christ into stupefaction. This strange
figure (assumed by the Jewish priests to be a heavenly being,
an angel of some order) proceeded to push away the stone
blocking the tomb's entrance with superhuman might. It was
later revealed that two unearthly-looking men dressed in
white clothes had been seen at the entrance of the tomb by
Mary Magdalene, Mary the mother of James, and Salome.
The three women said one of the eerie figures said: "Be not
affrighted; ye seek Jesus of Nazareth, which was crucified. He
is not here . . . he is risen. But go your way, tell his disciples
and Peter that he goeth before you into Galilee; there shall ye
see him, as he said unto you."

The enigmatic men in white later vanished into the skies as
mysteriously as they had appeared. Did they return to some
mothership in Earth orbit? – the ship that had been
interpreted as the Star of Bethlehem?

The resurrected Jesus later reappeared to his faithful
disciples, but seems to have undergone a "transfiguration".
Although he was apparently solid and tangible enough to eat
food and to allow the disciples to touch his wounds, doors did
not have to be opened before he could enter a room full of
people. He bi-located on several occasions (allowed himself
to be seen in several places at once simultaneously), and

seemed slightly different. Some people who had been familiar with him prior to the crucifixion did not recognize him immediately; in fact even Mary Magdalene mistook him for a gardener. Luke mentions this intriguing facial metamorphosis when he relates the two disciples' walk to Emmaus, seven miles outside Jerusalem. Christ joins them but says "Their eyes were holden that they should not know him." The disciples told the bemused Jesus about the crucifixion and of the empty tomb he had been laid in. Jesus then revealed his identity by expounding the scriptures concerning himself. The overawed disciples shared their evening meal with him, and he blessed them and broke the bread. He subsequently performed a vanishing act, and the disciples hurried back to Jerusalem to tell of their emotional and heart-lifting encounter with the risen Christ. The 11 Apostles, meanwhile, were giving their accounts of meetings with the returned Jesus, when their Lord suddenly appeared in their midst.

After the ghost-like Christ had instilled faith into his followers, he is said to have "ascended" into heaven. The Christian Bible doesn't go into any detail about what this ascension was like, but we possess thought-provoking accounts of the event in the Apocryphon Jacobi, and the Epistle of the Apostles. These books, which were suppressed by the Church for centuries, give us a full description of the Ascension. They tell us that at the ridge east of Jerusalem, known as the Mount of Olives, where Jesus often prayed and meditated in the evenings, there was a great stir. The resurrected Jesus of Nazareth was talking to his followers, when his words were interrupted by a clap of thunder and lightning. The roll of rumbling thunder shook the entire mountain, and a chariot descended through the clouds. The Jews of old called this chariot a *merkaba* – a celestial vehicle of the angels which is mentioned in the ancient Kabbals. The texts describe how Jesus entered the *merkaba* and was welcomed by the angels within, who were dressed in "white apparel". One of these heavenly beings said to the apostles: "Men of Galilee, why stand ye gazing up into heaven? This same Jesus, which is taken from you into heaven, shall so come in like manner as ye have seen him go to heaven." And the Apostles watched in wonderment as Jesus rose higher and higher into the heavens until he and his angels in the *merkaba* were lost to sight.

Today, the Christians assert that Jesus was God incarnate, while the Jews maintain that he was merely a prophet. Whoever Jesus was, there can be no doubt that he was a most extraordinary, and possibly extra-terrestrial, being. How else can we explain the miracles he performed, the transfiguration, and eventually regeneration after being executed on the cross? Then there is the futuristic philosophy Jesus propounded, which predates the doctrines of Communism formulated by Marx and Engels by centuries. Jesus said that it would be easier for a camel to pass through the eye of a needle than for a rich man to enter the Kingdom of Heaven, and he also said that in his Kingdom the underdog and the wretched would be put first (which enraged the self-righteous Pharisees). He told his astonished followers that pacificsm was the only way to live; if their enemy should strike them, they must turn the other cheek, ready to be hit again. This seemed to be the exact opposite of the Old Testament's suggestion of "an eye for an eye" and more in keeping with Gandhi's philosophy of non-violence which lay 19 centuries in the future. Jesus also preached that those who wished to follow him would have to love their enemies and pray for them, and abandon all worldly wealth. The strange philosophy of Christ seems so alien to the selfish nature of the human race; was this because Christ was an alien? Because the whole subject of Jesus and his teachings is still surrounded with so many blind dogmas and taboos, it is difficult to see beyond the religion and analyze just who or what the carpenter from Nazareth really was. The extra-terrestrial interpretation does not denigrate Christ in any way, but shows him in another, wider role in the cosmos. The next time you gaze up into the night sky at the stars, consider that somewhere out there, for all we know, an interstellar Christ may be preaching the word of Yahveh to the multitudes of some alien world.

Ten Reports of Historical UFOs and Possible Extraterrestrial Visits

1. In the Hunan Province of China there are rocks with 47,000-year-old carvings of cylindrical objects flying through the sky above a hunting scene.

2. On 21 September 1271, in Japan, a priest was spared from being beheaded when a gleaming silvery ovoid-shaped craft hovered over the scene of the intended execution and began to pulsate with a blinding light. The executioners panicked and fled, and the priest was released in the ensuing hysteria.

3. On 22 March 1870, Captain F. W. Banner and his entire crew on the British ship Lady of the Lake, sighted a circular vaporous object with a "semi-circle divided into four parts, and a central shaft running from the centre of the disk and extending far outward and curving backward". The disc-shaped craft moved against the strong winds and played tag with the ship until nightfall.

4. On 24 January 1878, Texan farmer John Martin dropped his tools in utter amazement when he saw a dark circular craft whizzing through the air across his farm. The strange flying machine was so enormous that its shadow covered the entire field Farmer Martin was toiling in. When local journalists asked Martin to describe the strange ship in detail, he said it had the "shape of a saucer". This was almost 70 years before Kenneth Arnold would christen modern UFOs "flying saucers" in his description of the nine strange objects he saw flying over America's Cascade Mountains in 1947.

5. An ancient cave drawing known as "The White Lady of Brandenburg" in South Africa depicts a lady dressed in a tight-fitting costume and wearing gloves. Behind her in the scene is a modern-looking man wearing a helmet with a tube in his hand. Their identities have never been established, but they were apparently revered by a tribe thousands of years ago.

6. Throughout the 1700s, settlers in America learned from the Indians that before the white man came there were men from ☞

the stars who paralyzed their people with a power which came from a tube. These star people even married some of the Indian women and took them into the skies.

7. At Alençon in France, in June 1790, peasants watched in awe as a huge red metal sphere descended from the sky and crashed into farmland. Shortly afterwards a man in close-fitting overalls crawled out of the globe and shouted out something in a language no one present understood. He then ran off into a nearby wood, and the peasants scattered when they heard a rumbling sound emanating from the sphere. Seconds later the spherical craft exploded with a muffled sound and created a miniature mushroom cloud. Pieces of shrapnel from the craft made a sizzling sound in the grass and disintegrated. A thorough search for the man from the globe began, but he was never found.

8. In 1851 a man calling himself "Vorin" was found wandering the streets of Frankfurt-an-der-Oder in Germany. When the authorities asked the stranger where he was from, he told them he came from "Laxaria", a country "on the continent of Sakria". Vorin was shown a map of the world and asked to point to his unheard-of country, but the enigmatic traveller smiled and said: "It isn't on this world." Vorin – whoever he was – was dismissed as a crank, but those who had conversed with him said he was a strange man who talked about planets he'd visited.

9. In 1905 a young man who was arrested in Paris for stealing a loaf was found to speak an unknown language, and after a lengthy conversation through sign language and drawings the thief managed to convey that he was from a "far-off place" called Lizbia. Thinking he meant Lisbon, the man was shown a map of Portugal, and a Portuguese man was brought in to talk with him. But it was soon established that the young offender was not from Lisbon, and the unidentified language the youth spoke was not an invented babble either; it had all the consistent syntactical rules of a language similar to Esperanto. Eventually, the man from an unknown nation was released – never to be seen again.

10. At Mexico in April 1883 Professor Jose Bonilla, Director ☞

of the Astronomical Observatory at Zacatecas was observing sunspots when a formation of several hundred circular objects crossed the sun's disc. No sooner had Bonilla recovered from this surprise when another formation crossed the solar disc on the following day. Professor Bonilla even managed to record the UFOs on a camera fitted to the telescope. This was the first time UFOs had been photographed.

Star Trekkers of the Middle Ages

Jerome Cardan (1501–76) was a noted Italian mathematician, naturalist, physician and philosopher. He was Professor of Mathematics at Padua and of Medicine at Pavia and Bologna. In his lifetime he wrote over a hundred treatises on physics, mathematics, astronomy, astrology, history, ethics, semantics, dialectics and natural history. He was even considered to be an equal to his great contemporary Leonardo Da Vinci. On the evening of 13 August 1491, at Milan, Jerome Cardan's father, Facius, had just completed his evening devotions when something strange took place. The nature of this recorded incident is still argued over today, and continues to defy an explanation. Seven men in strange uniforms materialized in his room. Facius recorded the eerie episode:

> *When I had completed my customary rituals, about the twentieth hour, seven men appeared to me, dressed in silken garments resembling togas, with glittering boots. They also sported a type of armour and beneath this armour one could see purple undergarments of an extraordinary splendour and beauty. Two of them seemed to be of a more superior rank than the others. The one with the most commanding air had a face that was tanned dark red. They said they were 40 years old, but none of them seemed more than 30. I asked who they were, and they replied that they were a kind of men, made of air and*

subject like ourselves to birth and death. There life-span was longer than our own and could extend as long as three centuries. When questioned on the immortality of the soul, they replied that nothing survived. When asked why they did not reveal to men the treasures of their knowledge, they replied that a special law imposed the heaviest penalties on them in the event that they did this.

The seven strangely clad men stayed in the company of Facius Cardan for three hours, and during this time one of the visitors, who seemed to be "their chief", heretically denied that God had made the world for all eternity. On the contrary, the leader of the visitants added, the world was created at each instant, so that if God were to "become discouraged" the planet would perish immediately. The seven men suddenly dematerialized, leaving the shocked Facius alone with an unbelievable tale to record.

In the Middle Ages the seven visitors were quickly branded as angels, but Cardan asked why angels would deny the immortality of the soul and explain the existence of the world with a sort of continuous-creation theory. In that case, the narrow-minded medieval thinkers reasoned that the unearthly guests had been demons. A similar religious interpretation was applied to explain the identity of three men "in bright apparel" who appeared in the year AD 696 to King Sebbi of the East Saxons as he lay on his sickbed. The men were dressed identically to the seven visitors who would later appear to Facius Cardan, right down to the glittering boots and metallic purple body armour. Three days after King Sebbi reported the apparitions, he passed away in his bed. It was assumed in those days that the mysterious trio had been deathbed hallucinations. Who were the seven visitors? Were they time-travellers from some future age, visiting the Middle Ages? Or could the seven outlandish-looking men and their "chief" have been a landing party of extra-terrestrial explorers who had beamed down from some starship – not unlike the *USS Enterprise* in the *Star Trek* TV series? We may know more about the mysterious visitors one day.

The "Devil of Eudora" Mystery

In June 1999 the US government declassified files on a weird incident which took place at the Arkansas town of Eudora in August 1949. According to the declassified but still partially

Ancient statute of god "Malachim"

censored files, in August 1949 a strange-looking creature described as a "devil" was captured in desert land near Eudora by the town's sheriff and deputy. The weird creature was human-shaped, 5 feet 3 inches in height, with grey scaly skin, a large globular head and enormous dark eyes. The sheriff had the creature locked up in the cells and wired government officials in Dallas to come and look at the animal, but before anyone came to look at the creature, a mob in the town stormed the jail, and after holding the deputy as hostage, they forced the sheriff to let the so-called devil out of its cell. The sheriff did, and the unfortunate creature was impaled with a hayfork, shot to death by the mob, then had kerosene dowsed over it before being torched. The crowd was led by a self-ordained minister who convinced the people of Eudora that the weird-looking creature from the desert was a demonic lackey of Satan. For years an American country singer named Tony Joe White claimed that his family had witnessed the strange incident at Eudora, but it was generally assumed that the story was a legend. Now several UFO investigation groups are looking into the incredible story.

The Modern UFO Era
From 1947 to the 21st century

As we have seen in the earlier chapters, UFOs seem to have been around for thousands of years, but ufologists have noticed a marked increase in UFO activity since 1947. That year is an important milestone in the study of UFOs, because it was the year of the Roswell Incident, when it was alleged that an extra-terrestrial craft crashed in the New Mexico Desert, and a month earlier in that same year the term "flying saucer" entered the English language when an American pilot had a close encounter with nine flying objects in the skies over Washington State. The pilot was Kenneth Arnold. On 24 June 1947, shortly before 3 p.m., Arnold was flying his Callair light plane over the Cascade Mountains at an altitude of 9200 feet, when he was startled by a tremendously bright flash ahead of him. Arnold quickly assumed the light had been

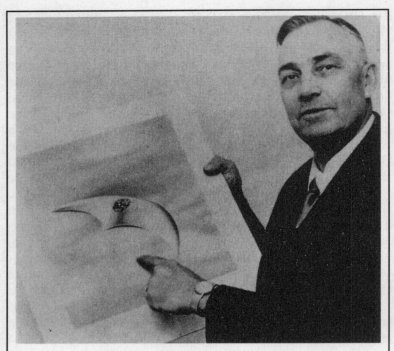

Kenneth Arnold with drawing of craft seen over Mt Rainier, 1947

reflected off an aircraft somewhere in the vicinity, and he looked around for any craft in case he was on a collision course. Behind the light aircraft there was a DC4 airliner flying at an altitude of 5000 feet, but to the north, Arnold was surprised to see nine peculiar-looking aircraft closing in on him at a frighteningly high speed (which he estimated to be around 1700 miles per hour). The objects were flying in tight formation with the leading craft – which was crescent shaped – slightly higher than the other eight, which were all lens-shaped. Arnold watched the futuristic-looking aerial convoy for two and a half minutes until they vanished into the distance, south of the peak of Mount Adams, towards Oregon.

Hours after the encounter with the UFOs, Kenneth Arnold was quizzed over the incident by journalist Bill Bequette of the *East Oregonian* newspaper. Asked to describe the flying objects, Arnold remarked that they had flown across the sky the way a flat stone or a saucer skipped across water if thrown at a certain angle. Bequette's imagination was fired by the mention of a "saucer" and within seconds one of the most popular and controversial terms of all time was born: "flying saucer".

Arnold later wrote a letter to a commanding general at a US airbase saying that he believed the UFOs he had seen over the Cascades had not been extra-terrestrial spaceships at all, but advanced experimental military aircraft financed by the Pentagon, but the US government denied the claim. However, there was a creeping paranoid suspicion in the American press that the flying saucers were just another secret weapon being developed by the US military. After all, just a couple of years before, no one had suspected that city-vaporizing atom bombs were being perfected in utmost secrecy at Los Alamos in New Mexico.

But seven months after the Kenneth Arnold sighting, a terrifying fatal encounter with a UFO took place in the airspace over Kentucky, and on this occasion the victim was a member of the US military.

The drama began on 7 January 1948 at 1.20 p.m. A flight of four National Guard P-51 Mustang aircraft were flying from Marietta, Georgia, to Standiford Field, Kentucky, when the flight leader Captain Thomas Mantell received a curious order from Colonel F. Hix, the commander of the nearby Godman airfield base: he was to investigate an unidentified craft hovering over their military installation. Mantell and the other pilots soon saw the UFO; in fact it was so large and bright, it was being seen by people over a 100-mile area. The enormous disc-shaped ship was hanging in the sky over Godman airfield base at an altitude of about 25,000 feet.

By 2.45 p.m. Captain Mantell and his flight of Mustangs roared into the skies over the military airbase, ready to confront the menacing spaceship. Thousands of feet below, Colonel Hix and scores of military personnel watched with baited breath to see how the UFO would react. The giant ship just remained stationary in the air as the P-51s climbed to challenge it. One by one the planes were forced to turn back as they hit 15,000 feet, simply because the craft were not equipped with an internal oxygen supply.

All of the planes landed at Godman air base except Captain Mantell's. Mantell was determined to get a closer look at the UFO, and he continued to climb to 22,000 feet, but the saucer-shaped craft suddenly started to ascend after giving off a brief flash of light. The brave captain radioed an intriguing message to the Godman air base. He commented: "It appears to be a metallic object! Tremendous in size . . . directly ahead and slightly above. I am trying to get closer for a better look."

Minutes later, radio contact with Captain Mantell was lost. The glowing UFO moved upwards and out of the atmosphere at such a speed that it was hard for the human eye to follow it.

The anxious radio operator at the air base transmitted several messages to Mantell but received no reply, so a search was launched for the wreckage of Mantell's Mustang plane. Just after 5 p.m. the wreckage of the P-51 Mustang was found scattered over half a mile of farmland near Franklin, Kentucky. Mantell's body was still in the cockpit. Some reports said the wreckage was riddled with strange tiny holes. The US Air Force and Naval Intelligence launched an investigation into the incident, and later concluded that Captain Thomas Mantell had died from anoxia (oxygen starvation) while chasing the planet Venus. This ludicrous explanation was later changed: they stated that Mantell had been chasing a weather balloon.

The microfilm copy of the joint Naval and Air Force investigation was mysteriously damaged, although some heavily censored documents referring to the inquiry were declassified in 1985. Everyone who had served under Captain Mantell was outraged by the claim that he had died chasing a mirage. All who knew Mantell said he was much too good a pilot to be depicted as some naive aeronautical idiot. The inquiry's verdict, then, smelt like a blatant cover-up. What's more, there were rumours circulating in America that six months earlier in New Mexico the US government had also covered up another UFO incident, only this time the casualties had been the "ufonauts" themselves. These rumours were referring to the famous Roswell Incident which has been the subject of much debate over the years.

The basic "facts" of this alleged event are as follows. At 9.50 p.m. on 2 July 1947 a luminous discus-shaped craft was seen flying at high speed in a north-westerly direction over Roswell, New Mexico. The next day the wreckage of what seemed to have been a flying saucer was found by Grady Barnett, a civil engineer with the US Soil Conservation Service working in Socorro, New Mexico. He was situated in a desert area near the plains of San Agustin, 250 miles west of Roswell, when he had noticed sunlight glinting off some object in the distance. Barnett thought it was a crashed plane, but when he arrived at the crash scene, he saw that it was an unfamiliar "metallic disc-shaped object", 25 to 30 feet in diameter. As Barnett cautiously approached the craft, he came upon a group of sombre-faced archaeology students from the University of Pennsylvania who were standing about the wreckage. They had also noticed the glinting object. What Barnett and the students came upon at that scene of the crashed UFO sent shivers up their spines. Scattered about the craft were bodies, but they were not human corpses. These bodies were about three feet in height, and had large overdeveloped globular heads. Their eyes were very small and oddly spaced, and the bodies were devoid of hair. The clothing they wore was one-piece and grey in colour, but there were no seams, fasteners or zippers on the clothing.

As Barnett and the students were inspecting the crashed spacecraft, a truck roared up to the unearthly scene and a stern-looking military officer got out of it. He told Barnett and the students that the Army was on its way and that they would have to leave the area immediately. Within minutes, more military personnel arrived and a cordoning-off of the crash site began. Barnett and the university students were warned not to speak to anybody about what they had seen and that it was their patriotic duty to remain silent.

On that same day 75 miles north-west of Roswell, local rancher William "Mac" Brazel and his son and daughter found fragments of a foil-like material that couldn't be dented – even with a sledgehammer. A reporter from the local radio station heard of Mac Brazel's discovery and tape-recorded an interview with him – before going to the military. Soon afterwards, Brazel was held for questioning by the Army while troops invaded his farm for a thorough search which soon located the strange foil. Local residents were at first bemused to hear that rancher Brazel was being interrogated by the military, but when they tried to visit him to see if the rumours were true, they found all roads to the ranch blocked by troops who had thrown a cordon around the surrounding area. It was several days before Brazel was allowed home.

The local newspaper, the *Roswell Daily Record*, declared in banner headlines on Tuesday, 8 July 1947: "RAAF Captures Flying Saucer on Ranch in Roswell Region". The story was even backed up by the press statement from the Army Air Force which admitted that a "flying disc" had been examined at Roswell Army Airfield and was now in the hands of "higher headquarters". The full statement was:

> *The many rumours regarding the flying disc became a reality yesterday when the intelligence office of the 509th Bomb Group of the Eighth Air Force, Roswell Army Airfield, was fortunate enough to gain possession of a disc through the co-operation of one of the local ranchers and the sheriff's office of Chaves county. The flying object landed on a ranch near Roswell some time last week. Not having phone facilities, the rancher stored the disc until such time as he was able to contact the sheriff's office, who in turn notified Major Jesse Marcel, of the 509th Bomb Group Intelligence Office.*
>
> *Action was immediately taken and the disc was picked up at the rancher's home. It was inspected at the Roswell Army Airfield and subsequently loaned by Major Marcel to higher headquarters.*

Yet shortly afterwards, the Army backtracked on its statement and denied any disc had crashed at all. The Public Relations Officer at Roswell Army Airfield issued another statement declaring that the Roswell UFO had been a downed weather observation balloon.

Armies of ufologists have tried to get to the bottom of just what happened at Roswell in 1947, but the US government has never declassified the truth. The main current theory is that several UFOs of extra-terrestrial origin crashed at

Roswell, possibly after a freak mid-air collision. If this was so, did the military manage to salvage the wrecks of the UFOs? It has been noted how shortly after the Roswell Incident, the transistor was suddenly "discovered" by Shockley, Brattain and Bardeen at the Bell Laboratories in America. Not long after that came the maser and the laser. Were these genuine scientific discoveries or the fruits of advanced technology plundered from the remnants of the Roswell spaceships?

In the political turmoil of the post-war years, it was certainly obvious that a physically and economically ruined and bisected Germany – the old enemy – was not producing the mysterious flying saucers, so some in the West surmised that the Soviet Union was the culprit. It was public knowledge that the Americans and the Russians had captured German rocket installations at Peenemunde and Nordhausen in 1945, and had reaped the military benefits of the advanced technologies plundered there. Some military minds in America and Western Europe started considering the possibility that the Russians had captured experimental flying saucer weapons from the Germans, and were in the process of testing them out in preparation for World War III. This anxiety in high places regarding the UFOs is apparent in the questions that Sir Winston Churchill asked in a letter addressed to the Secretary of State for Air, dated 28 July 1952: "What does all this stuff about flying saucers amount to? What can it mean? What is the truth? Let me have a report at your convenience." The Air Ministry replied to Churchill's queries, stating that flying saucers didn't exist and could always be explained away as unusual effects of the weather, mistaken identifications of aircraft, or meteorological balloons, optical illusions, hoaxes, psychological delusions, etc.

Despite the assurance of the myopic debunkers at the Air Ministry, the UFOs continued to make spectacular appearances in the skies of the world, and, ironically, one of the earliest post-war UFO incidents occurred at RAF Dishforth, Yorkshire, which must have embarrassed the Air Ministry officials. The encounter took place in broad daylight on the morning of 19 September 1952 – during a NATO exercise.

At 10.53 a.m. Flight Lieutenant John Kilburn and four other witnesses were watching a Meteor jet crossing the sky, when Kilburn suddenly noticed a silvery disc-shaped craft following the military aircraft.

"What the hell's that?" he remarked.

One of the witnesses answered that the object could be a parachute, but that interpretation was soon disproved when the silver UFO stopped dead, started to rotate, then accelerated at a phenomenal supersonic speed towards the western skies until it was lost to sight. The whole incident lasted 15 seconds.

A couple of months earlier that year, on 19 July, there was a spate of mass UFO sightings directly over the American capital of Washington. Five ovoid-shaped lights zigzagged across the sky over the White House as thousands of citizens watched in a state of near panic. The same lights returned a fortnight later to buzz the White House, only this time they brought reinforcements; there were at least 12 of the nocturnal objects zooming back and forth over the capital. Three F-94 jet fighters were scrambled to confront the intruders but the mystery deepened when two of the pilots said they could see no UFOs, while the third one said a cluster of blue and white lights had travelled alongside him for 15 seconds before flying off at an incredible speed. The press called the incident the "Washington Invasion" but the intelligence service stepped in and ordered the newspaper editors to play down the episode in the interests of national security.

Two years later, in 1954, there were several unexplained intrusions into the skies over northern Britain. The first took place on 4 February when 14-year-old Stephen Darbishire spotted a circular craft with a conning tower hanging in the air at Coniston, Lancashire. Stephen was lucky enough to be carrying a camera at the time, and quickly snapped the UFO. When experts inspected the photograph, they were not only amazed to see that the camera had captured the image of the craft; they were highly intrigued at the resemblance the UFO bore to the spaceships described by the American contactee George Adamski.

Because the Coniston photograph was unusually clear as UFO photographs go, the sceptics denounced the whole incident as a schoolboy hoax. But later, the negative of the Coniston snap mysteriously disappeared, and has never been recovered.

Just a fortnight after the Coniston sighting, a man named Cedric Allingham claimed he had talked to a UFO pilot in Scotland near Lossiemouth, in the Grampian region. Allingham had been out walking when he encountered a human-looking entity who emerged from a landed space-ship which – according to his descriptions – looked just like the Adamski UFOs. Allingham discovered that the visitant could not speak English, so he resorted to drawing symbols on paper in an attempt to communicate with the stranger. The spaceman would nod or shake his head at Allingham's symbols, and from this primitive form of communication Allingham concluded that the "man" was from the planet Mars. The stranger later entered his spacecraft and took off, leaving Allingham with an unbelievable tale for the sceptics.

Another UFO incident took place north of the English border on 4 April 1957 when a radar station at RAF West Freugh tracked a large unidentified craft over western Scotland. Even today, the Ministry of Defence remains tight-lipped over details of the incident, but from information that leaked out at the time, it seems that as soon as the UFO was tracked at the Scottish air base, radar stations all over Britain were put on red alert and told to watch out for the myste-rious disc-shaped craft, which was flying over the UK at 60,000 feet. With tensions between NATO and the USSR running high, the UFO was probably regarded as an incoming nuclear missile from the Soviets. Luckily, at the last minute, the UFO changed course and quickly vanished from radar screens.

That same year, scores of people saw a huge circular object flitting across the skies of Wardle in Lancashire. Some who witnessed the craft at close quarters claimed they could see "egg-headed" figures staring at them through circular portholes. A couple of months after the sighting all of the witnesses were visited by a sinister man who claimed he was a government-appointed UFO investigator. The man warned all the witnesses to keep quiet about the UFO sighting, and when several of the people he had visited complained to their local MP, the government denied that they had any individuals appointed to look into flying saucers. It seems, therefore, that the man had been one of the infamous "men in black".

In the following year, questions were asked in the House of Commons. George Chetwynd MP grilled the Under-Secretary of State of Air about the number of UFO sightings during 1957. The Under-Secretary admitted that during the period in question there had been 54 UFO incidents. Meanwhile, the concept of flying saucers was capturing the imagination of the British public, but the scientists and astronomers of the day were keen to deflate the idea of space visitations. A majority of these same "experts" had denied the credibility of any form of space travel only two years previously. In 1956 Dr Richard Wooley, the Astronomer Royal, had declared that: "Space travel is utter bilge." A year after that remark, the Russians launched Sputnik I, the world's first artificial satellite, into orbit, opening the Space Age. Wooley later put his foot firmly in his mouth yet again when he confidently predicted that man would never set foot on the Moon – as NASA was designing the Saturn V rocket which would take Armstrong to the lunar surface in 1969.

With such a disastrous track record, it's amazing how "specialists" like Wooley had the audacity to try and explain away the UFO phenomenon.

Despite all the debunking attempts, the flying saucer sightings persisted. In October 1958, American, Soviet and British astronomers were shocked when their radio and optical telescopes picked up a massive unidentified inter-planetary object out in space, heading towards the Moon at 25,000 miles per hour. The object emitted radio signals but no one on Earth could interpret them.

The arrival of the 1960s heralded an unprecedented under-standing among mankind of Earth's place in the cosmos. On 8 April 1960, Project Ozma, the search for radio transmissions from other worlds, was launched. Frank Drake, a young American astronomer, and his team of dedicated scientists at the Greenbank Radio Astronomy Observatory pointed the 85-foot-wide receiver dish at Tau Ceti, a star 11 light-years distant which is very much like our own sun. For hours Drake and his team listened for any radio emissions from the star, but none came. Drake decided to train the radio telescope on another star. He chose Epsilon Eridani, another sun-like star, and this time he heard strange pulsing signals that nearly blasted the indicator needles off their dials. Drake and his team were ecstatic. They were hearing signals from another civilization. For three months Drake listened to the signals, as did the scientists of US Naval Research Laboratory, then suddenly, and inexplicably, Project Ozma was terminated and the military claimed that the signals Drake heard had originated from a US military experiment. Many scientists refused to buy this explanation and thought the claim was just an attempt at a cover-up.

On 16 May 1963 more extraterrestrial signals were received. This time the listener was US astronaut Gordon Cooper, orbiting the Earth in his Mercury space capsule. Cooper was chatting to ground control on a special frequency when weird-sounding voices broke in on the channel. Ground control taped the voices, and when they played the recording back, the language spoken could not be matched with any known language on Earth, despite extensive linguistical analysis. Similar alien chatter was later picked up by several Moon-bound astronauts during the Apollo programme.

In May 1964, a year after astronaut Cooper heard the strange alien conversation, another eerie extra-terrestrial manifestation took place, but this time it occurred on Earth. Jim Templeton looked into the viewfinder of his camera and focused on his young daughter Elizabeth, who was holding a posy as she sat in a picturesque field near the Solway Firth in Cumbria. Mr Templeton photographed his daughter, and later, when the film was developed, he was intrigued and a little shocked to see an enormous white space-suited figure standing behind his daughter in the photograph, apparently watching the proceedings through a dark visor. Mr Templeton knew there was no one else in the field as he took the snap, and was at a loss to explain the unearthly figure's presence. Could it be that the fast camera shutter somehow enabled the capture of the alien's otherwise invisible image? If that is the case, it is chilling to imagine there could be such unseen aliens in our midst at this very moment, shielded from our narrow range of vision by some invisibility device. These transparent observers could even be responsible for many of the reports of poltergeists and ghosts that we often read of.

In the early 1970s the short-lived euphoria of the manned Moon landings opened up many people's minds to the real possibility of interplanetary and interstellar travel. It was reasoned that if mankind could travel to the Moon just 66 years after the first sustained powered flight by the Wright brothers in 1903, then what could much older civilizations "out there" be capable of with their technology? Throughout the world in the 1970s, it seemed that even the leaders of nations and other political figures were becoming more open-minded to the possibility of alien life. In 1973 Jimmy Carter, the governor of the American state of Georgia (and future thirty-ninth President of the USA) was sitting on a veranda with over 20 other people after an official dinner at Thomastown, when a spectacular-looking UFO as wide as the Moon passed overhead. Everyone present, including Governor Carter, watched in amazement as the enormous globular glowing craft went through the colours of the spectrum. The UFO slowly moved off then vanished. Carter promised that if he became president, he would do everything in his power to declassify all the secret files the military and FBI were alleged to have on UFOs. Alas, when Carter became President of the United States in January 1977, he never kept his promise and even refused to discuss the UFO he had seen four years previously.

The year Carter saw the UFO over Georgia, NASA astronauts Jack Lousma, Alan Bean and Owen Garriot were orbiting the Earth 270 miles up in Skylab 2 when they saw and photographed a globular flashing object which tagged along with the space station for over ten minutes. UFOs in Earth orbit are continuing to be seen by the crews of the space shuttles which routinely circle the world nowadays.

Astronauts are highly trained people, so the debunkers are having a hard time citing the usual explanations to dismiss the UFOs, such as misinterpretations of the planet Venus, and so on. What's more, many UFOs encountered in low Earth orbit have been captured by the astronauts' video cameras – which rules out subjective hallucinations.

Sightings and encounters with UFOs are continuing into the 21st century on a daily basis. The UFO enigma is a mystery which is refusing to die, but there is a growing consensus among the ufologists of the world that contact with aliens will be made soon. How and when this will happen is anyone's guess, but it has been conjectured that the human race may now have advanced sufficiently to be accepted into a federation of worlds; a type of "Galactic United Nations". This alliance of intelligent life forms would be quite accustomed to the emergence of new civilizations and would probably be careful not to destroy an emergent civilization by contacting it too early in its evolution. There are many examples in our terrestrial history of primitive cultures being destroyed and endangered by contact with more advanced societies, so perhaps it is just the same on a grander cosmic scale. Could some of the UFOs seen in our skies today be probes from the Galactic Federation monitoring our progress? The idea of a celestial commonwealth should seem particularly appealing to us inhabitants of a planet burdened with an out-of-control population explosion, various ecological disasters, belligerent nations with newly acquired nuclear weapons and chemical warfare technology, an unprecedented global crime rate, morally bankrupt and drug-dependent youngsters, and many other modern ills and scourges. Perhaps in this new millennium we will witness the arrival on planet Earth of representatives of the Union of Worlds; teachers from the stars who could help us through the most dangerous period in the history of human civilization. It could happen in your lifetime.

The Inter-galactic Tramp?

In May 1955 a 74-year-old vagrant Charles Jevington went missing from the English village of Thursby on the outskirts of Carlisle. "Old Charlie", as he was affectionately known by the locals, was a well loved character who was highly independent, yet partial to having a pint of ale bought for him at two pubs in the area. The Cumbrian police searched almost 25 square miles looking for Charlie, but he was nowhere to be found. The last person to see him was Meg Crompton, the daughter of a local farmer. She saw him hurrying across a moonlit field towards woodland with a haversack on his back. Police combed the woods, but there wasn't a sign of Mr Jevington's presence anywhere. It was assumed that he had perhaps hitch-hiked back to relations he was thought to have in York, but when the police alerted their colleagues in that city, they could trace no such relatives. Then five years later, events took a sinister turn. In August 1960 Charles Jevington turned up alive and well at one of his local pubs near Thursby, and he had an amazing tale to tell the villagers. He explained his absence by revealing that he had been on board "one of those flying saucers" for the previous five years. To the bemused yet curious drinkers, the tramp explained how aliens had invited him aboard their ship for "a long ride" after he saw them collecting plants in the nearby woods. Old Charlie said he had accepted their invitation and claimed that the spacemen even waited for him while he went to collect his basic possessions. Charlie and the spacemen then embarked on an incredible adventure-filled voyage across the galaxy to many weird and wonderful worlds. An amateur astronomer present scoffed at the far-fetched tale and asked Charlie if he had "dropped in on Saturn" during his interstellar wanderings.

"Oh no, sir," the tramp replied, "we only passed Saturn and saw its beautiful rings." And Charlie added, "All those planets out there by Saturn have rings."

"That is utter nonsense," said the amateur stargazer, "Saturn is the only ringed planet in the solar system."

All the drinkers sneered at the old tramp, but he maintained that the other planets had rings too.

When Charles Jevington then declared that he was returning to space in a fortnight, the drinkers howled with laughter, and the embarrassed itinerant slammed his pint glass down on the counter and left the pub saying, "You'll all see! I shouldn't have come back!"

Meg Crompton, the farmer's daughter, ran after Mr Jevington and asked him to return to the pub so she could buy him a meal, but the tramp was too proud and pointed to the sky, saying, "I'm going back."

Strangely enough, a fortnight later, Old Charlie went missing once again. This time for good. Around the time of the disappearance, there were five sightings of a huge disc-shaped craft flying silently across the starry skies over Carlisle.

Charlie Jevington's claims were ridiculed because in 1960 it was thought that the planet Saturn was the only world in the solar system to have rings. But nowadays, thanks to the photographic data beamed back from NASA's interplanetary space probes, we now know that Jupiter, Uranus and Neptune also have rings around them; these rings are not as prominent as Saturn's, and are not visible to Earth tele-

Giants in the Park

This bizarre story hit the world's headlines in 1989. If the report had appeared in the pages of the sensationalist tabloid newspapers, the tale would have been dismissed as a ridiculous gimmick to win the circulation battles. But the following story came out of the old Soviet Union in October 1989, and the news agency that issued the strange report was Tass, which is still one of the most sedate and serious news agencies in the world. The incredible story it wired to Reuters and other Western news centres was intriguingly entitled: "Giants in the Park".

According to the detailed news report, in October 1989 an enormous saucer-shaped UFO caused widespread panic by landing in a suburban park at Voronezh, which lies some 300 miles south of Moscow. Scores of witnesses , including soldiers and ☞

policemen, bravely gathered around the towering silvery craft, expecting it to take off again. But the ship remained where it was – then a huge door like the door of an aircraft hanger slid open. What emerged from the ship was described as looking like something out of a Japanese science-fiction movie of the 1960s. Three enormous robot-like figures stepped out of the spaceship. People screamed and ran for their lives, because the figures were around 25 feet in height, and the ground of the park shook as the massive metallic boots of the visitors stomped down. One of the robots ran after a crowd of twelve people and some accounts say the mechanical titan stooped down and picked up one of the terrified witnesses. It was an old man of around 75, who screamed as enormous tubular fingers wrapped around him. A policeman who hid behind a tree said the robot raised the man to its visor and started scanning him with a laser-like beam. The gigantic machine then thundered across the park and a deafening unintelligible voice boomed out from the machine, as if it was talking to its robotic comrades.

Then something even more bizarre happened: a huge globe, about 12 feet in diameter, floated out of the spaceship. It was metallic purple in colour and had various lights and small aerials on its hull. The globe whizzed about the park and chased an Alsatian dog, which ran off yelping. The globe gave out a series of bleeps and made a warbling noise. Witnesses said it behaved like some sort of pet. The globe discharged a massive electrical bolt into a tree, destroying its trunk. One of the robots then seemed to shout out a command at ear-splitting volume, and the globe whizzed across the park and zoomed back into the UFO. Some accounts said that the old man who had been picked up by the unearthly machines was never seen again. Over the following months, the enormous UFO buzzed several military missile bases in Russia and some parts of western China. It is said that a Chinese tracking station almost interpreted the enormous UFOs' blip on radar as an incoming strategic bomber from Russia. Seconds before the Chinese were about to fire missiles at the intruder, it shot off into space at an estimated velocity of 7 miles per second! Even today in Russia, the people of Vornezh cower or run for cover when low-lying aircraft pass over their park – just in case it is the giants returning . . .

scopes, but they do exist. So what are we to make of the old vagabond's story? Was it just a lucky guess in a contrived tale? Or did Charles Jevington go on an interstellar trip across the galaxy? If he did, could he still be out there somewhere in the cosmos?

A Space Oddity

Anyone who has ever looked up at the thousands of stars in the night sky has probably wondered if our Earth is the only inhabited planet in the universe. The believers say there must be life out there because all those countless stars are distant suns with planets going round them, and even if the chances of finding an Earth-type world were one in a million, that would still mean that there were billions of planets out there teeming with life. But the sceptics say that if that is so, why haven't we received one signal from one of these inhabited worlds? A good point, but there have been many strange, seemingly intelligent signals from outer space which have reached Earth since the dawn of radio telecommunication, although scientists have always explained away these space oddities from the cosmos as radio static from the stars. And yet, scientists must have some hopes that we are not alone in the universe, because they have attached to several deep space probes gold and platinum plaques which carry diagrams of human beings and messages of goodwill. Radio messages have also been transmitted from Earth to any extra-terrestrial civilizations that might be listening in the depths of space. One such signal was transmitted in 1974 from the enormous Arecibo radio telescope which is 1000 feet in diameter and is built into a natural convex hollow of the terrain in Puerto Rico. The message from the Arecibo telescope was aimed at the Hercules cluster of stars which lie 24,000 light-years away, so don't hold your breath for a reply. The message contains mathematical data, pictures of the human form, and a map of where we live.

Some scientists think this is a big mistake, as some of the civilizations out there might not be very friendly. They cautiously believe we should keep quiet, but mankind has already announced its presence to any extraterrestrial eaves-droppers who live within a hundred light-years, because the radio waves from the pioneering days of Marconi have now travelled that far out into space. It is also known that the megawatt radar beams of World War II have long radiated out into space and may have already attracted the attention of aliens. After the Sun, the planet Earth is now the most powerful radio source in the solar system, and even medium-wave stations can propagate radio waves in a vertical direction across interstellar space. Three years after the Arecibo radio telescope beamed its message of greetings to our hypothetical interstellar neighbours, an extremely powerful signal of unknown origin broke through on the radio and TV wavebands of southern England. This signal seemed to come through the upper layers of the ionosphere from interplanetary space and focused on the counties of Hampshire, Wiltshire, West Sussex and Surrey. The trans-mission began at precisely 5.12 p.m. on 26 November 1977, and lasted for almost six minutes. The signal was of such intensity that the aerials of several radio stations overheated with the power and seized up. The powerful signal swamped out Southern Television's news programme, and a strange deep artificial-sounding voice said: "This is Gramaha of Azkah speaking to you. For many years now you have seen us as lights in the sky. We now speak to you in peace and wisdom. We come to warn you of the destiny of your race, and urge your leaders to listen to this message."

The rest of the message concerned the nuclear arms race, the instability of a future Russia and China, the scientific exploitation of animals for food and the epidemic it would cause across Europe. And the message was particularly intriguing, because in 1977 although most people hadn't heard of the hole in the ozone layer, the narrator of the strange message said humans were causing havoc with the ozone layer because of industrial plants discharging gases into the skies. The message ended with Gramaha warning that a false prophet would appear at the beginning of the 21st century, and that he would be like another Hitler. In fact, the strange message seemed to make sense and spoke much good, so the authorities immediately denounced the intriguing transmission as a student hoax. Engineers ruled out a prank, especially from students, as the signal strength had been one of the order of gigawatts, and had even interfered with NATO's radio network. It was also pointed out that television stations are heavily guarded and almost impossible to tap into. The sophisticated equipment needed to swamp out an area covering several counties would not be available to students or normal pranksters, so, predictably, Russian propagandists were blamed. But what would the Soviets have gained from a message which warned of instability in the future Soviet Union? Questions were asked in the House of Lords, but the elderly peers seemed confused about the matter, and the debate about the message turned into little more than a humorous pantomime. The whole incident was gradually forgotten. It seems that no one ever considered that the message was not a hoax at all, but a genuine warning from our interstellar neighbours who are perhaps becoming concerned at our suicidal destruction of the environment and our preoccupation with war and violence. It seems that if it was a genuine message from above, it has fallen on deaf ears . . . perhaps it is now too late to even heed the warning.

What Goes on at Area 51?

Situated approximately 90 miles north of Las Vegas in the secluded stillness of the Nevada Desert lies the Nellis Air Force Range, which covers 3,026,700 acres. This land encompasses the controversial US Air Force base at Groom Lake – more commonly known as Area 51 to ufologists the world over. Just what goes on in Area 51 is not known to the public, as the base has been out of bounds to the civilian world since the 1950s.

Area 51 was, in effect, created when the US military asked Tony Levier, a Lockheed test pilot, to find a remote range that would be geographically appropriate to test out the U-2 spy plane. Levier settled for the dry lake bed in the Nevada Desert, which was already off limits because of its proximity to a nuclear test site. Construction soon began on project

Area 51, Nevada: Groom Lake

"Paradise Ranch", and the site was finished in July 1955 at a cost of $800,000. Paradise Ranch had a runway, two enormous hangars, a control tower, a mess hall and several mobile homes. The month the new test site opened a C-124 transport plane landed there with a U-2 plane in its hold. Even back then, the press were warned off with serious threats of imprisonment to photographers and reporters. This cloak-and-dagger secrecy naturally created an aura of mystery and intrigue around the US Air Force base. From vantage points around the desert, reporters with high-powered binoculars and telephoto lenses watched many weird and wonderful-looking experimental aircraft landing and taking off at the top secret base, including the SR-71 Blackbird high-altitude reconnaissance plane and the Northrop XRB-49A "flying wing" plane. As far back as 1975, there were scores of sightings of a strange-looking aircraft flying to and from the base, which is now known to have been the F-117A Stealth fighter. Military chiefs stepped up security measures around the base to keep out the prying pressmen and even purchased the land surrounding Area 51. In April 1991 a peculiar disc-shaped craft was seen flying into Area 51 from the north at an altitude of 9000 feet. Observers said the craft was so large as to dwarf the two F-16 fighter planes that were escorting it in. Video footage has also been released that purports to show high-velocity craft taking off from the Nevada base at speeds in excess of five times the speed of sound. One video was even shot from the space shuttle *Atlanta* which shows Area 51 from low Earth orbit. A fast-moving pinpoint of light is seen moving up from the base and out into space. The official explanation from NASA was that the light was just an ice crystal from the Shuttle's exhaust nozzles reflecting sunlight.

Ironically, the only detailed pictures of Area 51 that are available to the public are on the Internet, and they were all taken over a decade ago by Russian spy satellites, because military chiefs in the former Soviet Union were apparently obsessed with the clandestine goings-on at the Groom Lake Air Force base.

It is now virtually certain that a number of breathtaking aeronautical experiments are taking place at Area 51. In the 1990s it was widely reported that prototypes of a high-altitude hypersonic reconnaissance plane, known as the Aurora, were flying from Area 51 to RAF Machrihanish – a remote NATO air base situated on the Isle of Kintyre, to the west of the Scottish mainland. The Aurora's predecessor, the Blackbird (which was suddenly scrapped in 1990) set an absolute world speed record in July 1976 by flying at 2193 miles per hour at an altitude of 85,069 feet. But reports from reliable witnesses who have seen the Aurora – the Blackbird's successor – in action, claim the new plane was travelling at a phenomenal speed of almost 7000 miles per hour. What's more, unlike the Stealth bomber, which presents a small detectable radar target, the Aurora is almost completely invisible to radar and gives off negligible infrared emissions.

Another prototype aircraft seen in the skies over Area 51 is a triangular-shaped vehicle which can not only levitate and flit about at phenomenal speeds, it can also apparently "teleport" from locations miles apart at the speed of light.

According to alleged leaked reports from the Groom Lake base, the flying triangle is a nuclear-powered craft which uses three superconducting magnets at each point in its triangular frame to interact in such a way as to warp the space-time continuum. The resulting effect allows the craft to vanish and reappear miles away instantaneously. The military advantages of such a revolutionary vehicle are obvious, so the project will no doubt remain under a cloak of secrecy until the Pentagon is ready to release the facts. That was certainly the case when the existence of the B-2 Stealth fighter was denied by military chiefs for years, until the US model-making manufacturers Revell brought out the model kit of the B-2 in the early 1990s.

In 1998 two former workers at Area 51 claimed that drums of hazardous toxic waste of some sort had been carelessly incinerated at the base. For the first time ever, the existence of Area 51 was officially acknowledged by President Clinton in a press release from the White House Office on 29 January 1999. In Clinton's letter to the Speaker of the House of Representatives, he states:

Dear Sir

Presidential Determination No. 98–36 exempted the United State's Air Force operating location near Groom Lake, Nevada, from any Federal, State, interstate, or local hazardous or solid waste laws that might require the disclosure of classified information concerning that operating location to unauthorized persons. Information concerning activities at the operating location near Groom Lake has been properly determined to be classified, and its disclosure would be harmful to national security. Continued protection of this information is, therefore, in the paramount interest of the United States.

Sincerely,

William J. Clinton

Masters of Illusion

The following intriguing incident allegedly took place in England's Lake District, on the night of 22 September 1988, just four miles east of Kendal.

A plumber from Wrexham named Noel Harrison and his girlfriend Maxine Williams were travelling up the M6 in a Transit van on their way to see Noel's cousin in Grayrigg. Noel had travelled along the route to Grayrigg many times over the previous two years and was well acquainted with the area around Kendal and Windermere. He left the M6 as usual and joined the A685, which was deserted at that time of night, 11.15 p.m. Noel left the "A"-road and took his van down a country lane which wound its way round woodland to the town where his brother worked in a dairy. As Noel turned down the lane, he saw that the road ahead was blocked by boulders. He stopped the Transit van and looked at the obstructions with puzzlement, because there were no mountains nearby that could have produced the landslide. Maxine told him he'd better turn the van around and find another route, but Noel thought there was something strange about the blocked road. He left his van and looked down the road. He thought the moonlight was playing tricks on his eyes because the boulders that were strewn across the road didn't look real; they looked flat and two-dimensional, as if they were just cardboard cut-outs. As the plumber walked towards the boulders, something curious happened. When Noel glanced down at the road again, he could no longer see the huge rocks lying about; the road looked perfectly clear. When he walked back to the van, the rocks appeared again. They were obviously some sort of illusion. Noel told his girlfriend about the unreality of the rocks and she too saw them vanish when she viewed them from another angle. But Maxine said the illusion was creepy and had the eerie feeling that someone was watching them, so she asked Noel to go by another route to Grayrigg.

But curiosity got the better of Noel, and he drove his Transit slowly up the rock-covered road and, as expected, the rocks seemed to have no solidity at all, since the van proceeded up the lane without encountering any physical obstruction. Noel was flabbergasted by the illusion, but upon turning the sharp bend at the end of the lane, he and Maxine witnessed a spectacle that was even more astounding than the phantom rocks. In a clearing in the woods to the left of the road Noel and his girlfriend saw something that looked straight out of a science-fiction film. A huge silvery saucer-shaped craft stood on four legs, and beneath this strange craft two figures wearing large helmets were apparently at work on some apparatus that hung from the underside of the saucer. As the van passed, the helmeted people, who seemed to be about seven feet tall, turned and looked at the vehicle with their blank visors, as if startled. A blazing beam of light shone on the van from a dome on the top of the saucer, and Noel realized what he had stumbled on. He put the van into third gear and accelerated up the lane away from the strange craft. He looked sideways at Maxine and saw she was trembling with fear at the strange encounter. Noel sped up the lane and turned the van around a bend so fast the vehicle tipped slightly. He raced non-stop to the farm at Grayrigg and told his cousin about the strange encounter, who told him that there had been an item on the local radio about a strange glowing disc that had been seen flying erratically over the nearby village of Middleshaw. One report said the disc had been seen diving into woodland near Kendal, but the astronomer Patrick Moore had said that a meteorite had probably been behind the UFO sightings.

On the following morning, Maxine, Noel and his cousin visited the woods where the strange saucer had been seen, and they saw that in a clearing there were four circular depressions, left by the landing gear of the unearthly space-ship. Noel then remembered the phantom rocks, and he surmised that they had been some sort of hologram projection from the UFO to divert traffic from the area so no one would come across what seemed to have been a spaceship in need of repair. Three days later a silvery disc-shaped craft was seen flying at high speed along the shoreline at Morecambe Bay – less than ten miles from the spot where Noel and Maxine had seen the UFO.

The Berwyns, at the Gwynedd/Powys/Denbighshire border, Wales.

Crashed UFOs

1. The Berwyn Mountains Crash, Wales, 1974

Besides the Roswell Incident, there have been many other well documented accounts of alleged UFO crashes, and one of these cases is known as the Berwyn Mountains UFO crash, which took place in North Wales in January 1974.

At 8.30 p.m. on 23 January 1974, a large disc-like craft was seen to fall from the skies over Clwyd in Wales. Dozens of witnesses across Lancashire and Cheshire had phoned the police earlier that evening after seeing a strange formation of green lights flying erratically over the skies of the north-west. At exactly 8.38 p.m., something impacted into Cader Bronwen, a 3000-foot peak in the Berwyn Mountains of Clwyd, Wales, and the resulting tremor (which measured 4.5

on the Richter Scale) was felt in Wrexham, Chester, Liverpool, Southport and even in some areas of Greater Manchester. Seismologists at the Institute of Geological Sciences in Edinburgh were at a loss to explain the impact tremor, but suggested that it might have been a product from the minor Bala fault line which runs near the epicentre of the quake.

One witness, named Anne Williams, who lived in the area had a very clear view of the object which fell to earth to cause such a tremor. She later told UFO investigators: "I saw a bright light in the sky. It had a long fiery tail which went dim, and then very brilliant – just like an electric fire which keeps coming to life. The object was like an electric bulb in shape, with rough edges. It fell behind the hills at the back of my bungalow and the earth shook."

Another witness – off-duty police officer Gwilym Owen – was drinking in his local pub the Dudley Arms when there was a flash of bright light and a roar, followed by a terrifying bang which rocked the premises, shaking all the bottles and glasses. Police stations within a 60-mile radius of the crash site were flooded with calls from worried members of the public who had seen the lights in the sky and felt the powerful seismic jolt.

Police immediately converged on the Berwyn Mountains, expecting to find a crashed passenger jet, but just what they did find has never been divulged. One witness – a local named Ken Haughton – reached the crash site 90 minutes after the impact and came upon what seemed like a crashed spaceship. From close quarters Haughton could see a luminous sphere approximately 400 feet across. The RAF Valley Mountain Rescue Team, based over 80 miles away on the Isle of Anglesey were scrambled and flew by helicopter to the area. However, prior to the team's arrival, many witnesses spoke of seeing sinister black unmarked helicopters buzzing the skies over the Berwyn Mountains. These unmarked choppers were seen to rake the mountains with powerful searchlights, as if searching for something or someone. Many UFO researchers now concur that the black helicopters were probably carrying rapid deployment teams dispatched to investigate the downed UFO in North Wales.

A convoy of army trucks passed through Chester that night and made their way to the epicentre of the crash site, then the army threw a cordon around the area. Even the police and crash investigators were warned off. A nurse who lived near the scene of the impact told a local newspaper that a pulsating luminous flying saucer "the size of the Albert Hall" had smashed into the mountainside, throwing debris and bodies for over a mile. She said she walked up to one of the bodies, and realized it wasn't human, but before she could describe what she had seen, the military intervened, and two Ministry of Defence officials ordered her to remain silent about the UFO because her comments "would constitute a threat to national security and the defence of the realm".

Amazingly, another UFO was seen hovering in the airspace over the Berwyn Mountains shortly after the crash incident. It has been suggested that the second spaceship was searching for possible survivors from the crashed UFO.

In 1980 an electronics engineer named Arthur Adams, who had worked on Concorde, visited the Berwyn UFO crash site and found strange green-coloured pieces of metal embedded in the rocks there. He took samples of the metal to his laboratory and discovered that a sample the size of a 1-inch cube gave off two kilowatts of electricity when wired up to a voltmeter. Mr Adams contacted the *Daily Express*, and they published a series of articles about the strange find, but the Ministry of Defence stepped in and killed the story.

Today, no one knows what crashed in the Welsh Mountains on that winter night in 1974; some think it was an experimental man-made top secret military aircraft (possibly a prototype Stealth bomber), others think it was an alien craft from another world. If so, what happened to the bodies that were seen scattered all over the mountain after the crash?

2. The Boscombe Down Crash, 1994

In August 1994 a number of people in Wiltshire, England, reported seeing a distinctive-looking UFO which had a fuselage similar to a plane, but no wings; just two tapering tails. The strange craft was seen to hover and fly over the Salisbury Plain area near Stonehenge over the space of a month before it suddenly crashed one evening at 11 p.m. on 26 September 1994. The twin-tailed aerial vehicle plummeted hundreds of feet and smashed into the runway of Boscombe Down. Local aviation enthusiasts who tuned into the airband radios to hear messages from the unidentified aircraft heard military chiefs trying to make contact with the sky intruder, but their requests for the mysterious pilot to identify himself were never answered. The airband eavesdroppers drove to the Boscombe Down airfield to see what was going on, but they only got a glimpse of the crashed craft, which was lying at the end of the runway, covered in tarpaulin sheets. There were rumours that the crashed object was an experimental US military plane known as the TR-3A, but an aviation expert who had been tracking the twin-tailed craft over the RAF base with high-powered binoculars said the downed object was "not a plane from this planet".

The unidentified "plane" was later transported to an unspecified US Air Force base in America.

3. UFO Crash, 1964, England and West Germany
Shortly before his death in 1994, retired US Air Force intelligence officer Leonard Stringfield admitted that in 1964 a specially rigged naval flagship received a coded radio message which stated: "Artefacts had been recovered with three dead personnel."

Stringfield later learned that the statement had been alluding to a UFO that had crashed in two parts. The larger section had fallen in Penkridge, Staffordshire, and the remainder had come to earth in West Germany. The wreckage sections and the three dead alien bodies were shipped to Wright-Patterson Air Force base in the United States.

4. The Crashed Foo Fighters
Throughout the latter days of World War II and during the Korean War, there were many sightings of mysterious metallic globe-shaped craft, nicknamed "Foo Fighters". These wartime UFOs often accosted American, German and British bomber crews during flights over enemy territory. Almost all reports of the objects stated that they could

change colour from a transparent silver to a luminous orange, and when they did so, some powerful electromagnetic pulse was emitted which often made the engines of the bombers cut out. The mystery of the Foo Fighters was never solved officially, but American journalist Dorothy Kilgallen claims she was once told by "a British official of Cabinet rank" that shortly after World War II, a Foo Fighter crashed in Britain – and alien corpses were retrieved from it. Kilgallen was told: "British scientists and airmen examined the wreck of one unearthly ship and ended up convinced that the strange aerial objects were not Soviet inventions but spaceships from another planet."

The identity of the British official is still unknown, but retired diplomat and intelligence officer Gordon Creighton believes Kilgallen's source was Lord Louis Mountbatten, who had a lifelong interest in UFOs. Respected Brazilian UFO researcher Dr Olavo Fontes has vindicated Kilgallen's story. He claims that in the 1950s, while he was researching the subject of crashed Foo Fighters, he was visited by two sinister-looking men who stated they were from Naval Intelligence. They advised Fontes to discontinue his research into the Foo Fighters, but revealed that during World War II, six of the UFOs had crashed. Three had come down in North America, one in the Sahara Desert, one in Scandinavia, and one in Britain. All of the crashed craft had contained humanoid pilots, 32 to 46 inches in height.

5. The Rendlesham Forest UFO Crash, Suffolk, England, 1981

Between 27 and 30 December 1980 there were scores of UFO sightings about twelve miles north of Ipswich. Strange lights were seen to dart erratically over the Suffolk countryside at night, and many of the lights in the sky were seen to hover over the nearby coastal town of Leiston, where a nuclear power station is situated. Early in 1981 a bizarre rumour was buzzing through the local village of Woodbridge, close to where the UFO flap had been going on. The rumour doing the rounds in the village claimed that a UFO had crashed in Rendlesham Forest, which lies just to the north of Ipswich. According to the widespread hearsay, the craft had come down just two miles from the US Woodbridge air base on the evening of December 30. The mystery surrounding the outlandish rumour deepened when several respected ufologists investigated the claims – and obtained scraps of tantalizing information from a high-ranking officer at the air base. The officer, who refused to be named, stated that he had visited the site of the UFO crash along with the base commander and a group of security personnel. None of them carried any weapons, as this was strictly forbidden. The commander allegedly chatted with three aliens from the crashed UFO. The occupants of the craft were all about three feet in height and wore silvery suits. What's more, throughout the conversation, the aliens remained suspended in mid-air in shafts of laser-like light which shone from the UFO. The aliens said their ship had malfunctioned and asked for technical help, but none of the engineers at the base could understand the advanced components that propelled the craft. In the end, the aliens managed to fix their troublesome ship, and, after taking off unsteadily, they were soon climbing through the sky, back to where they came from. The commander was outraged that some of his men had taken photographs of the UFO and the aliens, and he had the snapshots confiscated and handed them over to the Ministry of Defence.

Investigations into the alleged Rendlesham UFO crash uncovered many other incidents which apparently backed up the story. Forestry Commission workers found several scorched trees in Rendlesham Forest, close to the spot where the crash-landing is said to have taken place. Besides the UFO reports which preceded the incident, there were also intriguing accounts from airline radar operators in the area who spoke of strange targets performing amazing aeronautical manoeuvres at supersonic speeds on their screens on the night of 30 December. The Ministry of Defence routinely denied the UFO crash story, but refused to explain why an A-10 ground attack aircraft kept circling Rendlesham Forest the day after the incident, taking hundreds of pictures of the site and monitoring the area for unusually high radiation levels.

6. The Alençon Incident, France, 1790

One of the earliest reports of a possible visitant from another world crash-landing in Earth came from the little French town of Alençon, which is situated about 30 miles north of Le Mans. The town is nowadays solely famous because of its fine lace, but over two hundred years ago, Alençon became renowned for something much less mundane that occurred within its vicinity.

At around 5 a.m. on 12 June 1790 peasants watched in awe as a huge metal sphere descended from the sky, moving with a strange undulating motion. The globe crash-landed onto a hilltop, and the violent impact threw up soil and vegetation which showered the hillside. The hull of the globe was so hot (possibly from a rocket motor or because of the rapid descent through the atmosphere) that it ignited the surrounding dry flora, and a grass fire quickly broke out. The peasants rushed up the hill carrying pails of water and, within a short time, the fires were extinguished.

A large crowd encircled the crashed globe, and some of the more adventurous people present stepped forward to touch the hull of the unearthly craft to discover that it was quite warm. A physician, two mayors from nearby towns and a number of officials turned up to see what had descended from the morning sky, and these important witnesses arrived just in time to see something sensational.

A hatch of some sort slid open in the lower hemisphere of the globe, and a man in an outlandish, tight-fitting costume emerged through the hatchway and surveyed the observers with an apprehensive look. He started mumbling something in a strange language and gestured for the crowd to get away from him and his vehicle. A few people stepped back, and the man ran through the break in the circle of spectators and fled into the local woods. Some of the peasants ran away from the globe, sensing that something dangerous was about to happen. The remainder of the crowd decided to follow suit, and seconds after the last members of the multitude had retreated from the sphere, it exploded with a peculiar muffled sound, creating a miniature mushroom-shaped cloud. The debris from the craft "sizzled" in the grass, and gradually turned to powder.

A police inspector named Liabeuf travelled over a hundred miles from Paris to investigate the crash, and he quizzed many of the witnesses, including the mayors and physician who had been present at the strange spectacle. The inspector organized a thorough search of the woods where the oddly dressed man had taken refuge, but the hunt resulted in nothing. The stranger seemed to have vanished as mysteriously as he had arrived.

In the report to his superiors, Inspector Liabeuf put forward the suggestion that the man who had landed in the globe could have been "a being from another world" – but the high-ups in Paris dismissed the intimation as "a ludicrous idea".

UFO Zones

One of the most unusual aspects of the UFO phenomenon is the apparent existence of specific geographical areas where sightings of UFOs and paranormal activity seem to be unusually regular. These so-called "window areas", as the ufologists call them, are thought to be in the vicinity of dimensional gateways or portals through which UFOs pass from their home planets. Some think that the UFOs do not travel through normal interstellar space on their journeys, but take an instantaneous short cut by traversing a region of higher-dimensional space that science-fiction writers have termed "hyperspace". The term was invented in 1934 by sci-fi pioneer John W. Campbell, who needed a convenient solution to the awkward problem of long-distance travel between the stars. Like most science-fiction concepts, hyperspace was later adopted by physicists and mathematicians as a theoretical possibility. Hyperspace is currently defined in scientific text books as "any space of more than three dimensions". To envisage travelling through hyperspace is virtually impossible, as it entails moving at right angles to every possible direction in our familiar space, but here's a good analogy to aid visualization. Imagine a map of the stars. We have to travel from, let us say, our own planet to a planet circling the nearest star to us – Proxima Centauri, which is about 4.2 light-years away. To cross such a vast distance through normal space would take hundreds of years by today's technological standards, and even if we moved at a velocity close to the speed of light, the journey would still take years. But imagine if we could somehow "fold" space to bring the points of departure and arrival together. This would be like folding our star map so that the solar systems of Sol (our sun) and Proxima Centauri are so close that we can simply "hop" a few hundred thousand miles instead of millions of millions of miles by the conventional route.

Until fairly recently, the idea of a hyperspatial region was not taken too seriously, but in 1962 Professor John A. Wheeler (the co-inventor of the hydrogen bomb) and Robert Fuller published a controversial scientific paper entitled "Causality and multiply connected space time". This paper introduced the concept of "superspace" – which was described as an immense but separate version of space that permeated every part of the universe. Journeys taken through superspace would, due to its nature, be much more rapid than the usual route, because the ordinary laws of physics would be considerably altered there.

The exciting possibility of this spatial region akin to hyperspace is strengthened by the fact that Wheeler and Fuller were not just surmising the existence of superspace in their paper; they were actually logically extrapolating from Einstein's General Theory of Relativity. Furthermore, there have been many inspiring discoveries about the space we assume to be nothing but emptiness. Quantum physicists have ascertained that on the scale of the sub-microscopic it is not the nice smooth nothingness it seems. Even the highest vacuum contained within a one-centimetre cube of space contains fluctuations and ripples of energy equivalent to a mass of 10^{91} kilograms. Considering that the devastating blast of a 20-megaton H-bomb results in just one kilogram of mass being converted into energy, there is a frightening amount of energy in just a cubic centimetre of space – if only we knew how to tap it. Within the subatomic turmoil of empty space, there are also subatomic-sized tunnels, just centimetres long, that connect different parts of space.

Physicist who have studied these tunnels, which they have nicknamed "wormholes", are baffled by their complex geometry, because some of these minute corridors seem to run "outside" of space and back again. The latest theory is that the wormholes connect every part of space to every other part, even across light-years, and if we were small enough to travel down these subways of superspace, we would have instantaneous travel to any point in the universe. Strangely enough, Einstein was incredibly far-sighted enough to make allowances in his theories of rela-tivity for the wormholes, and their existence would not violate Einsteinian laws or the laws of causality. At the moment, no one can even send a radio message down the wormholes, because their apertures are too small. Even an electron is about 100 billion times to large to enter a worm-hole. However, if some physicist finds a way to stretch the openings of wormholes to allow a spacecraft to enter them, the road to the stars would be ours and the true Space Age of interstellar exploration would commence.

It has been suggested that the only thing in nature which could widen the entrances to wormholes would be a black hole, and there are controversial plans to create mini-black holes here on Earth. Scientists at New York's Brookhaven National Laboratory (BNL) have spent over 700 million dollars creating the world's most powerful particle acceler-ator. The Relativistic Heavy Ion Collider was tested on 16 July 1999, but was promptly shut down by the BNL director John Marburger, pending an enquiry into fears that it might cause "perturbations of the universe". In other words, the super-accelerator was closed down in case the experiment accidentally created a small black hole on Long Island. The black hole could be formed because the gigantic machine has the power to create "strangelets" – a new type of recently discovered matter made up of quarks. Once strangelets form, they start an uncontrollable chain reaction, converting anything they touch into more quarks. The resulting mass could reach such a density as to form a small black hole. The black hole would be drawn by gravitational forces to the centre of the Earth, where it would devour the entire planet within minutes.

If there are technologically advanced races out in the universe who have long ago discovered how to manipulate wormholes with home-made black holes, they would have a long-established interstellar and intergalactic space subway system linking various worlds they are exploring or possibly colonizing. Wordsworth was probably right when he remarked that "the starry heavens have goings on"; space may be criss-crossed with a network of passages created by the superior civilizations of the cosmos.

Could the UFOs we see in our skies travel via the wormholes? It would certainly explain the way they seem to appear and disappear. Perhaps visiting extra-terrestrials use a network of hyperspatial routes that are rather similar to our extensive motorway systems. Could there be dimensional highways and relativistic roundabouts out there? If there are, then surely there must be junctions from which there are routes to Earth. Perhaps the spaceships which take these routes emerge from superspace into the normal space in the skies of Earth. Such spacecraft would no doubt have a device on board that enables the pilot to open and close the wormhole so that terrestrial aircraft cannot accidentally enter it. But perhaps, from time to time, planes have strayed into these sky portals. Maybe this was the fate of Flying Officer Brian Holding.

On 7 March 1922 Holding took off from the airfield at Chester, England, on what was intended to be a short flight over the border to an airstrip in Wales. On the return journey from Wales, Holding's plane was spotted by scores of witnesses droning through the skies back towards Chester. That plane and its experienced pilot never reached the airfield and was never seen again. A massive search for the wreckage of the missing plane was launched but not a trace of the craft was ever found. Stranger still, weeks before Holding flew into limbo, peculiar lights were seen flying in formation over North Wales. The region where Holding's plane vanished has been the backdrop to many unexplained occurrences over the years, and is now regarded as a major window area. The epicentre of this window area is said to be the Welsh coastal town of Barmouth, where geologists have detected zones of complex magnetic anomalies which are of unknown origin. The first reports of unearthly goings-on in this region date back to 1692, when a fiery object landed near Harwich and proceeded to terrorize the town's inhabitants for several months until it finally zoomed back into the skies. There were also reports of strange blue and white lights descending to Earth in the same locality in the years 1869, 1875 and 1877, but the most remarkable incidents occurred in 1905, when there was an outbreak of concentrated UFO activity. At the time of the sightings, a Welsh Methodist revival was happening in the area, and the strange aerial lights seen in the skies by many of the converted were naturally interpreted as religious signs.

One of the first reports of a UFO in the area of North Wales that year came in January from a train driver who saw ten bright lights hurtling across the early evening sky above a chapel at Egryn, which is a hamlet that lies between Barmouth and Harlech in Gwynedd. A plethora of other sightings of nocturnal lights followed, and one night an enormous glowing arch, which resembled the northern lights, appeared in the sky. One end of the arch was in the sea and the other end touched a local hilltop. Shortly afterwards, over one hundred witnesses sighed in awe as they watched a brilliant star-shaped object fly out of the arch and swoop down over the rooftops of Egryn. The brilliant light hovered over several houses then flew off at a phenomenal speed. The luminous arch gradually faded away into the night.

News of the nightly light displays soon spread, and a journalist and photographer from the *Daily Mirror* newspaper turned up to investigate the mystery. They too saw the lights. The *Daily Mirror* reporter wrote:

> *It was close to midnight and we were nearing Barmouth when suddenly, without the faintest warning, a soft shimmering radiance flooded the road at our feet. Immediately it spread around us, and every stick and stone within twenty yards was visible, as if under the influence of the softest limelight. It seemed as though some large body between earth and sky had suddenly opened up and emitted a flood of light from within itself.*

It was a little suggestive of the bursting of a firework bomb and yet wonderfully different. Quickly as I looked up, the light was even then fading away from the sky overhead. I seemed to see an oval mass of grey, half-open, disclosing within a kernel of white light. As I looked it closed, and everything was once again in darkness.

Throughout the rest of that summer until late July, the same almond-shaped mass was seen to open in the skies of North Wales to admit several lights and circular-shaped craft into the airspace over Barmouth. On one occasion, during a thunderstorm, forked lightning struck a lenticular mass in the sky, and the flash lit up three saucer-like objects which emerged from the mysteriously recurring lens-shaped cloud. A farmer who observed the cloud over an entire week may have been near to the truth when he remarked that it was, "A gateway for something from somewhere else."

The Barmouth window area, like other UFO zones all over Britain, Europe and the Americas, is dotted with ancient mounds and landmarks. Curiously, in that area of northern Wales there are many megalithic monuments. Some ufologists see a link here, and some have hypothesized that men living in the Barmouth area during the Neolithic period were also aware that the region was unusual and had probably erected their mighty stone markers to indicate the fact. If that were true, then these UFO windows must be thousands of years old, and possibly even older. Strangely enough, Stonehenge, the most famous megalithic construction in the world, is situated right next to the Wiltshire town of Warminster, where a major UFO window exists. Etymological analysis of place-names often reveals that a high percentage of window areas coincide with names beginning with "Devil", such as Devil's Elbow, Warwickshire, where many strange lights have been seen in the sky for years. On Lord Bath's estate at Longleat in Warminster, there is an area known as "Heaven's Gate". These names seem to echo the uncanniness and unearthly history of the places they name.

Another UFO "hot spot" that has been featured in the

media in recent years is the picturesque town of Bonnybridge in Scotland. Bonnybridge has a population of just 9000, one hotel, two pubs and a dozen shops, but since 1995 a steady stream of documentary-makers from the United States, Japan and Europe have invaded the town to film the strange aerial spectacles which the UFOs put on, almost on a daily basis. Some 5000 Bonnybridge inhabitants (more than half of the town's population) have witnessed bizarre and often terrifying UFO activity in the skies above their homes. At first, sceptics cited Bonnybridge's proximity to the flight paths of both Glasgow and Edinburgh airports as the reason behind the mass sightings, but independent qualified UFO investigators with high-magnification video cameras and telephoto cameras have recorded lights and objects which not only look nothing like terrestrial aircraft, they also perform aerobatic manoeuvres (such as right-angled turns) which cannot be executed by any aircraft made on this planet. As I write, the UFO activity over Bonnybridge is continuing, but scientists down here continue to turn a blind eye to the phenomenon.

Without a doubt, the most infamous window area on the planet is the so-called Bermuda Triangle, also known as the "Limbo of the Lost", the "Hoodoo Sea", the "Devil's Playground" and the "Graveyard of the Atlantic". Inside this vast triangular area, which stretches from Puerto Rico to Florida, and has its apex near the Azores, thousands of unexplained disappearances and incidents have taken place, dating back to the time of Columbus, who actually witnessed strange red globular lights which buzzed his ships on the historic approach to San Salvador in 1492.

The term "Bermuda Triangle" was coined by the writer Vincent Gaddis in 1964, and in recent years the Triangle has been dismissed by sceptics as an imaginary region of purely random sea and air disasters; a purely mythical zone, the result of exaggerations and sensational media reports. Yet no one can explain why so many uncanny aeronautical and maritime mysteries have taken place in the "imaginary" triangle. For example, in 1872, the *Mary Celeste* was found drifting near the apex of the Triangle.

Most unsolved mystery buffs know the basic story of the

Mary Celeste. She left New York in November 1872 under the command of Captain Briggs with 1700 barrels of crude alcohol in her hold, bound for Genoa in Italy. On board were Briggs's wife and two-year-old daughter, and a crew of eight.

Almost a month later, Captain David Moorhouse, master of a ship called the *Dei Gratia,* saw a speck on the horizon 500 miles east of the Azores. When he looked through his telescope, he saw it was a ship that was sailing erratically. He sent a boarding party over to investigate, and they saw that the deserted ship was the *Mary Celeste.* The only lifeboat was missing, but the ship was completely seaworthy. There were six months' worth of food and water on the ship, and the crew's oilskins, boots, pipes and tobacco had been left behind. It was obvious that everybody had left in a hurry. Only navigation instruments had been taken. Someone had struck the ship's rail with an axe, and in the cargo hold one of the barrels had been opened. The captain's sword was found on his bed in his cabin. On a slate, someone had chalked "Fanny my dear wife, Frances MR". Captain Moorhouse took the derelict ship to Gibraltar and after a lengthy court of enquiry Captain Moorhouse was awarded a salvage cheque for £2000.

Another ship which met a mysterious fate in the triangle eight years later was the British frigate *Atlanta,* which left Bermuda for England in January 1880 with a crew of 290 on board. The *Atlanta* never reached England and was never seen again. The British Navy seemed baffled by the frigate's disappearance, and conducted an exhaustive search of the Atlantic with six ships of the Channel Fleet. The ships combed the waters in a line over the entire area in which the *Atlanta* had been lost, yet not one stick of wreckage from the missing vessel was ever found. By May, the Navy were forced to call off the search, and to this day the *Atlanta*'s vanishing act has never been explained.

In August of the following year Captain Baker of the *Ellen Austin* was halfway between the Bahamas and Bermuda, bound for Boston, when he sighted an unidentified schooner. The vessel remained in sight for two days, and on 20 August 1881 the ship drifted within hailing distance. Receiving no reply to his signals, Captain Baker and four of his crew rowed over to the seemingly uninhabited schooner. Baker climbed on board the deserted ship first, then took out his loaded Colt revolver and motioned his men to follow him with it. Baker cried out, "Halloo thar? Anybody aboard?" and received no reply. The vessel was entirely seaworthy and in a well maintained condition. "My, she will make a fine prize, this one will," remarked Baker gleefully, thinking about the salvage award for such a decent ship. Two of the crewmen inspected the "ghost ship's" hold and saw that it contained a well packed cargo of mahogany. From this find, Captain Baker speculated that the schooner had probably been *en route* from Honduras, bound for England or possibly a Mediterranean port. He searched for the ship's log but it was missing, and so were the trail boards which would have informed him of the vessel's name. The fate of the ship's captain and crew was a real baffler, as there was no evidence of any violence on board the schooner, and she was well stocked with provisions and supplies.

Captain Baker returned to the *Ellen Austin* and hand-picked a prize crew to man the schooner he had found. Baker instructed them to bring the ship to Boston with the *Ellen Austin*. The men were put on the salvaged derelict ship and soon had her on her way to Boston. For two days the ships were so close they were within earshot, but later they became separated by a fierce Atlantic storm which was being generated by a hurricane which was tearing through Georgia, Alabama and Mississippi. Two days later, the storms died and an unusual calm descended. The sea was almost as flat as a mirror, but there was no sign of the prize ship. Then a sharp-sighted lookout pointed to a spot on the horizon. Through his spyglass, Captain Baker could just make out the sails of the prize schooner. He barked orders to change his ship's course, and the *Ellen Austin* was soon converging on the schooner. Everyone on board Baker's ship knew something was wrong, because the schooner was sailing so erratically; it took hours to catch her up. When the captain and crewmen from the *Ellen Austin* finally did board the schooner, they were confronted with yet another mystery. There was no one on board her. None of the prize crewmen were there, and what's more, for some strange reason, the bunks had not been slept in, none of the food and drink had been consumed, and the new logbook was nowhere to be found.

After hours of careful negotiation, Captain Baker convinced his superstitious seamen that there was a rational explanation for the disappearance of his prize crew, and he persuaded another group of his men to become the new prize crew. They expressed their fears that something evil was at work on the ship, so Baker allowed them to carry firearms. Once again, the two ships set sail for Boston, and once again the weather was against them. This time, a watery haze enshrouded the prize schooner, which was travelling behind the *Ellen Austin* at a close distance of just ten ship-lengths. But hours into the voyage, a lookout screamed frantically, "She's gone!"

Captain Baker came on deck and asked him what he was talking about. Then he too saw that the prize schooner was nowhere to be seen. She had been there one moment, but now suddenly vanished. And the schooner and the crewmen who had been persuaded to pilot her to Boston were never seen again.

If there is some unearthly force at work in the Bermuda Triangle that is responsible for these disappearances, then it seems it can extend its eerie influence into the skies above the Atlantic as well. On the afternoon of 5 December 1945, five Grumman Avenger torpedo bombers took off from the US Naval Air Station at Fort Lauderdale in Florida on a training flight. The five planes were Flight 19, and their mission was to fly due east from the coastline of Florida for 160 miles to the Chicken Shoals in the Bahamas, where the bombers were to fly north for 40 miles before heading back to Fort Lauderdale. The mission was very straightforward and should have gone smoothly, but something sinister happened that day which has never been resolved. At 3.45 p.m. Lieutenant Charles C. Taylor, leader of the flight, radioed a bizarre distress call to the Fort Lauderdale base. His frantic voice stated: "Calling tower, this is an emergency. We seem to be off course. We cannot see land. Repeat: we cannot see land."

The astounded staff in the tower radioed back: "What is your position?"

The strange reply that came back made no sense at all: "We are not sure of our position. We can't be sure just where we are. We seem to be lost."

The concerned staff at the tower consulted their charts and attempted to guide Lieutenant Taylor back to the base. "Assume bearing due west," was the simple order broadcast to the bombers from the senior flight instructor at Lauderdale.

However, Taylor replied, "We don't know which way is west. Everything is wrong . . . strange. We can't be sure of any direction. Even the ocean doesn't look as it should."

Word of the weird predicament of Flight 19 spread like wildfire around the base at Fort Lauderdale. At 4.25 p.m. the last transmissions were heard from the doomed flight. The mystifying last comments were: "It looks like we are entering white water. We're completely lost."

That was followed by silence and crackles of static. Tension mounted in the crowded tower at Fort Lauderdale. The radio transceivers were retuned and the volume turned up, but the men of Flight 19 never radioed back.

There were claims by some of the staff at the tower that the last transmission from one ill-fated pilot of Flight 19 was the chilling statement: "Oh my God. They look like they're from outer space . . . don't come after us."

A Lieutenant Crone flew out to the last estimated position of Flight 19 in his Mariner flying boat with a crew of 13. This plane, with its 124-foot wing span, was larger than a Flying Fortress, and carried enough fuel to remain aloft for over a day. But within 20 minutes, radio contact with the Mariner flying boat was lost. No traces of the flying boat was ever found, nor was a single piece of wreckage from any of the five Avenger bombers ever found. On that fateful December day, six US Navy planes and 27 men had vanished without a trace. There was a Naval Board of Inquiry, but the members were unable to reach an official verdict. One member of the board later commented that Flight 19 and the Mariner flying boat had, "vanished completely as if they'd flown to Mars".

Scores of other planes, both military and civil aircraft,

vanished and malfunctioned while flying over the Triangle, and even satellites passing over the accursed region have been known to suffer technical glitches. In November 1969 Apollo 12 was in Earth orbit, its crew making preparations that would rocket their ship to the Ocean of Storms landing site on the Moon. Before they embarked on that historic trajectory, the astronauts took several snapshots of the Earth, and captured photographic evidence of a phenomenon which has only deepened the mystery of the Bermuda Triangle. The astronauts had photographed streaks of apparently white or luminous water in the area of the Bermuda Triangle, chiefly near to the Bahamas. These unusual streaks of luminosity were one of the last terrestrial things that the astronauts could discern from interplanetary space, but no one has ever explained the white waters phenomenon. Could this meteorological anomaly throw some light on the puzzling comments of the doomed Flight 19 crewmen, who spoke of entering "white waters" shortly before their transmissions ceased?

Even today, the Bermuda Triangle area still has an unusually high incidence of disappearances, and there has been talk of tackling the problem by conducting a study of the region, but as usual, the problem is scientists who are afraid to stick their necks out to admit that the Triangle exists. Japanese scientists have recently proposed leaving buoy-like probes in the Triangle. These weatherproof probes would have robust video cameras and an array of scientific measuring instruments to relay information back to a ship or land-based data-gathering centre. Of course, electronic and mechanical instruments have a tendency to malfunction in the Triangle, so it would be a risky venture, but at least the Japanese are making a noble attempt at understanding the phenomenon instead of uneasily dismissing it.

The "Men in Black" Mystery

One of the most sinister sub-cultures of the UFO phenomenon is the strange "men in black" who allegedly turn up at the homes or workplaces of people who have had an encounter with a UFO. Long before the modern UFO era, which commenced with Kenneth Arnold's sighting of UFOs in the skies over Washington State, it seems that the men in black were at large, threatening people who had witnessed unearthly spectacles to remain silent. For example, in 1905 North Wales was gripped by a tremendous religious revival when there was a spate of spectacular UFO sightings in the area. One woman named Mary Jones observed strange luminous globes and craft at very close quarters, but could not divulge her experiences, because she was visited on three successive nights by an eerie "man in black" who warned Mrs Jones to keep quiet about her close encounters or she'd be very sorry. There are many similar accounts further back in time, but the modern "men in black" scenario most UFO buffs are familiar with can be precisely dated back to a chilling incident which is alleged to have taken place in the early 1950s.

In January 1952 Albert K. Bender, a dedicated American UFO investigator, founded the International Flying Saucer Bureau in Connecticut. Bender spent an intensive year studying the UFO phenomenon from every conceivable angle, and then, one night, the "solution" hit him. Bender later stated, "I went into the fantastic and came up with the answer."

But no one ever got to know just what this answer was, for, according to Bender, he was silenced by three sinister men who appeared in his bedroom. The UFO investigator had typed an article about his findings for his own non-profit journal, *Space Review*, when he experienced a sudden dizzy spell. He went to lie on his bed, and was terrified at the sight of three black silhouettes materializing in his bedroom. When the shadows became solid, Bender saw that they were three men dressed in black clothes. Their faces were partly shaded by the Homburg-style hats that they wore. Bender said he felt the strangers probing his mind, and one of the visitors told the investigator that his speculation about the UFOs was correct, and Bender suddenly noticed that this man in black was holding the typescript of the article that had been written for the UFO journal.

A strong voice in Bender's head told him, "You are not to

tell anyone the truth; it is your duty as an American citizen. We have a special assignment down here and must not be disturbed by your people. We are among you and know your every move."

Moments later, the odd trio were nowhere to be seen; they'd vanished into thin air. Naturally, Bender was ridiculed when he told his colleagues about the etheric visitants but, unknown to most UFO researchers at the time, Bender's encounter with mysterious men in black was by no means a unique occurrence – reports of identically dressed visitors have been cropping up since the flying saucer era began in 1947. In the early days it was assumed that the strangers were CIA or FBI personnel because of their clandestine behaviour. In all the early reports, the men in black were said to wear outdated black suits and trilbys, and were always seen to arrive in a black Cadillac bearing number plates that turned out to be bogus. The visitors' faces, invariably described as oriental-looking, were often said to be crudely daubed with make-up. The victim who was harassed by the men in black was always a person who had encountered a UFO, and this person was always alone at the time of the visitation, as was Albert Bender.

In November 1961 office worker Paul Miller and three companions were on a homeward journey to Minot, North Dakota, after a hunting trip, when they noticed a 50-foot-long cylinder hovering in a field. The cylinder was glowing with a whitish-green light. Two figures descended from the underside of the strange object. From his stationary car, Paul Miller watched them advance, and panic seized him. He grabbed his rifle, got out of the car, and fired at the creatures, wounding one of them. He jumped into the car with his friends and they tore away from the area, but when they arrived at Minot, they felt strange, and learned that they had somehow lost three hours. Then they started to recall how they had all suffered a strange blackout simultaneously while travelling down a secluded road. Still, the four men agreed to keep their experience of the UFO encounter a secret.

The next morning, three men arrived at the office where Miller worked. They said they were government officials, but never showed their credentials, and asked to see Paul Miller. They quizzed Miller in private about the UFO encounter, but did not mention the shooting incident for some reason. The men – described as sallow-skinned and dressed in black – took Miller to his home and asked to see the clothes he had worn on the previous night. One of the men kept examining the soles of the shoes Miller had worn on the hunting trip. Miller asked the men how they had found out about the UFO sighting, but he received no reply. After probing the house for an hour, the men suddenly left and the Air Force later told Miller they too were in the dark regarding the identity of the visitors.

In August 1965 a Californian highway inspector named Rex Heflin saw a metallic disc-shaped object floating across the sky over the Santa Ana freeway. Heflin had a Polaroid camera at hand (for his job), and took four photographs of the UFO. The fourth picture was taken of a doughnut-shaped ring of smoke that the UFO left behind when it manoeuvred off into the heavens. The sighting attracted widespread media attention, and Heflin got a call from a man who said he was from the North American Air Defence Command (NORAD). An individual in typical "men in black" attire turned up at Heflin's home and persuaded him to hand over the Polaroid snaps of the UFO. Luckily, Heflin had taken the trouble of copying the photographs, because the man in black never returned the original UFO snapshots. NORAD denied any knowledge of the "representative" who had visited Heflin's home. Two years later, another suspicious-looking official turned up on Heflin's doorstep one night. Mindful of his last encounter with a dubious visitor, Heflin asked the stranger to show him some form of ID, and the stranger presented his credentials: a number of cards and documents that suggested that the caller was a Captain C. H. Edmonds of the Space Systems Division.

"What's your business?" Heflin asked Edmonds.

"It's about the photographs you took of the UFO. Are you going to try to get the originals of them back?" Edmonds asked.

"No", replied Heflin, and he noticed how his answer seemed to make the visitor smile slightly. Heflin suddenly noticed a black Cadillac parked in the street nearby. A silhouetted figure in the back of the vehicle was pointing a small device at Heflin and the visitor. This device was not unlike a modern camcorder, and Heflin felt he was being filmed with it.

The "captain" then started to ask Heflin if he had heard about the so-called Bermuda Triangle, and Heflin nodded, but the stranger then digressed into mundane talk, before saying goodnight.

A subsequent investigation proved that there were four Captain C. H. Edmonds on the Air Force's list of officers, but none of them resembled the man who had visited Heflin, and none of the captains had any connection with the Santa Ana UFO case.

Heflin returned home one day and two of his neighbours told him that they had seen men in military uniform sneaking around the back of Heflin's house. One of the mystery men seemed annoyed and resorted to knocking heavily on the front door of the house – before storming off to a Cadillac. On several occasions, Heflin found that the envelopes containing his mail had been tampered with, and whenever he used his telephone, he heard strange clicks which convinced him that he was being bugged.

While driving at night in July 1967, Robert Richardson of Toledo, Ohio, was negotiating a bend in a road when he found himself confronted with a strange circular craft that was blocking the road ahead. Unable to stop in time, he rammed the unearthly-looking object, which somehow "faded away" seconds after the impact.

Richardson told the police about the strange collision, but when they accompanied the driver to the scene of the crash, the officers could only make out the skid-marks of Richardson's car. Richardson returned to the crash scene the next day, and was surprised to find a small irregular-shaped lump of metal that looked as if it had come from the UFO. Richardson informed the Aerial Phenomena Research Organization (APRO) and told them that he had been in a collision with a UFO. A member of APRO recorded the time and date of the alleged incident and filed it. Richardson later took the strange piece of metal to APRO for analysis.

Three days later, at 11 p.m., two men in their late twenties confronted Richardson at his home and, without identifying themselves, they asked a series of questions relating to the UFO encounter. For some unexplained reason, Richardson felt peculiar, and had no desire to ask the visitors for their credentials. The strangers were very pleasant, and when they'd finished with their inquiries, they left the house and climbed into a black 1953 Cadillac. Richardson scribbled down the car's number, but when the registration was checked it was found that no such number had ever been issued in the United States.

A week later, two different men visited Richardson. They were dark complexioned, and one spoke in a perfect English accent, while the other had a similar accent with a slight, indeterminable foreign intonation. The men tried to persuade Richardson that he had imagined the UFO, but they later demanded that Richardson hand over the lump of metal. Richardson said that APRO had the metal, and one of the men in black warned, "If you want your wife to stay as pretty as she is, then you'd better get the metal back."

APRO concluded that the metal contained an unusually pure proportion of magnesium and iron, and when they handed the sample back to Richardson, he waited for he men in black to return for the metal lump, but they never did.

Another classic "men in black" incident took place at Maine, USA, in September 1976 at the home of Dr Herbert Hopkins, a 58-year-old doctor and hypnotist who was acting as a consultant on an alleged UFO abduction case. Early in the evening, a man phoned Hopkins and identified himself as the vice-president of the New Jersey UFO Research Organization. The caller asked Hopkins if he could come to his home to discuss the abduction case, as it was of immense interest to him. Dr Hopkins said he was welcome to come over. After putting the phone down, Dr Hopkins walked to the porch of his house – and there was the caller, walking up the porch steps. There was no car to be seen, and even if the man had travelled by car, Hopkins knew that the stranger couldn't possibly have reached the house that fast from any phone (in 1976 personal mobile phones were not in use).

Hopkins later said that the caller looked like an undertaker. The hat, suit, tie and shoes he wore were a funereal black. His shirt was white, and his suede gloves were grey.

The visitant was admitted to the house, and he and Dr Hopkins discussed the abduction case for about twenty minutes, when the visitor suddenly suggested something that made the doctor suspicious. The man in black told Hopkins, "Erase the tapes you have made of the hypnotic sessions with the UFO witnesses. Have nothing further to do with the case."

The suggestions made the doctor uneasy. The man in black put his gloved hand to his mouth and wiped what appeared to be a thick layer of lipstick. Upon seeing the red smear on his glove, the stranger quickly took off his gloves and put them in his inside jacket pocket. Hopkins watched in fear as the visitor stood up and approached menacingly. He said, "You have two coins in your pocket. Give me one of them."

The doctor reached into his pockets and discovered that the visitor was right. He did indeed have two coins. Hopkins placed one of them on the visitor's outstretched hand. Seconds later, the coin on the man's palm seemed to go out of focus – and then vanished before the doctor's unbelieving eyes.

"Neither you nor anyone else on this plane will ever see that coin again," the man in black said.

A few minutes later, the caller became unsteady on his feet, and his speech faltered. He enigmatically commented, "My energy is running low . . . must go now . . . goodbye."

The visitor staggered out of the house and descended the porch steps with great difficulty. Dr Hopkins saw a bluish-white light flashing in the driveway, but was too afraid to see what it was.

Later that night, when the doctor's family had returned from visiting relatives, someone noticed strange markings on the driveway. The black streaky markings ran along the centre of the driveway – where no wheels could have been. On the following morning, the markings had vanished, yet there had been no rain to wash them away.

Dr Hopkins was naturally reluctant to tell anyone of the "man in black" episode, but three days later, on 24 September, the mystery deepened when Maureen, the daughter-in-law of the doctor, was herself involved in a "men in black" type of incident.

Maureen received a telephone call from a man who said he was a friend of her husband, and he asked if he and his girl-friend could come to visit. Maureen asked her husband John who the caller was, and he explained that he had met an odd man a couple of days back at a fast-food restaurant. Maureen told the caller he was welcome to come over with his companion.

When the couple arrived, Maureen saw that they both appeared to be in their mid-thirties, but wore curiously old-fashioned clothes. The woman's breasts were set very low, and she walked in a peculiar way which seemed to originate with a hip problem. Both visitors took slow, short steps, as if they were frightened of falling.

John and Maureen offered them two bottles of Coca-Cola. The couple accepted the cola with enthusiastic nods but never even bothered to taste the drinks.

John and Maureen surveyed the way the couple sat awkwardly on the sofa. There was something artificial about the visitors; they almost seemed to be robotic in their move-ments. The man started to rub his partner's breasts with his hands. He looked at John as he did this and asked, "Is this the way it is done?"

John and Maureen were flabbergasted at the man's behav-iour.

"Do you and Maureen watch television much?" the man suddenly asked, and stopped fondling his partner.

"Yes, I suppose so. Why?" John answered. He was becoming intrigued with the couple.

The man continued to quiz John and Maureen. He asked if they read books. What did they read? What did they talk about?

The male guest then put two audacious questions to

Maureen: "Do you have any nude pictures of yourself? How were you made?"

Enough was enough. Maureen ordered the couple to leave immediately.

The man and woman stood, but the former seemed unable to walk. This seemed to frighten the woman, and she turned to John and said, "Please move him; I can't move him myself."

The man suddenly became animated, and walked directly to the door in a straight line, followed by his female companion. They both left without saying goodbye.

The reports of these strange individuals who pop up at the home and workplace of a UFO witness are still being reported. The FBI has shown an interest in the "men in black" phenomenon, and has frequently attempted to track down the "impostors" – but to date no one has been arrested. The men in black are always a step ahead of the authorities, and they now seem to be changing their mode of transport. The reports of black Cadillacs have now almost entirely been superseded with accounts of black unmarked helicopters buzzing the neighbourhood of UFO witnesses. In early 1994 George and Shirley Coyne, directors of the American UFO investigation organization MUFORA, actually presented the FBI with a videotape that clearly shows a black helicopter tailing the car that the couple were travelling in. The couple have allegedly received threats from the men in black, but Shirley Coyne says, "We're not afraid. They haven't done anything to us yet."

Since the collapse of communism in the former Soviet Union, the Russians have released many top secret reports of "men in black" incidents that have occurred in their country. In April 1992 one female witness who observed a UFO at close range near Moscow was later harassed by three mysterious men in black. One of the men actually paralyzed the woman by simply touching her. Throughout the intense paralysis, the woman felt as if her mind was being ransacked by the "oriental-looking" man. For months after the traumatic incident, the woman exhibited a strange bio-magnetism; pots and pans, anything metal, would stick to her as if she were a magnet, and people who touched her hands often experienced a severe electric shock.

Who are the sinister black-clad stalkers? Suggestions that they are secret service men sowing the seeds of disinformation – a typical CIA practice – just doesn't stand up when we realize that these unearthly thugs have been reported in countries like the USSR and China, where Western intelligence agents cannot operate. That leaves us with only one other possibility: that the men in black are from another planet – perhaps another dimension, even. But what is their purpose here on Earth? Time will tell.

PART TWO

Mysterious Creatures
• •

Werewolves

> *Even he who is pure of heart*
> *And says his prayers by night*
> *May become a wolf when the wolfbane blooms*
> *And the Moon is full and bright.*
>
> *Anon.*

Werewolves – men and women who have been transfigured into wolf-like creatures – may seem nothing more than a grim folk tale from the Dark Ages, but long before the time of Christ there were well documented reports of sinister human-wolf hybrids being at large. Some of these creatures were said to have been ordinary people transformed through black magic into enormous wolves or fur-covered bipeds who retain some of their human characteristics. If only these reports were unreliable, sensational products of a superstitious or unbalanced mind; then we would be able to dismiss them. But a majority of the accounts and descriptions of werewolves come from level-headed soldiers, doctors and lawyers. The ways a man or woman can become a werewolf are not known with any certainty, but it was once claimed that eating the wolfbane plant or drinking from a stream from which a wolf has drunk will induce the transformation. Then there is the transforming power of the malevolent curse inflicted by those well versed in occult science. This was thought to have been the case in eighteenth-century France, when a libidinous nobleman named Count Getulio Vargo attacked a beautiful young gypsy woman near the Auvergne mountains in southern central France.

Count Vargo raped the 20-year-old woman one moonlit night but he was apprehended by her brothers as he dragged her by the hair through the woods. The brothers dealt the young nobleman a severe beating and chased him through the woodland. One of the Romany brothers swore a strange curse at the fleeing aristocrat, which seemed nonsensical. In the jinx, the gypsy said all of nature would be against the count; all the animals would turn against him and that he would never rest. The lustful count laughed nervously as he fled, but 30 minutes later, a wood chopper saw a strange grey-furred overgrown beast, like a wolf, but standing on its hind legs, watching him from a forest clearing. The beast roared and charged towards the woodman, who was too terrified to run. Thankfully, the huge animal – which was larger than a bear – ran past him and closed in on a caped figure who had been strolling down a lane. This figure was the Count Vargo, just five minutes away from his home. The lupine monstrosity seized its terror-struck human prey with its huge foaming jaws and shook the body as if it were a rag doll. The wood chopper suddenly regained the power of movement in his legs and ran off to the sanctuary of his abode, which was little more than a log cabin.

As the woodman opened the door to his mountain home, his sole companion, an old Alsatian shepherd dog, bolted past its trembling master and ran at the strange creature attacking the count. The hound bit the rear of the ravenous beast, and the grizzled fiend reacted by twisting swiftly from the heavily lacerated body of the count. In one swift deadly reflexive movement, the monster tore out the throat of the old Alsatian with its powerful razor-toothed jaws. The wood chopper watched what happened next from a gap in the window shutters of his bolted home. The unidentified animal reared up on its hind legs and released a stomach-turning howl which echoed through the mountains. The animal then turned to face the woodman's dwelling, and for one heart-stopping moment, the wood chopper expected the demonic bipedal brute to come for him, but the animal ran off into the forest. The wood chopper refused to budge from the safety of his home until well after dawn, when he finally ventured out with a wood axe to survey the carnage. His old dog lay in a wide pool of blood, but Count Vargo was still alive and moaning, despite a heavy loss of blood from a neck and chest wound. The wood chopper carried the nobleman to his wooden shack and then went to the count's brothers to tell them of the traumatic incident.

Count Vargo made a miraculous recovery, but a month later he went missing from his home. His cook had thought it strange that during the past fortnight the count had repeatedly asked him to undercook the meat and poultry of his meals. One of the servants had even witnessed Count Vargo eating a raw leg of lamb in the pantry during the night.

The brothers of the count surmised he had been driven insane by his horrific encounter with the ursine-like monster, so they paid the local villagers to patrol the region, but the missing aristocrat was nowhere to be found.

Then one Sunday night a month later, in June 1764, a bloodcurdling howl reverberated through the nearby Margeride mountains in the neighbouring district of Gevaudan, and so began a nightmare saga which is still talked about in that part of France to this day. The howling that caused the peasants of Gevaudan to shiver in their beds came from the Mercoire forest near Langogne. One brave woman who went out to locate the eerie animal came upon a sight which was to haunt her for the rest of her life. She described the animal to the terrified villagers:

> It was the size of a cow with a very wide chest, an enormous head and neck, pointed ears that were like erect horns. Its long snout was akin to that of a greyhound, and four long fangs protruded from the monster's mouth, which was foaming. The tail of the animal was long and very thin, and a black stripe ran from the space between the beast's eyes, along its back, down to the tail. It had big claws which looked like a man's hand only three times larger, and its eyes glinted red and contained so much evil. For as long as I live I shall never forget the malicious way the creature regarded me. Those eyes were not those of an animal; they were the eyes of something that had once been a man.

The woman went on to describe how the strange-looking

Wild Beast of the Gevaudan, France

animal had circled the cows, but two bulls had kept the creature at bay with their horns. After a few tense moments the freakish animal ran off at high speed in 30-foot bounds.

In the months following the sighting, the "Beast of Gevaudan", as it became known, went on a killing spree; and humans as well as livestock were the victims. The beast slaughtered men, women and children in the region and often left the victims barely alive minus their torn-off limbs. The people of Gevaudan and the farming communities of the Margeride mountains barricaded themselves indoors as soon as twilight was falling, but the marauding beast still found more victims. One young milkmaid was literally torn apart within 20 feet of her two brothers, who attempted to beat off the Beast of Gevaudan with cudgels studded with spikes, but it was useless. The animal seemed invulnerable and hardly reacted to the two men beating it on the head and back as the screaming woman's head was torn off by the lion-sized mouth. One of the brothers fled and the one who stood his ground had four fingers on his hand bitten off by the satanic creature. When the brothers returned at first light to the spot of the attack, they found the shredded corpse of their sister. It was only recognizable because of the ring visible on the remains of a mutilated hand. An old man who visited the site of the butchery trembled and remarked, "This is not the work of a wild animal. It is the work of a werewolf. There were werewolves in these woods and mountains when I was a child."

The elderly man's comments struck a chord of terror in the minds of the people gathering to see the torn-apart remains of the milkmaid.

On 8 October 1764 it became apparent that the Beast of Gevaudan was no ordinary animal when two professional hunters tracked down the animal and blasted it with powerful muskets from a mere ten paces. The beast dropped but got quickly to its feet. The hunters reloaded their rifles and moved closer, thinking they would be able to finish it off, but after they fired at it again, the animal fell down for a few seconds, rose once more and ran into a wood. The hunters reloaded and gave chase. The men managed to discharge two rounds into the animal, but the Beast of Gevaudan seemed impervious to the musket shot and escaped.

The hunters assured the terrified locals that the bloodthirsty creature had been fatally wounded and would be found dead soon.

Even more victims were killed by the demoniacal carnivore in the following week, bringing the death toll to 40. The Beast of Gevaudan generated so much mass hysteria with its horrific and audacious attacks that news of its horrifying assaults reached the ears of a Captain Duhamel, who decided to draft 57 of his dragoons into the animal's killing grounds.

Forty men patrolled on foot and 17 mounted soldiers scoured the countryside after dark, but still the Beast managed to carry out its horrifying attacks right under the dragoon's noses. Duhamel was greatly embarrassed by the boldness of the creature, and added fuel to the werewolf rumour by saying that the Beast of Gevaudan suspiciously showed an almost human intelligence, which made him ponder upon its nature.

Even when the cracksmen of the dragoons had fired repeatedly at the Beast, it seemed invulnerable and simply turned to run without suffering a scratch. This seemed to back up the claims of a deranged local peasant suffering from religious mania who warned the people of the region that Beelzebub had been sent among them in the form of the Beast, as punishment for their iniquities.

The news of the eerie ravenous animal spread throughout France and the other countries of Europe, and soon every professional and amateur hunter was converging on Gevaudan, spurred on by the promise of a large reward which had been put up by the farmers being terrorized by the voracious killer. King Louis XV was mortified by the failure of the dragoons to kill the Beast of Gevaudan, so he enlisted the services of a man named Denneval who was reputed to be the greatest wolf hunter in Europe. Denneval had killed 1200 wolves during his career and was said to have an almost supernatural talent for tracking down animals. The hunter turned up at Gevaudan in February 1765 with six of his best bloodhounds and attempted to track down the Beast, but the dogs became quivering wrecks and began to yelp when they approached the area where the creature had recently been seen.

A month afterwards, the Beast carried out a particularly violent attack on the Denis family of Malzieu. Julienne and Jeanne, the young daughters of Farmer Denis, were looking after the livestock in a field with their 16-year-old brother Jacques when the Beast came out of hiding and struck.

Jeanne, Jacques' 20-year-old sister, suddenly let out a scream. The boy turned from the fire he had just lit in the field and saw the enormous wolf-like animal seizing his sister's head with its jaws. Jacques was so enraged by the animal's attempt to kill his sister that he ran over to it and somehow managed to grab the animal by its throat and pull it away from Jeanne, who was screaming hysterically.

Jacques squeezed the Beast's throat as hard as he could, and the animal snapped at him with its enormous mouth, but the muscular young farmhand used his fear and anger and summoned an inner strength. He threw the Beast onto the fire he'd just built and the animal howled in agony, before running off back to where it had sprung from.

Jeanne Denis was still screaming, with blood pouring from two deep perforations behind each ear, made by the fangs of the Beast. Jacques tried to calm his older sister down but she never recovered from the attack and went insane.

A month later the gruesome remains of a woman and her child were found in a wood. The grisly find incited Denneval to track down the creature, but it always seemed one step ahead of him and continued to evade capture.

In April 1765 the Beast approached a nobleman called de la Chaumette and acted very strangely. De la Chaumette said the animal wagged its tail as if to exhibit some sort of affection for him. It whined and approached the nobleman, who was on horseback, but he reacted by firing his pistol at the creature. It ran off and kept glancing back before it vanished into a wood. That same day the Beast was seen crossing a ravine just a mile from the curious encounter with de la Chaumette.

Around this time, an old Jesuit priest made a startling accusation about de la Chaumette's placid encounter with the Beast of Gevaudan. The priest maintained that he had discovered that the Beast had been the nobleman's close friend Count Vargo in the form of a werewolf; that was why the animal acted so affectionately towards de la Chaumette.

De la Chaumette was outraged by the holy man's claim, but secretly confided to friends that the Jesuit might have hit on the awful truth behind the Beast of Gevaudan. After all, no one had yet been able to find the missing count. The Jesuit was later interrogated by de la Chaumette, who was curious how the Roman Catholic priest had deduced that Count Vargo was the Beast of Gevaudan, but the elderly divine would only say that he could no longer comment on his allegation because his superiors had instructed him to refrain from discussing werewolves and other unholy creatures.

In May 1765 the creature terrorizing Gevaudan killed several people in one day and also killed the rumours that the Beast had been killed by troops. The King of France had been confidently informed by his emissary Denneval that the creature had been killed and was probably lying dead in a wood. When the king heard that the Beast was still at large and again on the rampage, Denneval was unceremoniously sacked by the monarch, and Antoine de Beauterne, the king's personal gun carrier, was assigned to rid Gevaudan of its monster.

De Beauterne was more methodical in his pursuit of the Beast. He drew up detailed maps of Gevaudan, analyzed the common routes the animal took on its people-hunting expeditions, and hatched meticulous plans to entrap the creature. All the plans hinged on a gut feeling de Beauterne had about a ravine in the area which he suspected of being the Beast's lair. By 21 September of that year, the plans were ready and rehearsed to a T. Forty hunters and a dozen dogs encircled the Beal ravine. The circle of men and canines closed in slowly and, sure enough, the Beast appeared in a clearing. It turned slowly, surveying the armed men closing in as they beat the thicket with canes. The hunting dogs barked furiously at the unearthly creature, which was looking desperately for a break in the human link to make its escape. Suddenly, the Beast charged at one of the hunters but Antoine de Beauterne shouldered his heavy calibre musket and fired. The shot blasted the Beast's eyeball open and exited through its skull. Another shot from a gunman struck the animal in its right shoulder. The Beast reared up on its two legs, then fell down. One of the hunters cheered and sounded on his horn in triumph.

Then the Beast got up with blood dripping from its eye socket. It bounded at de Beauterne, but another hunter shot it in its thigh. The animal yelped and turned towards a break in the circle, then raced off to make its escape. Antoine de Beauterne and the hunters watched in disbelief as the ultra-resilient creature once again cheated death and evaded capture, but this time the animal was too seriously wounded, and as it ran off, it stumbled and fell. It refused to get up again, and when the hunters gathered around the Beast with their muskets trained on it, they saw that the animal was motionless. At last, the Beast of Gevaudan was dead.

The carcass was measured and weighed. It was over six feet in length and weighed 143 pounds. No one could decide just what the animal was, although some naturalists claimed it was a rare type of overgrown wolf. The Beast of Gevaudan was stuffed and taken to the king's court. It was later exhibited at the Museum of Natural History at Paris, but was lost at the beginning of the twentieth century.

The people of Gevaudan regarded Antoine de Beauterne as

their saviour, and were almost ready to venerate him as a saint, but in the winter of 1766 something started killing and mutilating the locals again. The word went round that the Beast had been resurrected, while other rumours had it that there was a family of werewolves at large in the area.

In the summer of that year, several villagers from Gevaudan made a pilgrimage to Notre-Dame de Beaulieu, which was located at the foot of Mount Chauvet. After celebrating mass and taking holy communion, the pilgrims had a gun and several cartridges they had brought along blessed. When they returned to Gevaudan, a man named Jean Chastel was given the blessed gun and cartridges to kill the new Beast. This took place on 19 June 1767 at the scene of the last Beast-slaying – the Beal ravine. Chastel read out passages from the Bible, and everyone present heard the rustling of leaves. An enormous animal which looked identical to the Beast came out of the shadows of a wood and stood staring at Chastel. The latter raised his blessed musket and ammunition and pointed it at the creature. After saying, "You will kill no more," he opened fire and hit the animal in the head. The gigantic wolf-like animal fell dead instantly. Some accounts say the second Beast was thrown on a bonfire, and that on the spot where it was killed, the grass refuses to grow.

Count Vargo was never found, and his fate remains a mystery.

The Welsh Werewolf

As most horror film buffs know, a werewolf is a person who changes into a wolf-like creature when the moon is full. This is a myth, as most country-dwellers who know their folklore will tell you. A real werewolf is said to be a large unidentified species of wolf which has no tail and is usually quite long; often over seven feet in length, the animal carries out most of its hunting at night when the moon is full, but these strange creatures also go on the prowl most nights regardless of whether the moon is full or not. Most people have heard of the Beast of Bodmin Moor and the Surrey Puma: strange unidentified animals which have been tearing hundreds of sheep and cattle apart for years, but there is another violent creature roaming parts of the United Kingdom which has also killed people, and this animal is known as the Welsh Werewolf.

Records of an enormous wolf-like animal in North Wales date back to 1790, when a stagecoach travelling between Denbigh and Wrexham was allegedly attacked and over-turned by an enormous black beast almost as long as the coach horses. The terrifying animal tore into one of the horses and killed it, while the other horse broke free from its harness and galloped off into the night whining in terror. The attack took place just after dusk, with a full moon on the horizon. The moon that month seemed blood red, probably because of dust in the stratosphere from a recent forest fire in the Hatchmere area. The locals in North Wales and Cheshire thought the moon's rubrical colour was a sign that something evil was at large and the superstitious phrase "bad moon on the rise" was whispered in traveller's inns across the region.

In the winter of 1791 a farmer went into his snow-covered field just seven miles east of Gresford, and he saw enormous tracks that looked like those belonging to an overgrown wolf. With a blacksmith, he followed the tracks for two miles, and they led to a scene of mutilation which made the villagers in the area quake with fear that night.

The tracks led into a farmstead where every single animal had been either literally torn to shreds or mortally wounded. One snow-covered field was just a lake of blood dotted with carcasses of sheep, cattle, and even the farmer's dog. The farmer was found locked up in his house in a terrible state. He wasn't harmed physically, but he was terrified. He had barri-caded himself in after witnessing an enormous black animal that resembled a wolf ripping the throat out of his sheepdog. The animal had then gone for the farmer, but he had just managed to run in the farmhouse in time. He had bolted the heavy oaken door and hid under a table in the kitchen armed only with a pitchfork. The farmer said the wolf pounded on the heavy oak door, almost knocking it off its hinges. The weird-looking animal then stood up on its hind legs like a human and looked in through the windows of the farmhouse.

Its eyes were blue and seemed intelligent and almost human-like. The beast foamed at the mouth as it peered in, then bolted from the window to commit wholesale carnage on the farm. Each of the sheep were left as pelts of wool with a head attached, lying flat on the snow like a woollen mat. The animal had even eaten sections of the animals' spines, and no one had ever seen a predator do something like that before. The church set up patrols in search of what was suspected to be an evil werewolf, and bands of villagers braved the freezing blizzards with lanterns, muskets and pitchforks in search of the ravenous beast, but only its tracks were ever seen.

Seven years later, two men walking across the Bickerton Hills in Cheshire saw something that sent them running for their lives. The full moon had just risen, and as it peeped over the hilltop, the travellers saw the silhouette of an enormous unidentified animal against the lunar disc. The animal lifted its head and let out a bloodcurdling howl which echoed through the Cheshire hills. The two men rushed into an inn and refused to continue their journey until morning. At dawn on the following day, the mutilated bodies of two vagrants were found in a wood just five miles from the inn. It didn't seem to be murder, because their bodies had been literally slashed to ribbons by something which had claws like knives. One of the victims had tried to cross a stream as he had fled the scene of the slaying and had been pounced upon in the waters. His head was never found, and seemed to have been torn off. The head of the other victim was found stripped of its face and ears in another part of the wood. The jaws of the animal that killed the man must have been powerful because the victim's skull had been cracked and splintered during the gruesome attack.

Someone wrote an anonymous letter and posted it to the local minister. The letter-writer said the beast that had killed the men had been a werewolf which had been on the loose in that area of Cheshire and Wales for over a hundred years. The letter-writer said that the attack had happened during an eclipse of the moon, when the moon passes into the earth's shadow and seems to turn dark red, and he claimed that he had heard the terrible screams of the tramps who were slaughtered by the animal. The writer told the minister to paint crosses on the doors of each dwelling in the village because the werewolf was driven in its bloodlust by the evil spirit of a Welsh warlock who had been burnt at the stake by the ancestors of the villagers in the year 1400.

The attacks by the large black wolf gradually died out, and the people of Cheshire and Wales breathed a sigh of relief.

But two centuries later, attacks by a large unidentified animal were reported once more. In February 1992 a Welsh newspaper called the *Western Mail* reported sightings of a strange bear-like animal that had been seen across Wales. In the north of the country, a farmer who had spotted the animal on the night of a full moon said he had afterwards found two of his full-grown 70-pound lambs ripped apart. One of the lambs was flattened as if it had been run over by a farm tractor. There were around 70 further sightings between 1992 and 1994, and London Zoo gave the farmers in the area advice for trapping the unknown predator.

Cages baited with steaks and special trapdoors were installed on the farms in the hope that the beast would venture into one of them. The thing did go into one cage, but when the door sprung shut, the animal pulled two steel bars open and escaped. London Zoo said some lunatic must have helped the animal escape, but the farmer said that the animal had pulled the bars apart itself. London Zoo experts said no known animal could have done something like that, even a grisly bear. One pathetic explanation was that a wolverine was on the loose, but the tracks left by the violent animal seem to indicate that it is a large variety of wolf. One American expert on animal tracks said the prints left by the animal strongly resembled fossilized tracks left by the long extinct sabre-toothed tiger. But the sabre-toothed tiger has not roamed Britain since the Pleistocene Era over 2 million years ago. From the pattern of sightings made after 1995, it seems that the so-called "Welsh Werewolf" is steadily moving eastwards towards Cheshire and Merseyside.

The Giant Spider of the Ukraine

The following creepy tale has been buzzing around the Internet for years and has also appeared in various tabloids in Europe, but has never been reported in the British or American press.

In the summer of 1990 police in Russia found a resident in a block of flats in the Ukraine area dead on the floor of an elevator. The man had two holes in the side of his neck – which was badly bruised yellow and blue. At the post mortem, the coroner discovered that the man in the elevator had died through shock and loss of blood. About 1.5 litres of blood were missing, yet there had been no bloodstains in the elevator. It was as if a vampire had sucked the blood out of the dead man, but the Russian police couldn't accept that outlandish explanation.

A month later, police were called to the same block of flats because a girl of thirteen was trapped in the elevator, which was stuck between the fourth and fifth floor. Residents heard the girl screaming frantically, and when the police arrived with three members of the local fire service and gained access to the elevator, they found the girl lying on the floor of the elevator. The girl was dead, and two small puncture marks were later found on the girl's left breast, which was heavily bruised. The residents refused to use the faulty elevator, and were convinced that a vampire was at large in the block of flats.

Police started to play down the seemingly unsolvable deaths, and one former KGB propaganda minister named Leonid Keernev suggested that the girl had died after injecting heroin, but the dead girl's parents threatened to sue the official, because their daughter had never taken drugs and no syringe was found in the elevator.

To get to the bottom of the matter, a Russian detective and a sergeant entered the lift and rode it continually up and down. The two men were armed with pistols and carried flashlights and two-way radios.

Three days later, the lift was travelling upwards when it halted in-between the fifth and sixth floors of the building. The lights went out, so the men switched on their torches and two-way radios to alert their colleagues who were playing cards in a police van in the street below.

The two trapped men waited, perhaps wondering if some ghostly vampire was about to materialize. There was a long silence for about three minutes; then they heard something scuttling above their heads. Something was moving along the roof of the elevator. The detective noticed a black square – almost a foot across – set in the roof of the elevator where an access panel had come away. The lift was so old that the panel had probably fallen off because of rust. The detective shone his torch through the square hole in the roof, and the beam from his torch lit up the lift shaft above and the steel cables supporting the lift. Something peered through that hole that made the detective's blood run cold. A small black hairy head the size of an orange with a bunch of black gleaming eyes the size of grapes looked in at him.

The sergeant was terrified by the freakish-looking animal and raised his Beretta and aimed it at the thing, but the detective calmly ordered him not to fire yet.

"What is it?" said the petrified police sergeant, trembling, and almost dropping his torch with nerves.

"Turn your torch off," the detective said to the sergeant.

"What? No way, sir," the sergeant protested, sweating heavily.

"That thing doesn't like light," said the detective. "You keep your torch on, then, and I'll turn mine off. Don't make any sudden moves, and tell the men downstairs to stand by."

The detective switched off his light, and watched the thing slide further into the lift. Suddenly, the sergeant's nerves got the better of him, because he had three phobias: fear of the dark; fear of enclosed spaces; and arachnaphobia – a fear of spiders – and that horrible thing hanging through the hole in the ceiling looked like an overgrown spider. So the sergeant freaked out and dropped his torch, and his nerves cost him his life. The torch hit the floor and smashed. Before the detective could switch on his torch, the enormous hairy black spider dropped into the lift with lightning agility and bit out at the only thing in the lift that was moving excitedly. The spider bit the unfortunate sergeant's face and hung on as it drew out his blood. The detective switched on his torch and saw the whole nightmarish drama. The sergeant was screaming, and the spider was like something from another planet. Its body was the size of a Jack Russell dog, and its six hairy legs were almost three feet long. The freak insect's mouthparts were embedded into the sergeant's face, and as it sucked out his blood, the spider's body turned red. The detective took aim and shot twice at the spider. The first shot missed, and the second bullet blasted one of the spider's legs off, but when the bullet ricocheted off the wall, it bounced back and smashed the torch bulb. The lift was once again in total darkness. The sergeant stopped screaming and his body hit the floor with a thump, and the detective could feel the bristly hairs on the insect brush against him as the huge spider ran past and climbed back up to the hole in the elevator's roof.

When the police and firemen opened the elevator, they found the dead sergeant, whose terror-stricken face was bruised and bloody – and on the floor in the corner, sat the traumatized detective. Nearby on the elevator floor was a long hairy black leg of the spider, still twitching. The detective remained speechless for a while then blurted out the incredible story. The authorities quickly hushed up the incident, but news of the story got out via the Internet, and a version of the story also appeared in a Turkish newspaper, but was quickly denounced as an exaggeration. It was claimed that the giant spider was a deformed black widow spider that had been mutated by the radioactive fallout from the recent Chernobyl nuclear plant disaster. Later reports on the Internet said Russian troops had destroyed the spider with a flame-thrower, then discovered the insect had laid eggs at the top of the lift shaft.

Four Weird Unidentified Creature Reports

1. The **Chupacabras** (pronounced Chew-pah-kahb-rahs) means "goat-sucker" in Spanish and is the name of a strange-looking creature which has allegedly been killing livestock and pets all over the world since the late 1970s. Those who claim they've encountered the unidentified animal say that it

Chupacabras (goatsucker), mysterious creature responsible for killing animals in Puerto Rico and Mexico during 1990s – based on eye-witness descriptions

stands between four to five feet in height and has red eyes, long fangs, powerful legs and a dull grey skin. Many witnesses have also stated that the Chupacabras has spinal quills that double as wings. The creature was first reported in 1975 at Rio

Grande Valley, South Texas, when something began killing cattle in the area and draining every drop of blood from the carcasses. A condor was initially blamed, but several people in the area said an unusually large wolf-like creature was seen at the time of the attacks on livestock and managed to avoid capture.

After something of a hiatus, the bloodsucker came out of retirement and was at large in Puerto Rico in 1995, where it caused the baffling deaths of around 1200 animals, including turkeys, rabbits, goats, cats, dogs, cows and even horses. The most bizarre sighting of the Chupacabras took place in November of that year when the strange entity entered a house in the north-central city of Caguas and pounced on a stuffed teddy bear. The creature was described as being similar in appearance to a wolf but three times the size.

The Chupacabras has also allegedly been seen in Europe and the suburbs of Moscow, but cryptozoologists are split in their opinions as to what type of creature it is, and, in the meantime, the bizarre animals remain at large.

2. The **Wisconsin Werewolf** has a long history which is said to date back to the legends of the American Indians, but in modern times the legend of the Canadian wolfman can be traced back to the early 1930s. One night in 1936, just east of Highway 18, in the vicinity of Jefferson, Wisconsin, Mark Schackelman came upon a tall humanoid beast that was covered in black hair and gave off a repulsive aroma which reminded him of rancid meat. The hairy man was clawing at the earth of an old Indian burial mound, and when it turned to face Schackelman, he saw to his horror that the anthropoid had a face which resembled a cross between a dog and an ape. Schackelman instantly had the gut-wrenching feeling that he was looking at something Satanic, and he had the urge to flee, even though his legs were numb with fear. The bipedal wolfman started to growl at Schackelman, then snarled a three-syllable word at him which sounded like "gadara". Seconds later, the hairy humanoid vanished. Schackelman later learned that "gadara" was the name of a Bigfoot-like creature that had been reported in the north-eastern USA. There were further major sightings of the Wisconsin

"manimal" in July 1964 and November 1968, and since then the werewolf has been seen by scores of people. Some cryptozoologists think that the so-called werewolf is probably an undiscovered species of indigenous ape – perhaps a cousin of Bigfoot?

3. The **Indiana Toxic Sludge Mutant** – it may sound like something out of a "B" movie of the 1950s, but both the US Environmental Protection Agency and the Indiana Department of Environmental Management have not only officially confirmed that this bizarre creature exists, they are also taking the matter very seriously. The strange animal was first reported in November 1996 when a 30-year-old employee of General Motors saw a squid-like creature, the colour of an earthworm, in the sludge pit of Delphi Interior and Lighting Systems Plant 9 at Anderson, Indiana. The pit, which had contained a swampy mixture of antifreeze, paint stripper, oil and polyal (a chemical cocktail used to make car bumpers), had just been cleaned out when a writhing tentacled creature was spotted in the pit. It was killed and placed in a jar for examination. It was about eight inches long with long tentacles and primitive eyes, but could not be identified. Then more of the creatures surfaced. Some of them were also killed and put in jars, but the others squirmed back under the chemical dregs. Sharon Morton, a spokeswoman for the Delphi company in Detroit, tried to play down the incident by telling the press that the so-called squids were a minor "bacterial growth" in the pit, but no one will ever know just what creatures were found in the pit of Plant 9 because US government officials confiscated all the specimens.

4. The **Giant Shrimp**. In 1948 a young woman named Virginia Staples of Washington State moved into an old apartment on Denny Street, Bremerton. The landlord told her that she could use the washing machine in the basement, where there were a number of clotheslines strung to dry her clothes. Miss Staples was using the crude washing facilities in the basement one day when she noticed several gaping holes in the walls. The landlord said these holes were rumoured to

be passages which led down to the sea, and no one knew why they were there. However, he intended to have them sealed up in the near future. Several tenants of the house told Virginia not to use the basement, as there was something creepy at large down there. Virginia didn't know what the tenants were referring to until a week later, when she was hanging up her clothes. Miss Staples had the intense unnerving feeling that she was being watched by someone – or something – and she finally turned around towards the back of the basement. What she saw would give her nightmares for the rest of her life.

A strange-looking creature, some five feet or more in height, emerged from one of the holes in the wall. It had a bright orange colour with little spidery legs and antennae on its head. It looked just like an enormous giant shrimp. The head of the creature moved in and out of some sort of shell and its emotionless beady red eyes surveyed the woman, making her skin crawl.

Virginia was paralyzed with shock and unable to cry out. Suddenly, the terrifying creature made a clicking noise and advanced towards her with four extended insect-like arms. Virginia suddenly recovered the power of movement and turned and ran out of the basement. She was so terrified that she left the house that day and went to live with a cousin in Seattle.

In the meantime, other residents heard strange clicking and scraping noises in the same basement, but, despite numerous complaints to the landlord and the local authorities, no investigations were undertaken, and the house was later torn down. During demolition, it was established that three passages in the house led to a sewer which drained into an inlet from the sea.

Out-of-Place Animals

At precisely 1 a.m. on a 18 July 1963 lorry driver David Black braked his vehicle at Shooters Hill in south-east London because he thought he saw an injured dog lying by the roadside. Black left his vehicle to go to the aid of the animal.

He later reported: "I walked over to it, and then it got up. I knew then that it wasn't a dog. It had long legs and a long pointed tail that curled up. It looked as if it had a mouthful of food. It ran off into the woods."

The police were naturally sceptical about Mr Black's story, but a patrol car was sent to the area soon after the alleged encounter. A large, fierce-looking cat, resembling a cheetah, charged at the police car and leaped clean over the bonnet. The police were no longer sceptical, and later that day the big-game hunt was on for the creature the press christened the "Beast of Shooters Hill". One hundred and twenty-six policemen were drafted in with 21 tracker dogs at their disposal. Thirty soldiers were also sent into the Shooters Hill area to track down the beast, and they were later accompanied by ambulance men, animal welfare officers and hundreds of citizens armed with pickaxe handles, air rifles and hatchets. During the hunt, the authorities believed the creature being stalked was a cheetah – the fastest land mammal, which can move at the phenomenal speed of around 70 miles per hour – so motorcycle police were brought into the hunt. Over 850 acres of woods and open common were combed by the hunters, but all they found was a set of large paw prints in a muddy stream bed. The Beast of Shooters Hill seemed to have vanished into thin air. The mystery cat was seen three times more that week, but was never captured. Just how a cheetah, if that's what the beast was, came to be in the Shooters Hill area of London has never been answered satisfactorily; the cat is indigenous to Africa and south-west Asia!

Another out-of-place animal that has been prowling the suburbs of London for over two centuries is the Surrey Puma. The earliest written record of a big unidentified cat in the Surrey area is to be found in William Cobbett's *Rural Rides*, published in 1830. In his book about the English countryside, writer and journalist Cobbett claimed that in 1770, when he was an eight-year-old, he saw a large fierce-looking cat up a tree near Waverley Abbey. The cat was seen irregularly over the two centuries, but in the 1960s there was an amazing spate of puma sightings that struck fear into the hearts of people living in the patchwork of commuter towns in the rolling countryside of Surrey. It all began in the summer of 1964 when strange bloodcurdling howling noises were heard one night near Crondall on the Hampshire border. The howling, described by one petrified pensioner as "the sound of a hundred cats being murdered", continued for weeks in different areas of Surrey, and in each area where the nocturnal ululation was heard, cattle would subsequently be found mauled by something with a large bite span and razor-sharp claws.

In August that year Farmer Edward Banks, the manager of Bushylease Farm in Crondall, saw the savage work of the Surrey Puma when he found a horribly mauled steer in the nearby woods. The young bullock had broken out of its enclosure with the rest of the herd on the previous night when the puma was circling its field. The big cat had evidently singled out the animal after frightening the rest of the herd into a stampede. All this was no surprise to Farmer Banks; he had seen the puma many times over the previous two years, and knew it would only be a matter of time before it attacked his livestock. Fortunately, the steer survived, but other farmers in the area read of the attack and decided to patrol the vicinity with shotguns, ready to blast the "Crondall Cougar". Billy Davidson, a Canadian ranger on holiday in the area, joined in the hunt, but the big cat wasn't caught. Davidson was a professional at puma tracking, and he vouched that the mystery cat was a puma, and he even identified its lair, but the enigmatic feline never returned to the den.

By September the Godalming police had logged 362 sightings of the puma in their daybook, and the authorities thought the sightings were the result of a mass break-out from a zoo. Checks were made at every zoo in the south of England, but no wild animals were absent.

On 4 September a blackberry picker named George Wisdom had an encounter with a huge snarling cat at Munstead, Surrey. Wisdom heard deep growling from bushes, and was terrified when a puma-like animal emerged from hiding. It was around five to six feet in length, excluding its long tail, and had a black stripe running down its dark golden brown body. Fortunately for Mr Wisdom, the cat turned away and disappeared back into the undergrowth. Three days later, a half-mile trail of paw-prints appeared overnight in freshly raked sand that had been laid down by the local racing stables for practice gallops. Each print was six inches across, and they were quickly identified as puma prints by experts from London Zoo.

Just a stone's throw from Munstead Common, on 24 September, a roe deer was found dead with a broken neck and deep multiple lacerations on its body. Nearby a heifer was found. It was badly wounded but alive. The pattern of sightings suggested that the puma was moving in a north-eastern direction – towards London.

Zoological experts were baffled at the presence of a cat that was native only to North and South America. In 1964 there were only 23 pumas in Britain, and they were all securely behind bars. There were many theories to explain the origins of the big cat. The favourite hypothesis at the time was that a puma cub had been imported illegally in the late 1950s; once it had grown, it had either escaped or been deliberately freed. In 1966 a rumour swept Surrey: a boy from London who had been attending the Guildford Show that year had been overheard to say that he knew of a family in Woking that had released three puma cubs into the Surrey countryside. The boy was never traced, leaving the story unconfirmed.

Later that year, on 4 July, the Surrey Puma was seen in a field in full view of scores of witnesses that included policemen, Post Office engineers, and villagers. For 20 minutes the cat roamed a meadow adjoining the home of the Reverend Andrew Elphingstone, the Queen's cousin, at Worplesdon, near Guildford. One of the first to see the cat was Inspector Eric Bourn of the Special Constabulary, who watched it from his garden from a distance of 100 yards, after hearing a Post Office engineer who was working close by yell, "Look at that puma!" Mr Bourn told a reporter from the *Times*:

> *I went to where the engineer was standing and sure enough, without any doubt whatsoever, there was the puma. I watched it come out of a copse, and walk along the side of the meadow, keeping to the cover of the hedge,*

to within 100 yards of the bottom of my garden. Then it lay out of sight. It was ginger-brown colour and the size of a Labrador dog. I rang the police. Just as they arrived it got up and sauntered back at a leisurely pace to the copse as I watched through field glasses. I do not know whether it saw us watching but it was in no hurry as it went to Mr Elpingstone's copse and disappeared. We went over to where it had lain in the grass and found a half-eaten rabbit.

A motorcycle patrol officer, PC Robin Young, also saw the puma. He told the *Times*:

The animal was in sight for 20 minutes and there was no doubt it was a puma. It was ginger-coloured and had a long tail with a white tip and a catlike face. It was just walking casually through the meadow. I had a good look at it through binoculars from 60 yards away. One of the villagers there had a shotgun and took a pot shot. Then the animal took off. We followed it for about half a mile then lost it when it reached the road.

Puma-mania peaked around 1966, with many pubs in Surrey and the south-east London suburbs unscrupulously selling "game permits" to every would-be puma hunter. Large-scale "safaris" were held almost every week, but they always failed to find their quarry.

Big cats are still being seen all over Britain. In 1994 they came under government scrutiny for the first time when an official conference on the Beast of Bodmin was organized by someone who had had an encounter with a big cat: Paul Tyler, MP for North Cornwall. The conference drew landowners, police officials, MPs, representatives from the National Farmers Union, and the Ministry of Agriculture. The concern expressed at the conference wasn't just for livestock; a number of people had been attacked by big cats in the previous year. One of these victims was 32-year-old Sally Dyke, a Midlands veterinary lecturer who had been trying to hunt the "Beast of Inkerrow" in Hereford with her husband. She received three deep five-inch-long lacerations to her ribcage, which bled profusely.

Not only were the big cats becoming violent towards humans, they were also making more intrepid forays into urbanized areas. On 20 January 1994 a traveller on the Underground saw a large puma-like cat roaming around waste ground near Northolt station in west London. Robert Delane stated that the animal was three feet tall and around four feet long, with a velvety biscuit-coloured coat. He told a reporter from the *Evening Standard*: "I watched for about two minutes as it walked through the brambles and then it went into some coal bunkers." Animal expert Doug Richardson of London Zoo commented: "The description is of a mountain lion. Railway land would suit it perfectly. The animal would be undisturbed and have a plentiful food supply."

On 11 March that same year there were eight independent sightings of a lioness stalking the Winchmore Hill area of north London in broad daylight. The first report to police came in around noon from Mrs Lisa Bostock, who sighted a large cat with "short golden hair and big padded paws" in Firs Lane, which runs parallel to the A10. Mrs Bostock said the animal was strolling along a canal towpath. The police switchboard was later flooded with hysterical calls from residents in the Winchmore Hill area who described a giant cat, some three feet in height, that was slinking through their back gardens. Thirty police officers were drafted into the area equipped with megaphones to warn the public to keep their children and pets indoors. They also contacted the local school, and pupils were ordered to stay behind after classes until the "Beast of Winchmore Hill" was caught.

A police helicopter buzzed the skies over Palmers Green and Winchmore Hill, and on the ground a London Zoo marksman with a tranquillizer gun waited patiently for a reliable sighting of the animal. Plenty of sightings came, but none of them reliable. Every corpulent sandy-coloured domestic cat in Winchmore Hill triggered a false alarm. Even a docile bull mastiff was mistaken for the lioness!

Alas, in the hysteria that followed, the lioness managed to slip out of the area without being captured, leaving the police with egg on their faces and the newspapers with an incredible story to report.

The next big cat scares that year occurred in Chiswick

throughout June to August, and at Connnaught Waters, Epping Forest, on 24 July.

Pumas and lions aren't the only out-of-place animals that have been seen in the London area. On 27 December 1981 four youngsters aged nine to thirteen claimed they had encountered "a giant great growling hairy thing" wandering about on the snow-covered Hackney Marshes. Tommy Murray, 13, watched in complete terror as the beast raised itself into the air on its hind legs. The young teenager turned on his heels and raced through the snow, slipping several times. His friends scattered in all directions. Earlier that day Tommy and his mates had seen curious footprints unlike anything they'd seen before. Tommy had traced them to the strange beast. When he reached home he cried the story out to his parents, and within the hour, 50 policemen with dogs and a team of marksmen invaded Hackney Marshes. A police helicopter soared high above them carrying officers with high-powered binoculars. Only tracks were found, and experts deduced that they had been made by a bear. The newspapers learned of the story and after investigating the bear paw-prints, they asked the chief inspector who had organized the hunt if he thought the whole affair had been a hoax. The chief inspector replied: "Although I didn't see the boys myself, I'm reliably informed that they were very frightened by what they saw. They were not hoaxers, although, of course, they may have been hoaxed. The search itself was interesting; it was winter and there was about two inches of snow. I saw three sets of prints that to me were strange. One of the prints was on an island which had a perimeter fence and a locked gate. The other two lots were near marshalling yards. All three were on virgin snow and could not have been made by a hoaxer because no other prints were near them or led to or from them."

Nevertheless, the chief inspector had a theory; he thought the boys had been frightened off Hackney Marshes by someone who had dressed up as a bear. But information that wasn't made public at the time suggests something more sinister was going on. During the previous December the mutilated remains of two bear corpses were found in the River Lea at Hackney. Both animals had been decapitated and skinned. How the bears came to be in that area was a puzzle to the police. A similar conundrum confronted the police in March 1962 when a "four-footed sandy reptilian animal", around three feet long and weighing ten pounds, was run over by a car in Friern Road, East Dulwich, in south-east London. The corpse was examined by RSPCA officers and a zoological expert, but no species like it had ever been seen before. Being an embarrassment to the police, the RSPCA and a London Zoo expert, the unidentified lizard-like creature was given a prompt secret burial.

Hampstead Heath in north-west London is another unlikely setting for out-of-place creatures. In the summer of 1926 scores of people reported seeing a strange creature in the Vale of Health pond. Several dogs that were present when the creature emerged from the water whimpered and turned to flee with their tails literally between their legs. Some witnesses who got a good look at the aquatic being claimed that it was a seal, but no one was sure what it was until the night of 25 August 1926, when an angler at the pond caught something. He reeled in his line with the help of an old fisherman, because whatever had taken the bait was extremely powerful and quite frenzied. After struggling for several minutes, the two anglers watched in bewilderment when they saw what was at the other end of the line; a small seal. It splashed about and barked at them. It made desperate attempts to return to the pond but the two anglers overpowered the creature and took it to the local Vale of Health hotel. The hotel proprietor, a Mr Fred G. Gray, put the seal in a large fish tank and exhibited it to guests. The *Daily Chronicle* got wind of the strange catch and sent a reporter to investigate the bizarre story. Hours later, the surreal story was also taken up by the *Evening News*, which sent a reporter and a Mr Shelley from London Zoo to look into the matter. Shelley identified the amphibian as a wild seal, but could not believe that it had originated in the Vale of Health pond. The reporters heard that there were more seals in the pond, and Fred Gray claimed that he had seen seals at the pond himself two years previously. Gray believed there was a simple rational explanation for the seals' presence; the creatures had swum up the Thames and reached the pond via the River

Fleet which runs into it. But Shelley dismissed the theory as ludicrous, for no one had ever reported seeing seals swimming up the River Fleet.

On 2 November that year, the *Daily Chronicle* reported the sensational capture of a second seal at the Vale of Health pond. The day before, an astonished angler had caught a seal (larger than the first one) which "fought like a lion and barked like a dog" with a rod and line. As he hauled it in the animal screamed in agony as the hook tore through its mouth and nose, and a few minutes after being landed, it died. The carcass was taken away by the angler to be stuffed for his private collection. In the meantime, the seal at the Vale of Health – now christened "Happy" – had put on weight and appeared to be in good health. The *Daily Chronicle* article ended by reiterating Mr Gray's theory about the marine mammals swimming up the River Fleet from the Thames into the pond. The theory was quickly ridiculed by zoologists, and when the seal sightings at the Hampstead Heath pond diminished, the columns on the phenomenon got smaller, and the whole affair was soon forgotten. Some 66 years later, on 7 April 1992, the *Daily Telegraph* reported several sightings of an eight-foot grey seal swimming in the River Thames, yards from Westminster!

On 5 October 1994 the *Evening Standard* disclosed that a 100-strong colony of tube-web spiders – cousins to the bird-eating tarantula had been discovered in an isolated part of Hampstead Heath. The colony was discovered by Edward Milner, the Spider Recorder for the London Natural History Society. He said, "I was walking across Hampstead Heath and I noticed there was something different around here. Then I started scrabbling around in the grass and I saw these webs. On a wet, miserable autumn day I was exhilarated." Milner was exhilarated because, according to the textbooks, the tube-web spider became extinct over a century ago, so the origin of the spider colony is proving to be an unsolvable mystery for natural historians.

Finally, another mystery from Hampstead Heath was reported on 9 August 1994 in the *Big Issue* magazine. An article revealed that a strain of dangerous crayfish found only in America has been found in the men's bathing pool. The freshwater crustaceans, known as Louisiana reds, are the size of small lobsters, but can deliver a nasty nip. Marine biologists have discovered that they are also carrying a virus which could eradicate native crayfish. How the American crayfish arrived in the pool is still a complete mystery.

PART THREE
Mysterious Lands and People
● ●

The Vanishing Eskimo Folk

There are three dimensions of space: they are length, breadth, and width; or backwards and forwards, side to side, and up and down. Einstein proved that there is another dimension: the fourth dimension is time. The three dimensions of space specify *where* an object is, and the fourth dimension specifies *when* an object is. Seems complicated, but scientists now believe that there are more than four dimensions, and that these unchartered dimensions may be interwoven with our own and may sometimes even become accidentally accessible to ordinary human beings. This would explain the thousands of bizarre disappearances which are reported worldwide each year. Every year over 1 million people go missing in the United States alone. Some of the disappearances are mundane, like the teenage runaway, but there are so many baffling cases of people disappearing literally into thin air, as in the following true story, which has been thoroughly investigated over the years.

In November 1930 Joe Labelle, a Canadian fur trapper, snowshoed into a thriving Eskimo fishing village situated on the shores of Lake Anjikuni in Canada. Labelle was greeted with an eerie silence. He thought this was very strange because the fishing village was a noisy settlement with 2000 Eskimos milling back and forth to their kayaks. But there wasn't a soul about. Labelle visited each of the Eskimo huts and fish storehouses but none of the villagers was anywhere to be seen. Labelle saw a flickering fire in the distance and approached it gingerly, sensing something evil was afoot on this moonlit night. Upon the fire was a smouldering pot of blackened stew. To make matters more mysterious, Labelle saw that not a single human track had left the settlement. Labelle knew something bizarre had happened to the 2000 people, and so he ran non-stop to the nearest telegraph office and sent a message about his findings to the Royal Canadian Mounted Police. The Mounties turned up hours later, and they too were baffled by the mass vanishing act. An enormous search party was sent out to look for the missing villagers, but they were never found, and the search party unearthed some strange findings. All the sleigh dogs that had belonged to the Eskimos were found buried 12 feet under a snowdrift at the perimeter of the camp. All of them had starved to death. The search party also established that all the Eskimos' provisions and food had been left in their huts, which didn't make any sense at all. Then came the most chilling surprise of all: the search party discovered that all of the Eskimos' ancestral graves were empty. Whoever or whatever had taken all the living villagers had also dug up the dead as well, even though the icy ground around the graves was as hard as iron. Later on that unearthly silent night the Mounties watched in awe as a strange blue glow lit up the horizon. The eerie radiance was not the northern lights, but seemed steady and artificial. As the Mounties watched, the light pulsated then faded. All the newspapers of the world reported the baffling disappearance of the 2000 Eskimos. Although many believed that a rational explanation would eventually come to light, the Anjikuni mass disappearance is still unsolved.

What Happened to Madoc's Expedition

Every schoolchild knows that it was Christopher Columbus who discovered America over five hundred years ago in 1492, but it is now an accepted historical fact that Columbus only rediscovered America that year. Others had reached the long-suspected western continent before him.

Some of the earliest visitors to America were Chinese and Japanese seafarers who landed on the west coast between 3000 and 2500 BC to establish short-lived settlements on the Valdavian coast of Ecuador. In the 1970s pottery from the Jomon region of Japan was unearthed at the site of the Valdavian settlement, and two stone anchors of Chinese origin were discovered off the coast of California. Further evidence that the Far Eastern peoples reached America first is found within China's oldest manuscript, the *Shan Hai King*, which contains an accurate description of the Grand Canyon.

On the Atlantic side of America, in the sixth century AD, another pre-Columbian explorer turned up – St Brendan the Navigator, an Irish monk who had sailed from Kerry in the year 540 in search of a mystical "Land Promised to the Saints" in a 36-foot-long wooden-framed boat covered with greased oxhide. St Brendan and a crew of fourteen monks reached the shores of Newfoundland after encountering a huge crystal island – probably an iceberg.

After St Brendan, Leif Erickson, the hot-tempered son of Viking Erik the Red, sailed across the Atlantic in 1001 AD with a crew of 35, and, despite having no maps or a compass to guide them, they reached the coast of Labrador via a northerly route past Iceland. Erikson established a Norse settlement in the Cape Cod region where he found grapes growing, so he called the newly discovered country Vinland. However, the Viking community didn't last long, and according to the Icelandic chronicle *Flateyarbok*, this was because the native American Indians drove the bellicose Vikings out of the country.

The next people to discover the North American continent were the Welsh, and, unlike all the previous explorers, they established a permanent settlement, and some members of the colony evidently married several of the native Indians.

In 1170 Prince Madoc ap Owain Gwynnedd landed on the shores of Mobile Bay, Alabama. Madoc had made the transatlantic voyage after being driven into exile in North Wales by his brothers after causing the death of his father during a battle. With no estates of his own, the banished Welsh prince decided he would go in search of unknown lands to conquer, and so he built the *Gwennan Corn*, a wooden single-masted vessel, and sailed for Conway. The North Equatorial Current took him to the Gulf of Mexico, and after a short stay in the strange new land, the Gulf Stream took the far-travelled Celt back to his own waters. When the prince recounted his tales of the new world, many scoffed and doubted him, but some were curious enough to join Prince Madoc on his second voyage to the unknown continent. Three ships sailed from North Wales for America – and were never seen again. But that isn't the end of the story. Centuries later, other European explorers discovered the ruins of three medieval Welsh-style fortresses near Chattanooga in Tennessee, and in the same region there lived

Mysterious Island

In 1938 three Irish fishermen were feared dead when their fishing boat failed to return to Valentia Island, off the coast of Kerry, after a storm. Despite an extensive search of the waters off the Irish coast, the three fishermen could not be found, nor could a trace of their boat. Four days later, the missing men turned up at Valentia Island with a bizarre tale to tell. They said that their boat had smashed into uncharted rocks during the storm, and that they had gone ashore on an island, which they could not identify. The stranded fishermen then spotted a monastery in the distance, and they set off towards it. The monks there were very helpful, but said that the fishermen would not be able to stay on the island. The monks said they were of the Order of Saint Brendan, and were very reclusive. They went down to the shore at first light and set about mending the hull of the fishing boat. The three fishermen sailed from the island in the early morning mist and headed for the south-east as the monks had directed. Within a minute, the mysterious island was no longer visible in the mist. When the fishermen related this story, most people doubted them, but over the centuries there have been scores of sightings of a mysterious island off Ireland's western coast. Many folklorists believe it is the phantom island that the Irish monk St Brendan said he'd visited in the fifth century.

a tribe of curious Indians known as the Mandan, a fair-haired people who responded immediately to the explorers who spoke in a Welsh tongue. The Mandan tribe also used boats that were almost identical to Welsh coracles. Unfortunately, the Mandan are now virtually extinct because white fur-traders started a smallpox epidemic among them in 1838 which almost decimated the tribe.

Who Was Jack the Ripper?

The Romany people believe that an approaching tragedy casts a warning shadow ahead of itself, and, strangely enough, in the August of 1888 the dusky skies over London turned a vivid blood red at sunset over three consecutive nights. The unusual meteorological phenomenon was mentioned in the *Times*, evoking an avalanche of letters from people offering explanations. Some thought the crimson twilight was an omen of a war in Europe, while others believed the dark rosy hue was being caused by dust from a forest fire which had drifted up into the stratosphere. On the last night of the red sky, a serial killer known as Jack the Ripper struck in the East End of London, carving out a place for himself in the history of infamy. According to a recent poll held by Madame Tussaud's Waxwork Museum in London, 3500 visitors who were asked to name the three most feared people in history chose Adolf Hitler, Count Dracula and Jack the Ripper. The latter has inspired two operas, Alban Berg's *Lulu* and the *Threepenny Opera* by Bertolt Brecht and Kurt Weill, as well as a mountain of factual and fictional books, stage plays and films. So why are we fascinated by Jack? It could be because he was never caught, so every budding Sherlock Holmes is free to speculate on the identity of the Whitechapel Murderer. Another reason Jack is so popular is due to the way he is often portrayed as an almost folklorish character in his traditional costume – a black silk top hat, black suit, and flowing cape – devilishly carrying his little black doctor's bag through the narrow gaslit streets of Victorian London. But this image couldn't be further from the truth. If we were to travel back in a time machine to the night of the Ripper's first murder, we would experience the grim reality of Whitechapel's mean streets.

In the Whitechapel area alone in 1888, there were twelve hundred prostitutes, and a considerable percentage of these "fallen women" were in fact, fallen girls of ten and eleven years of age. In the 65 brothels of Whitechapel, there were occasional murders, but out in the streets, where the freelance whores plied their trade, murder was much more common. Punters who turned nasty were just another risk to the harlots of the East End, and one punter who turned very nasty on the morning of Friday, 31 August 1888, sent shockwaves of terror through the festering thoroughfares of Whitechapel, Spitalfields and beyond. This punter was Jack the Ripper. The time was 3.40 a.m., and Charles Cross, a Bethnal Green carter, was walking to work through Bucks Row (later renamed Durward Street) when he noticed what seemed to be a bundle of tarpaulin lying near the entrance of a stable yard. Upon taking a closer look at the bundle, Cross saw that it was not tarpaulin, but a middle-aged woman lying on her back with a slight grin on her face. Her frilly skirts were rolled up to her thighs, so the carter assumed that the woman had been raped and left unconscious by the attack, but another carter who came along took a closer look at the inert woman and felt her face. It was stone cold. She was dead, but it was too dark to see just how she had died. The police were informed and a local doctor, Ralph Llewellyn, performed the post mortem on the dead woman, who was later identified as Mary Ann Nichols, a 42-year-old prostitute from Thrawl Street, Whitechapel.

The killer had evidently cut Mary Ann's throat (from left to right) after savagely ripping through her abdomen with a long-bladed knife. There were also several curious deep stab wounds around the genitals, and a small purplish bruise on the right side of the victim's face which seemed to have been caused by Jack's thumb as he held the victim's head steady before the throat-slashing. Dr Llewellyn deduced that the jagged incisions running from the bottom of Mary Ann's ribs to her lower abdomen were the work of a left-handed person with a basic knowledge of human anatomy.

The killer had not copulated with the victim, and there

were no traces of sperm on the corpse. It transpired that Emily Holland, a lodger from the same doss-house as Mary Ann Nichols, had been the last person to see the murder victim alive. Emily told police that she'd been on her way to see a blaze at Ratcliff Dry Dock when she saw Mary Ann in a drunken state in Osborn Street, walking towards Whitechapel. Emily urged her friend to come home with her to get some sleep, and she drew Mary Ann's attention to the nearby church clock, which was striking 2.30 a.m., but Mary Ann refused to accompany her friend back to the doss-house, and headed towards Flower and Dean Street, looking for clients.

Detective Inspector Abberline, former head of the Whitechapel CID, was drafted from Scotland Yard to coordinate the murder investigation. He had an unrivalled knowledge of the East End, and he imagined that the culprit he was seeking was just another run-of-the-mill cut-throat. Abberline and his men were still getting nowhere with their inquiries eight days later, when the killer struck again. The mutilated body of 47-year-old prostitute Annie Chapman was found in the backyard of a barber's shop at 29 Hanbury Street at 5.55 a.m. on Saturday, 8 September. Her stomach had been ripped open and her intestines pulled out and thrown over her left shoulder. In a neat line at Chapman's feet the killer had positioned all of the prostitute's personal belongings – two farthings, a comb and a piece of muslin. The killer had evidently taken two of Annie's rings from her, as the marks of the missing rings were still visible on the victim's fingers. Nearby, there were three curious clues: two pills and part of a torn envelope bearing the crest of the Sussex Regiment, but for some unknown reason, the pills, envelope and the arrangement of the prostitute's personal items were not mentioned at the inquest, and the police never explained why the information was withheld.

On 29 September a legend was born when a letter, signed "Jack the Ripper", arrived at the Central News Agency. It read:

Dear Boss,

I keep on hearing the police have caught me but they wont fix me just yet. I have laughed when they look so clever and talk about being on the right track.

I am down on whores and I shant quit ripping them till I do get buckled.

Keep this letter back till I do a bit more work, then give it out straight. My knife's nice and sharp and I want to get back to work right away if I get a chance. Good luck.

Yours truly,

Jack the Ripper

P.S. Don't mind me giving the trade name. Wasn't good enough to post this before I got all the red ink off my hands curse it. No luck yet they say I am a doctor now ha ha.

What seemed to be the Ripper's thumb print was faintly visible on the letter. Whether he had left the fingerprint in red ink deliberately will never be known, but the Victorian police had their chance there and then to file away the fingerprint for future comparisons with other prints, but Abberline's detectives were simply too ignorant to think along such lines, and the first fingerprint conviction would not take place until 1905.

Abberline and his murder squad were baffled by way the Ripper had been seen by no one in an area that never slept, and another puzzle was the way the victims were slaughtered without making a sound. The superstitious denizens of the East End had a field day with these strange facts. Only something supernatural could be responsible for the hideous crimes. The notorious black magician Aleister Crowley added fuel to the bogeyman tales by speculating that Jack the Ripper was a black warlock who had the power of invisibility, and the mystic said his theory would also explain how Jack was able to carry out his abominable work in total darkness.

And on the subject of the supernatural, Robert James Lees, one of the greatest psychics of his day, allegedly had intriguing premonitions of the Ripper murders – and the medium also said he once had an encounter with Jack in broad daylight in the heart of London. The chance meeting occurred in September 1888 as Lees and his wife were riding on an omnibus. The bus stopped at the top of Notting Hill and a distinguished-looking gentleman got on and sat within six feet of the medium, who started to feel an aura of evil emanating from the passenger. Lees whispered to his wife, "That is Jack the Ripper."

Lees's wife giggled, thinking her husband was joking.

"I am not mistaken," replied Lees, "I feel it."

Throughout the rest of the journey, Lees couldn't take his eyes off the man, and the passenger became very nervous when he noticed the medium's constant gaze. At Marble Arch the omnibus came to a stop, and the man Lees was watching like a hawk suddenly jumped up out of his seat and got off the vehicle. Lees did the same and followed the man down Oxford Street. Five minutes into the pursuit, the psychic called out to a passing constable and pointed to the man he was following, saying, "That man is Jack the Ripper. Quick! After him, Constable."

The bemused policeman looked at Lees and dismissed him with a warning: "Beat it. Go on, or I'll run you in."

"But I have supernatural knowledge. You must go after him," Lees insisted, but the policeman continued on his beat in the other direction. Meanwhile, the guilty-looking man was waving frantically to a cab. When Lee was a hundred yards from the man, a cab pulled up and the man who may have been Jack the Ripper got in. The cab was driven at breakneck speed down Piccadilly.

The Lees story has received a lot of criticism from sceptics over the years, but it should be remembered that Robert Lees was a highly respected medium who was frequently invited to Buckingham Palace by Queen Victoria. The Queen was very impressed by Lees, and often asked him to contact her late husband, Prince Albert. Lees was known for his integrity, and was a friend to both Disraeli and Keir Hardie. The medium was also a religious man, and he became the leader of the Christian Spiritualists in England. Everyone who knew Lees said he was not a liar and not one for embroidered tales, but Lees's account of his encounter with the Ripper was never taken seriously.

At 1 a.m. on Sunday, 30 September, the body of a Swedish prostitute, known around Whitechapel as "Long Liz" Stride, was found in Berner Street. Louis Diemschutz had been leading his pony and cart through the almost pitch-black darkness when the pony had suddenly stopped in its tracks. Diemschutz lit a candle and saw that the obstruction in front of his pony was Stride's body. With a shudder, he saw blood still flowing from the prostitute's slashed neck. Diemschutz had the eerie feeling that he had disturbed the Ripper, and he felt that the murderer was lurking close by in the darkness, cursing him for interrupting the gruesome work.

Upon learning of the third murder, the police stormed Berner Street, but Jack was nowhere to be seen. He had slipped out of the area and, unknown to the police, he was on his way to commit another murder.

In Long Liz's left hand a detective found scented lozenge sweets wrapped in tissue paper, and in the other hand he found a few grapes. This was strange, as the post mortem on Elizabeth Stride found that she had not eaten sweets or grapes, but the police thought the lozenges and grapes were of no significance anyway.

Forty-five minutes after killing Stride, Jack the Ripper found his fourth victim in Mitre Square, Aldgate. Her name was Catherine Eddowes, a 43-year-old prostitute. Jack's knife had torn a Z-shape in her chemise during the attack, which had left Eddowes horribly mutilated. The corpse was discovered by PC Watkins, who had only passed through the square 15 minutes before. When he shone his bull's-eye lamp on the body, he felt nauseous at the sight of the body, which he later described as "all ripped up like a pig at the market with the entrails flung in a heap about her neck".

The high-pitched sounds of police whistles were soon echoing through the streets around Mitre Square, but again Jack had vanished into the night – but not without leaving a clue first.

A blurred message, written on the black dado of a staircase wall at a block of tenements in Goulston Street, read: "The Juwes are The men that Will not be blamed for nothing."

The bizarre graffiti was discovered at 3 a.m. by PC Long, shortly after he had found a bloodstained piece of an apron that had evidently been cut from the Mitre Square victim's clothing. Presuming that the strip of cloth had been discarded by the Ripper, Long had gone to the nearest building – the Wentworth Dwellings – hoping to find more clues, and had stumbled on the most importan, yet enigmatic clue in the Whitechapel Murders case.

The chalked message was later erased by the hand of the Metropolitan Police Commissioner Sir Charles Warren. Sir Charles said the word "Juwes" would spark off an anti-Semitic riot.

For over a month the Ripper was inactive, and the inhabitants of the East End wondered if Jack had given up his satanic work, but the hiatus came to an end on Friday, 9 November. For almost 90 minutes Jack tore into the body of 25-year-old Mary Kelly in her little room at 13 Miller's Court. It was the first time the Ripper had struck indoors. He virtually skinned what was his last victim, and left the unrecognizable carcass of what had been a pretty young woman on her bed. A heart rested on the pillow, next to a head that was almost severed from its body.

The exact time of the murder was never determined, but around 4 a.m. Elizabeth Prater, who lived near Miller's Court was awakened by her kitten walking across her neck. As Prater awoke, she heard the distinctive voice of a woman screaming, "Murder!" and the woman shouting the word three times. The screams seemed to originate from the direction of Miller's Court, opposite Prater's window, but such cries were so common in the area that Prater took no notice and went back to sleep.

After the horrific murder of Mary Kelly, Jack the Ripper never killed again, and just why the murders came to such an abrupt end will probably never be known. Why did he stalk and slash the harlots of the East End? Was the motive sexual, or did he have a grudge against prostitutes? How did he manage to carry out his grisly operations in near-total darkness? What was the meaning of the cryptic message chalked on the wall? Over a century has passed since the heinous crimes were committed, and despite all the books and theories about the legendary killer, Jack the Ripper's identity is still a complete mystery.

Top 10 Jack the Ripper Suspects

1. Francis Tumblety – an American Ripper

A breakthrough by a team of British and American criminologists has discovered that a bogus New York doctor named Francis Tumblety arrived at Liverpool, England, on an Atlantic steamship at the beginning of 1888. It is thought that Tumblety (a seller of quack remedies and pornographic literature) had fled to England after being suspected of a string of Ripper-style killings in America. Tumblety openly admitted that he had an obsessive hatred of women because his mother had neglected him when he was a boy. Tumblety moved to London's East End a few months after his arrival at Liverpool, but he continued to pay the rent on his Liverpool lodgings so he would have a place to retreat to if the police got too close. In those times, Liverpool was the main port of embarkation for the States, so Tumblety only had to board a steamer to return to America under a pseudonym if Scotland Yard were on his trail.

In fact, recently discovered Home Office files reveal that at the height of the Ripper murders, in October 1888, a special team of CID men were sent to Liverpool to mingle with people at the docks who were embarking on the America-bound steamers. The plain-clothed officers had been briefed to keep a lookout for an American physician who had been arrested on suspicion of being the Whitechapel murderer. This doctor, who seems to have been Tumblety, was said to be a master of disguise and something of an embarrassment to Scotland Yard because he had somehow escaped from police custody.

In December 1888 the heavily disguised Francis Tumblety left his lodgings in Liverpool and took the train to London. From there he journeyed to Dover and boarded a ferry to France. Under the pseudonym of "Frank Townsend" he then boarded a steamship at Le Havre which took him back to America. The Ripper murders came to an abrupt end in London, but after Tumblety arrived in the States, someone started killing the prostitutes of New York.

After Tumblety's death in May 1903, the New York Ripper never killed again.

2. Dr Thomas Neill Cream

Cream was born in Glasgow, Scotland, in 1850, and at the age of 13 went to Canada with his parents in 1864. In 1876 he graduated as a doctor of medicine at McGill University in Montreal, and thereafter began a dark career in crime which by this time included arson, abortion, fraud, theft, blackmail – and attempted murder. Three women are known to have died under his care as a doctor, and while Cream was practising as a doctor of quack remedies in Chicago, he had an affair with a young woman and poisoned her elderly, epileptic husband. Between 1881 and 1892, Cream murdered five London prostitutes by strychnine, admitting that he had carried out the murders "for the sheer joy of killing". He was sentenced to hang, and on the gallows on the day of his execution – 15 November 1892 – he shouted out, "I am Jack the – " just before the trapdoor opened, and never got to finish the intriguing sentence. Many criminologists, however, have argued that Cream was under lock and key in Joliet Prison, Illinois, when the Ripper was stalking Whitechapel, but the debate continues.

3. Reverend Samuel Barnett

The Reverend Samuel Barnet was born in Bristol, England, in 1844 and educated at Wadham College, Oxford. In 1873 he went to a Whitechapel parish, where he sympathized with the poor of London, especially the prostitutes, whom he obsessively tried to "save". Barnett also took part in advocating far-sighted educational reforms, various poor-relief measures, as well as universal pensions. However, some Ripperologists have conjectured that Barnett may have had a darker repressed side, and have made much of the fact that the crusading reverend was virtually intimate with the local "fallen women" the Ripper slayed. Consider, also, that Barnett would have been familiar with the local geography of the Whitechapel streets and alleys. Police searching the streets of the East End would not have considered a clergyman as a suspect, as many priests and ministers were frequently called out during unearthly hours to perform the last rites. Furthermore, the much-loved and highly respected Barnett was well known to the local police constables of

Whitechapel and would automatically have been above suspicion. Barnett as a suspect would make sense of some unusual aspects of the Ripper murders: namely, that of the 1200 prostitutes in Whitechapel all the victims of Jack lived within a few hundred yards of each other and seemed to have known each other. Annie Chapman lived in 35 Dorset Street, and so did Michael Kidney, with whom Elizabeth Stride used to live. Mary Kelly lived just at the back of Dorset Street in Miller's Court. Could the Reverend Barnett, who knew all of these people, have been the common denominator in the highly localized grouping of victims?

4. Stephen Knight's "Unholy Trinity"

The late author Stephen Knight carried out extensive research into the Whitechapel murders in the 1970s and reached the startling conclusion that Jack the Ripper was not one man, but three. Knight called the three killers the "Unholy Trinity", and named them as the Royal Surgeon to Queen Victoria, Sir William Withey Gull, the artist Walter Sickert and the Duke of Clarence's coachman John Netley. Knight proposed in his fascinating book *Jack the Ripper: The Final Solution* (1976) that the three men carried out the Ripper murders in order to silence a gang of prostitutes who were blackmailing the Royal Family about an alleged secret marriage between the Duke of Clarence and a beautiful young Catholic artist's model. Fearing that a revolution would result from the scandal, Salisbury, the Prime Minister, ordered the elimination of the blackmailers and was even helped by police chiefs and freemasons who were anxious to preserve the status quo at any cost. Knight gives persuasive accounts in his book of how the victims of "Jack" were lured into a carriage with a promise of good payment, only to be killed, mutilated, then dumped at another location (thus explaining the mystery of how the Ripper worked in total darkness). History records that Sir William Withey Gull officially died in 1890, but there were strange rumours that Gull had not died at that time, but had been driven insane by a guilt complex, and a newspaper in Chicago claimed that the supposedly deceased Royal Surgeon had in fact been committed to a London asylum after a private trial presided over by 12 eminent Harley Street physicians.

5. Montague John Druitt

Montague John Druitt was born on 15 August 1857 at Wimborne in Dorset. He was educated at Winchester College, where he became a prefect and showed a remarkable talent for cricket. He won a scholarship to New College, Oxford, where he studied Classics and obtained a Third Class Honours Degree. He subsequently studied medicine, and held an avid interest in surgery which may have been sparked by his cousin, a Dr Lionel Druitt, who had a surgery at the Whitechapel Minories – just a ten-minute walk from the furthest Ripper murder sites. Druitt suddenly switched to studying law, and enrolled at the Inner Temple in May 1882. During his studies he worked as a teacher at a crammer's school in Blackheath. He was called to the Bar in 1885 but his legal career was a disastrous failure. In July 1888 Druitt's mother was certified as insane and Druitt himself apparently started telling several close friends that he was also going mad. Scotland Yard suspected the 31-year-old failed barrister of being Jack the Ripper but never made an arrest. Druitt was last seen alive on 3 December 1888, when he wrote on a piece of paper: "Since Friday I felt that I was going to be like Mother and the best thing was for me to die." That suicide note was found too late, because Druitt later filled the pockets of his overcoat with stones and either jumped or waded into the River Thames. His body was found floating in the river near Chiswick on 31 December 1888. Many in Scotland Yard thought Druitt's suicide explained why the Ripper's reign of terror had suddenly come to an abrupt end.

6. "Jill" the Ripper – the Whitechapel Murderess?

The notion that Jack the Ripper could have been a Jill – a woman – was first conjectured by Sir Arthur Conan Doyle, the creator of master detective Sherlock Holmes. Doyle used the same inferential logic Holmes would have applied to the case and speculated that the Ripper could have been a psychopathic midwife, or perhaps the embittered wife of someone who had contracted a venereal disease from a Whitechapel prostitute. There were many female abortionists practising in the East End who would have gone about after dark with splashes of blood on their clothing, and many of them carried crude surgical instruments and drugs. When Mary Kelly was murdered, police could not account for the female clothing and remains of a woman's hat which were burning in the fireplace. Was the clothing the discarded blood-spattered disguise of Jill the Ripper? The mad abortionist theory seems a possibility, considering the fact that Mary Kelly was three months pregnant when she was so brutally killed and mutilated. Nonetheless a majority of the victims were in their forties.

7. James Kenneth Stephen

James Kenneth Stephen, an English author of excellent humorous verse and parodies, was the cousin of Sir Leslie Stephen – the tutor of Prince Albert Victor (the Duke of Clarence) and the father of Virginia Woolf. By a dark coincidence, J. K. Stephen was a friend of John Montague Druitt – another Ripper suspect. Stephen suffered an accidental blow to the head and afterwards became something of a bitter woman-hater. Many of his warped misogynistic poems concern the harm womankind has inflicted upon men, and some verses are penned in the same acerbic and twisted style as the Jack the Ripper letters. Some criminologists have suggested a homosexual affair between Stephen and the Duke of Clarence, and have alleged that the former killed Mary Kelly in a fit of jealous rage because she had come between him and Prince Albert Victor. Supportive evidence for these outrageous claims, however, is still being sought by researchers.

8. Alexander Pedachenko, the Mad Russian Doctor

This theory has more substantial weight than most. One strong suspect mentioned by Scotland Yard's Ripper files is Alexander Pedachenko, referred to as "an insane Russian doctor", known by other *nom de plumes* such as Vassily Konovalov, Andrey Luiskovo, as well as Mikhail Ostrog. The Russian doctor was employed at a clinic in the East End where Martha Tabram (a prostitute who was killed and mutilated in the style of the Ripper in August 1888), Mary Nicholls, Annie Chapman and Mary Kelly received treatment early in 1888. Research has strongly hinted that Dr Pedachenko had already "ripped" a Parisian prostitute, and may have been deliberately introduced into England by the Okhrana – the Russian czarist secret police – to discredit and disgrace the Russian radicals who were living in exile in Whitechapel. When Pedachenko later returned to St Petersburg, he ended up in an asylum after murdering another woman. Many police officials vouched for the Russian Ripper claim, including the assistant head of the CID, Basil Thompson.

9. The Unknown Secretary
According to William Booth, the founder of the Salvation Army, a secretary he employed (a man he refused to name) once made a sinister prediction concerning a future victim of Jack the Ripper. This allegedly happened in London's East End in February 1891. Booth's secretary became twitchy and agitated when he heard people discussing the dreadful murders of the East End, and he suddenly said: "Carrotty Nell will be the next to go!" The secretary was referring to the nickname of a 25-year-old red-haired prostitute in Whitechapel named Frances Coles. Booth and his friends thought it was a strange and morbid thing for the usually timid secretary to say, but three days later, on 13 February, "Carrotty Nell" was found dead from multiple stab wounds in the East End. A drunken railway worker named Thomas Sadler was arrested for the murder, but later released through lack of evidence. The secretary of William Booth, who had predicted Carrotty Nell's grisly fate, vanished into obscurity before police could quiz him about his sinister foreknowledge.

10. The Duke of Clarence – A Royal Ripper?
Throughout the duration of the Whitechapel murders, Queen Victoria showed an unusually intense interest in the case, and constantly asked the Home Secretary to keep her informed of the latest developments. Around this period, an intriguing rumour circulated London from the mansions of Mayfair to the slums of Whitechapel and Bethnal Green: it was claimed that the Queen's eldest grandson, Prince Albert Victor – the

Duke of Clarence – was somehow involved in the murders. Various researchers have suggested that this gossip about the Duke may have leaked out of Buckingham Palace via the servants. The Duke of Clarence died in 1892; had he lived, he would have become king when his father, Edward VII, died.

In the autumn of 1889, the upper-class stratum of England was rocked by a scandal which came to light following a police raid on the premises of 19 Cleveland Street. That address was found to be a homosexual brothel, and an unprecedented cover-up operation by the authorities was soon under way. The landlord of the brothel was allowed to flee the country, while a number of male prostitutes were paid a fixed income for three years on the condition that they stayed in Australia. However, the newshounds of Fleet Street managed to obtain the distinguished names of some people who had been frequenting the brothel. They were Lord Arthur Somerset, son of the Duke of Beaufort (and assistant equerry to the Prince of Wales), Lord Euston (a son of the Duke of Grafton), and the Duke of Clarence – the Prince of Wales's elder son who stood in direct line of succession to the throne. The shamed duke – who was nicknamed "Victoria" in homosexual circles – was promptly sent to India with his grandmother Queen Victoria, while Lord Salisbury's government tried desperately to muzzle the press. Alas, the Cleveland Street Scandal never went away, and in January 1892, just months after it was announced that the Duke of Clarence was to be engaged to Victoria Mary of Teck, Prince Albert Victor suddenly died. The official version was that he had expired after catching a cold caught while courting in the grounds of Sandringham. The Duke's father decreed that there was to be no lying-in-state, no embalming and exhibiting of the body, and all of the dead prince's correspondence was to be burned immediately. There were rumours that the Duke of Clarence had been "removed" because he had been an embarrassment who stood in direct line of succession to the throne. Some said he was not dead at all, but imprisoned in Glamis Castle in Scotland. And still there were more whispers that the Duke had been involved in the Whitechapel murders, but to this day, no one has convincingly determined what the basis of these intriguing rumours was.

The Other Jack

Only one other "Jack" caused as much fear and mayhem as the Ripper. His true name will never be known, but during his 67-year reign of terror, the superstitious people of Victorian England called him "Spring-Heeled Jack", because of his amazing superhuman ability to leap over rooftops. Jack made his frightening debut one September evening in 1837 on Barnes Common, a secluded tract of land in London. A businessman who was taking a short cut across the common was shocked when a six-foot figure wearing a tight-fitting white suit and helmet jumped over the eight-foot-high railings of a nearby cemetery, shrieking with laughter. Understandably, the man turned on his heels and fled, convinced he had encountered a demon. On the following night, the leaping terror attacked three girls who were making their way home via the common. Two of the girls escaped, but the remaining one became so weak with fright that she collapsed, and found herself at the mercy of the unearthly assailant. As he leaned over her, the girl saw that her attacker resembled Satan himself. He had bright red eyes, a long prominent nose, and strange pointed ears. As the monster ripped the girl's clothes off with his claw-like hands, she passed out. A policemen later discovered the unconscious girl and revived her. When she started babbling about the devilish attacker, the policeman thought the girl had been drinking. But more and more assaults were reported as the weeks went by, and when the *Times* started to publicize the supernatural prowler's attacks, many Londoners refused to go out at night and barricaded themselves indoors. When the old Duke of Wellington read of the leaping man's cowardly attacks, he patrolled the city each night on horseback with two loaded pistols, but Spring-Heeled Jack was skilful at evading capture; whenever the police approached, he would simply bound off into the night

Jack eventually tired of frightening the denizens of the capital, and began a trek of terror in a northerly direction across the country.

By the turn of the century, Spring-Heeled Jack had turned up in the south of Liverpool, where he was first seen making a

Spring-Heeled Jack

40-foot leap over the reservoir building in High Park Street, Toxteth. A week later Jack performed his Grand Finale when he turned up early one Sunday evening at Salisbury Street, Everton, where he ran screaming along the rooftops. It is said that the members of a Bible study class at St Francis Xavier's school became hysterical, thinking that Jack was the Devil. The teacher told her pupils not to look out the window at the leaping figure, but to close their eyes so that they could pray for the Lord to intervene. Meanwhile, outside, a mob of Evertonians arrived with bottles and sticks, who had no intention of letting Jack molest their women, gave chase, and the leaping man bounded up onto the steeple of St Francis Xavier's. The awe-struck crowd looked on in disbelief as Jack jumped from the steeple down onto the roofs of Haigh Street, before he bounded away in the direction of William Henry Street. After that eventful night the strangest figure in occult folklore was never seen again.

Is the Boston Strangler Still at Large?

In June 1962 a sinister serial killer began strangling single women in Boston, America, thus sparking off one of the most notorious and mysterious murder cases since the Jack the Ripper slayings. The so-called Boston Strangler held the city in a grip of fear for 19 months. There was never a sign of forced entry at any of the victims' residences, and all the murdered women were invariably left in obscene positions. On the necks of most of his victims, who were aged 19 to 85, the killer left a distinctive calling card in the form of a flamboyant bow, tied with the women's own underwear. Police deduced that the Strangler was a suave-talking man who won his victim's confidence before throttling them, and assured the public that they were doing all they could to apprehend the madman. However, 13 people were murdered before the killing spree ended in January 1964 with the arrest of Albert DeSalvo, a former army sergeant of the Military Police. DeSalvo confessed to the murders and the whole case entered the annals of popular folklore. In 1968 director Richard Fleischer made a gripping film of Gerold Frank's book of the infamous case with Tony Curtis in the starring role.

What isn't widely known about the Boston Strangler case is that DeSalvo recanted his confession in 1968, and, amazingly, he was never actually charged with the murders because the prosecutors claimed they had insufficient evidence to convict him. However, DeSalvo received a life sentence for a series of alleged rapes, but was stabbed to death in his cell in 1973 at the age of 40. For many years there were unsettling rumours that DeSalvo had not been the Boston Strangler, but a mere braggart who craved attention and hoped to make money from his false confessions. It was alleged that DeSalvo had obsessively followed the Boston Strangler case in the newspapers and had collected enough clippings to gain an in-depth knowledge of the crime scene and other details. In fact many police officers involved in the case as well as some relatives of the murder victims believed DeSalvo was an egotist who dreamt of becoming rich from book and movie deals about the killings. Casey Sherman, whose aunt, Mary Sullivan, was the last victim of the Strangler, believes there was more than one killer at large. In August 1999 the Boston Strangler case was re-examined by professional serial-killer profilers who concluded that there may have been more than one murderer at work. Forensic experts are also using modern DNA technology to analyze evidence from the crime scenes of the renowned murder case to determine once and for all if DeSalvo was the Strangler. Until the results of the forensic examinations are known, we won't know if the rumours about the real Boston Strangler still being at large are true.

The Man from the Pru Mystery

William Herbert Wallace was born to lower-middle-class parents in Keswick in the English Lake District in 1878. His first job was a draper's assistant, but he found the occupation boring and developed an urge to travel. He visited India, then Shanghai, but wasn't impressed with what he saw. After contracting dysentery, he returned home to England, physically shattered, to re-evaluate his life.

Around this time, he was becoming an avid reader of the *Meditations*, a classic written by the Roman emperor and stoic philosopher Marcus Aurelius. Wallace strongly identified with stoicism, which advocates freedom from passions and desires, and he adopted the stoic creed, which in a nutshell is: Don't expect too much out of life, but strive to improve it by applying discipline and hard work.

Wallace later became a Liberal election agent in Yorkshire, where he met a pretty dark-haired woman named Julia Thorp. Julia was well read and, like Wallace, was familiar with the classics. She also spoke French, could execute the most exquisite sketches, and played the piano. At last William Wallace had a companion who could meet his intellectual level, and he married Julia at Harrogate in 1913.

The outbreak of World War I put paid to Wallace's political agent's job, and after trying a succession of unsatisfying occupations, he found stable employment as an insurance agent at the Prudential Assurance Company in Liverpool's Dale Street.

The Wallaces soon settled into their new home at 29 Wolverton Street, a quiet little cul-de-sac in the city's Anfield district. For 16 years Wallace held the same job without promotion, and during this period the couple led a rather humdrum lifestyle. They had no children, no real friends, and lived on less than four pounds a week.

When Julia was in her early fifties she became very frail and was helped once a week by a charwoman. Almost every week William Wallace played third-rate chess at the Liverpool Central Chess Club, where he was a member. While Wallace was on his way to the club on the evening of Monday, 19 January 1931, a man was making a twopenny phone call to set in motion a train of events that would lead to Julia's death and result in the insurance agent going on trial for her murder.

The time was 7.15 p.m. A man in a red public telephone box situated on the corner of Rochester Road and Breck Road lifted the receiver and asked the operator to connect him with Bank 3581, the telephone number of Wallace's chess club in town. There was a technical hitch, so the operator recorded the number of the caller's box: Anfield 1627. Moments later the same man called back and once again asked for Bank 3581.

"Operator," said the caller, "I have pressed button 'A' but have not had my correspondence yet."

The caller was then put through to the chess club, where waitress Gladys Harley answered the call.

"Yes?" said the waitress.

"Is that the Central Chess Club?"

"Yes."

"Is Mr Wallace there?"

The waitress looked around the room, which was almost empty, and called to Samuel Beattie, who was the captain of the chess club. "Mr Beattie, someone's on the phone for Mr Wallace."

"Well, he's not here yet," said Beattie, glancing up from his game of chess, "But he's down to play a game, so he should be along later."

As Beattie continued his game, the waitress interrupted him again, sighing, "Will you please speak to this man?"

Beattie reluctantly left the game and took the receiver from the waitress.

"Samuel Beattie, club captain here. May I help you?"

"Is Mr Wallace there?"

"No, I'm afraid not."

"But will he be there?"

"I can't say. He may or may not. If he is coming he'll be here shortly. I suggest you ring up later," replied Beattie, slightly ruffled.

"Oh no, I can't," said the caller, "I'm too busy. I have my girl's twenty-first birthday on and I want to do something for her in the way of business. I want to see him particularly. Will you ask him to call round to my place tomorrow evening at 7.30?"

Beattie replied that he would if he saw Mr Wallace, and asked for the caller's name and address.

"The name is Qualtrough. R. M. Qualtrough."

"And the address?" said Beattie, poised with a pen to scribble it down.

"25 Menlove Gardens East."

Later that evening, at 7.45 p.m., Wallace came into the chess club and Beattie informed him of the call from a Mr Qualtrough.

"Qualtrough? Who is Qualtrough?" Wallace asked blankly.

"Well, if you don't know who he is, I certainly don't," said Beattie.

"Is he a member of the club?" Wallace asked with a puzzled look.

"No," replied Beattie, "we've no one called Qualtrough."

"I've never heard of the chap," Wallace said, "what did he want?'

In response to this question, Beattie handed Wallace the piece of paper on which he had written down Qualtrough's address and the time of the requested meeting.

"Where is Menlove Gardens East?" said Wallace, scanning the address with his wire-framed spectacles.

Beattie didn't know, but went to ask a colleague who was well acquainted with the local geography of Liverpool's streets. A few moments later Beattie came back shaking his head. "No, he's not much help I'm afraid."

"I've got a tongue in my head. I'll find it," said Wallace, and he pulled out his pocket notebook and scribbled down Qualtrough's name and address. Already, the prospect of earning a 20 per cent commission on an annuity for Qualtrough's daughter was looking irresistible to Wallace.

At ten o'clock on the following morning Wallace left Wolverton Street and rode a tram to the Clubmoor district where he commenced his rounds, collecting a few shillings here, paying out benefit there. It was quite an uneventful day.

The insurance agent's last call was at Eastman Road, where a woman wanted to know how she could surrender her policy. After explaining the procedure, Wallace returned home to Wolverton Street at around 6.05 p.m. and had tea with Julia. Wallace then gathered several forms needed for the business transaction with Qualtrough and went upstairs to the bathroom. He washed his hands and face, then went into the bedroom where he changed his collar and brushed his receded hair.

At 6.45 p.m. Wallace patted his wife on the back and promised her he'd be back as soon as possible. As he left the house via the back door, he told Julia to bolt the door after him. That, he would insist later, was the last time he saw his wife alive.

Twenty minutes later, at 7.06 p.m., Wallace boarded a No. 4 tram and asked the conductor if it went to Menlove Gardens East. The conductor shook his head and advised Wallace to get a tram numbered 5, 5a, 5w or 7.

Wallace started to get off the tramcar but the conductor stopped him, saying: "Stay on the car. I'll give you a penny ticket for a transfer at Penny Lane."

Wallace thanked him and settled down in a corner seat in the tram's saloon. Four times during the journey Wallace reminded the conductor of his intended destination. At Penny Lane the insurance man boarded a No. 7 tram, and when it reached the top of Menlove Avenue, the conductor called Wallace to the platform and pointed to a road.

"That's Menlove Gardens West. You'll probably find the street you want in that direction," the conductor told him.

Wallace thanked the tram conductor, and as he stepped off

the car, he remarked, "I'm a complete stranger around here."

As Wallace strolled down Menlove Gardens West, he saw a woman coming out of a house. He quickly crossed the road and asked her about the location of Menlove Gardens East. The woman said she had never heard of the place. Wallace continued on his quest to find Qualtrough's home and asked another local. The man he questioned hadn't heard of the elusive address, so Wallace wondered if Beattie had misheard Qualtrough on the phone. Wallace therefore called at 25 Menlove Gardens *West*. He ran the bell at that address and an old white-haired woman came to the door

"Does Mr Qualtrough live here?" Wallace asked, tensely.

"There's no one of that name here," the woman told him.

"I'm looking for Menlove Gardens East, but they tell me there isn't any," Wallace explained, anxious to hear the old woman's reply.

"I don't know the name," she said, and she told Wallace she was certain that there were Menlove Gardens North, South and West only.

The Man from the Pru, as he was known to his customers, thanked the old woman for the information and bade her goodnight. Shortly afterwards, at 7.45 p.m., Wallace spotted PC James Sargent and he asked him if he knew the whereabouts of the mysterious address. The policeman knew the district very well and said there was no such place. Wallace thanked him and started to walk away, then stopped and turned around. He asked, "Is there anywhere that I could see a street directory?"

PC Sargent told him to try either the post office or the police station.

Wallace suddenly looked at his watch and said, "Will the post office be open? Yes, it's not eight o'clock yet."

There was no street directory available at the post office, so the counter clerk told him to try the newsagent's. At the shop, Wallace reiterated his account of the search for what appeared to be a non-existent address, and the shop owner handed him a street directory. After examining the directory and finding no Menlove Gardens East, Wallace left the shop after 8 p.m. and caught a tramcar home. Throughout the trip back to Wolverton Street, Wallace felt very uneasy about his fruitless odyssey, and remembered that there had recently been several robberies in his neighbourhood. He thought about his delicate and vulnerable wife Julia alone in the house.

At 8.45 p.m. John and Florence Johnston of 31 Wolverton Street were about to leave their house through the back door when they noticed their neighbour Mr Wallace walking down the alleyway towards them.

"Good evening, Mr Wallace," said Mrs Johnson.

In an uncharacteristically anxious tone, Wallace asked, "Have you heard anything unusual tonight?"

"No, why?" said Mrs Johnston curiously, "What's happened?"

Wallace told them how he'd been away from his home since 6.45 p.m., and that he had just discovered that the front and back doors of his home were locked from the inside. John Johnston told Wallace to try the back door again. If he found it still locked, Mr Johnson said he would try to gain entry with his own back door key.

Wallace returned to the back door and this time the handle turned without difficulty and the door opened. "It opens now," he mumbled and disappeared into the house, leaving the door ajar. The Johnstons remained outside, waiting apprehensively. They heard the insurance agent calling for his wife Julia, then, about three minutes later, Wallace hurried out of the house and into the yard.

"Come and see! She has been killed!" Wallace cried excitedly.

He led the Johnstons into the house. Close to the fireplace in the parlour lay the huddled corpse of Julia Wallace. Her head had been smashed into a bloody pulp, and parts of her brain had spilled out of the skull. Her left arm was outstretched towards the piano and her eyes stared lifelessly at the pedals.

Wallace stood trance-like in the middle of the room, gazing down at Julia's corpse. He stooped down and felt her wrist for a pulse. There was none but the body was still warm.

"I'm going for the police. Don't disturb anything," said a shocked Mr Johnston.

"Get the police and a doctor," Wallace said, then despondently added, "but I don't think that it's much use. They've finished her."

"As Mr Johnston hurried out of the parlour, Wallace and Mrs Johnston went into the kitchen, where it was ascertained that four pounds was missing from a cash box. However, upstairs in the bedroom, Wallace found a roll of pound notes left in an ornamental jar that had not been touched by the callous intruder. Wallace came back down the stairs and went back into the parlour with Mrs Johnston, where he tearfully surveyed Julia's battered body. He stooped down by the body and said, "They've finished her. Look at the brains."

Mrs Johnston shuddered at his words.

Wallace then walked around the corpse, scrutinizing it. He stopped and suddenly drew attention to something peculiar. "Why, whatever was she doing with my mackintosh?"

The garment in question was tucked under Julia Wallace's right shoulder.

At 9.15 p.m. PC Fred Williams arrived at the scene of the murder by bicycle. He propped his cycle against the low front wall of No. 29 and knocked on the door. A few moments later Mrs Johnston came to the front door but found the temperamental lock too much of a challenge. Mr Wallace came to her help and somehow managed to open the door effortlessly. Wallace ushered the policeman in, saying, "Come inside, officer. Something terrible has happened."

PC Williams entered the parlour and knelt by the body. After finding no pulse, the policeman listened to Wallace's story about the wasted journey to Menlove Gardens, then went on a tour of the house. Not long afterwards more policemen invaded the house. Hot on PC Williams's heels came Sergeant Breslin, then Whitley MacFall, a prominent Professor of Medicine from Liverpool University who had been summoned to examine the corpse. He was followed by Detective Inspector Gold, Detective Sergeant Bailey, a police photographer, and a fingerprint expert. Then, at 10 p.m., Chief Superintendent Hubert Moore, the head of Liverpool CID, arrived with another police sergeant.

Moore, a red-haired Irishman, took a quick look at the body

in the parlour and spoke to PC Williams. He then asked Wallace if either he or any of his neighbours had seen anyone loitering around the house before the murder. Wallace said that he hadn't, nor had his neighbours seen anything suspicious. Moore then left the house and drove to the local police station to telephone all the details of the murder to an inspector at Liverpool's police headquarters in the city centre. Moore alerted all police divisions in the county, instructing them to be on the lookout for a heavily bloodstained man.

At 10.30 p.m. Superintendent Moore returned to Wolverton Street and asked several detectives who were also arriving at the house to search for the murder weapon. Moore examined the recalcitrant but intact front door lock and deduced that no one had made a forced entry. He walked down the hallway and turned into the kitchen to quiz Wallace again. As Wallace described his search for Qualtrough, Moore's eyes scanned the insurance man's clothing for any traces of blood. There were none. Moore then reached out for the cash box and opened it. He looked at Wallace and said, "I can't for the life of me understand why a thief would go to all this trouble of putting the lid back on the box and putting it back where he'd found it."

Later that eventful night, Wallace found he could not make a proper statement in the crowded atmosphere of his home, so he was taken by a police car to the local police station where he could make some attempt to collect his thoughts in a quieter environment. At the station, Wallace was exhaustively interviewed by Inspector Gold and Sergeant Bailey.

At 4 a.m. Superintendent Moore finally left Wallace's home and drove to the station where the insurance man was being interviewed. When Moore arrived, Wallace asked him if there had been any developments in the case, but the superintendent had nothing further to report. Wallace asked if he could go home to bed, but Moore said that would be impossible. Instead he allowed Wallace to stay at his sister Amy's house in southern Liverpool.

On 2 February, at 7 p.m., a police car drew up outside Amy

Wallace's house. Superintendents Moore and Thomas and Inspector Gold got out of the car and called at the house. William Wallace's nephew Edwin answered the door and admitted the three detectives into the house.

"Someone from the police station wants to see you," Edwin told his uncle.

"Take a seat, gentlemen," Wallace said, but the detectives didn't respond. They stood there like statues without even removing their hats. Inspector Gold finally broke the silence. "Mr Wallace, you know who I am?" Gold intoned, sombrely.

Wallace nodded and was about to speak when Inspector Gold continued, "It is my duty to arrest you on the charge of having wilfully murdered your wife, Julia Wallace, and I have to caution you that anything you may say in reply to the charge will be taken down in writing and used in evidence against you."

"What can I say in answer to this charge, of which I am absolutely innocent?" replied a stunned Wallace.

Nobody answered. The sound of Inspector Gold scribbling Wallace's reply in his notebook seemed amplified in the silence.

To his startled nephew, Wallace said, "Edwin, they have come to take me away."

"I'm awfully sorry, Uncle; is there anything I can do?" said the young man in a broken voice.

The murder trial opened at the Liverpool Spring Assizes in St George's Hall on 22 April 1931. To the two prison officers standing on each side of the prisoner, the Clerk of Assizes shouted: "Put up Wallace!"

The officers immediately accompanied Wallace up the steps and into the dock. Within a few tense moments there was a call for silence, and everyone in the court rose as the sheriff and his chaplain entered the room, followed by Mr Justice Wright in his goat-hair wig. As the judge and clerks took their places, the pack of newspaper reporters up in the press box waited impatiently with their sharpened pencils and shorthand notebooks at the ready. The atmosphere was nothing short of electric because already the press had turned the case into something of a *cause célèbre*; in fact the murder was like something out the pages of an Agatha Christie detective novel. It had all the ingredients of a typical English whodunnit mystery: the mysterious telephone caller, the brutality of the killing, yet the apparent lack of motive.

The cold official voice of the Clerk of Assizes boomed across the packed courtroom: "William Herbert Wallace, you are indicted and the charge against you is murder in that on the 20th day of January, 1931, at Liverpool, you murdered Julia Wallace."

Wallace looked down from the dock with a numb, blank expression.

The Clerk then asked: "How say you, William Herbert Wallace, are you guilty or not guilty?"

In a resolute tone Wallace replied, "Not guilty."

The jury was sworn in, and Edward George Hemmerde KC began his opening speech for the Crown: "Members of the jury, the prisoner at the Bar, William Herbert Wallace, is indicted, and the charge against him is murder, in that on the 20th day of 1931, at Liverpool, he murdered Julia Wallace. Upon his indictment he has been arraigned, upon his arraignment he has pleaded that he is not guilty and has put himself upon his country, which country you are, and it is for you to enquire whether he be guilty or not and to hearken to the evidence."

For two hours the jury listened to Hemmerde's graphic account of the "real" events leading up to the murder. Hemmerde promised the jury "evidence which will not show you any motive, nevertheless what I shall suggest to you will carry you almost irresistibly to the conclusion that this woman was murdered by her husband".

Hemmerde commenced to throw doubt on the story of the Qualtrough telephone call, saying, "You might think it curious that a total stranger to the prisoner, speaking from a place 400 yards from his house . . . should have rung up the City Cafe [where the chess club met]; you would have thought that he might have called at the house; you might have thought that he might have written to the house, he might have left a note at the house!"

And of Wallace's expedition to Menlove Gardens, the prosecutor suggested it was illogical for an experienced insurance agent to "call the next night on someone he does not know, at an address which you will find does not exist". To the jury, Hemmerde said, "Do you believe a tale like that?"

Mr Hemmerde then drew the jury's attention to the curious way in which Wallace had drawn attention to himself to support his alibi on his way to the fictitious Menlove Gardens East: speaking to the tram conductors and members of the public, and, most blatantly of all, discussing the exact time of the evening with a policeman.

As for Wallace's alleged difficulty in gaining access to his home upon his return to Wolverton Street, Hemmerde suggested, "suppose you came to the conclusion that the doors never were shut against him . . . you then find a man who could perfectly well get in if he wanted to, pretending that he cannot get in."

The intimation was that Wallace had pretended he couldn't get into his house to ensure that he had witnesses not only to see him arrive home but also to observe his demeanour and his well exhibited concern and suspicion that all was not well.

Referring to the mackintosh found at the scene of the crime, Hemmerde offered the possibility that the raincoat had been used to protect the murderer from being splashed with blood. He told the court: "The history of our criminal courts shows what elaborate precautions people can sometimes take. One of the most famous criminal trials was of a man who committed a crime when he was naked."

Hemmerde was here referring to the Swiss valet François Courvoisier, who was naked when he cut the throat of Lord William Russell in 1840. Hemmerde went on, "A man might perfectly well commit a crime wearing a raincoat as one might wear a dressing gown . . . with nothing on, on which blood could fasten."

Summarizing, Hemmerde added, "This is not a case where you will be in any way concerned with other possible verdicts such as manslaughter. If this man did what he is charged with doing, it is murder foul and unpardonable. Few more brutal can ever have been committed . . . this elderly lonely woman literally hacked to death for apparently no reason at all. Without an apparent enemy in the world, she goes to her account, and if you think the case is fairly proved against this man, that he brutally and wantonly sent this unfortunate woman to her account, it will be your duty to call him to his account."

When the Crown Counsel finally sat down, his version of events seemed unshakeable to the jury. Wallace had telephoned the chess club, leaving a message for himself, and on the following night cold-bloodedly murdered his wife – perhaps, as Hemmerde had suggested, in the nude, or wearing only his mackintosh to prevent being splashed with her blood.

Mr Roland Oliver rose to open for the defence. He cross-examined Samuel Beattie, who had conversed with Qualtrough by telephone on the eve of the murder.

"Do you know Mr Wallace's voice well?" said Oliver.

"Yes," Beattie replied.

"Does it occur to you that it was anything like his voice?"

"Certainly not," said Beattie firmly.

"Does it occur to you now that it was anything like his voice?"

Beattie replied, "It would be a great stretch of the imagination for me to say it was anything like that."

Oliver then produced a witness who swore he had spoken to Julia Wallace at 6.40 p.m. on the evening of the murder. The witness was Alan Close, the 14-year-old milk boy who regularly delivered milk to the Wallace household.

But, despite Oliver's bold efforts, the case against Wallace seemed concrete, and on Saturday, 25 April, the trial reached its climax. The jury was out for only one hour. The verdict they returned was "Guilty".

Like a true stoic, Wallace showed no emotion as the black cap was placed on the judge's wig.

"William Herbert Wallace," Justice Wright proclaimed, "the jury, after a careful hearing, have found you guilty of the murder of your wife. For the crime of murder, by the law of this country there is only one sentence, and that sentence I now pass upon you. It is that you be taken from hence to a place of lawful execution, and that you be there hanged by the neck until you be dead, and that your body be afterwards buried within the precincts of the prison in which you shall last have been confined. And may the Lord have mercy on your soul."

Wallace was then led from the court to a waiting black Maria which took him to Walton Gaol. He was stripped naked at the prison and was soon wearing the grey gaol uniform. By now the stoicism had evaporated and Wallace was sobbing openly. He continued to cry as the warders led him to the condemned cell.

But Wallace appealed against the verdict, and in the following month the unbelievable happened: his plea was upheld by the Court of Appeal. It was the first time in the history of British Law that the court had overturned a conviction for murder – on the grounds that the verdict had opposed the weight of the evidence. Wallace was freed.

He was taken back at his old job, but many of his colleagues still had lingering doubts about his innocence, and backs were turned upon him. The whole affair haunted him so much that, in the end, he left his Anfield home and retired to a home across the River Mersey at Bromborough on the Wirral. On 26 February 1933 William Herbert Wallace died in Clatterbridge Hospital from renal cancer. He was aged 54, and had protested his innocence to the last.

Not surprisingly, armies of criminologists and crime writers such as Edgard Lustgarten, Raymond Chandler and Dorothy L. Sayers have tried to solve the Wallace case over the years, but to date, despite all the attempts, the case is still officially unsolved, and it looks as if it will remain that way for some time to come.

The Chilling Mystery of the "Zodiac" Murders

The sinister Zodiac Murders have been investigated and re-examined by many of the world's leading criminologists and serial-killer profilers but, as of yet, no one has solved the case. All the crime experts will agree on is that the killer who called himself Zodiac was evidently a cerebral yet outrageously daring egotist who carried out cold-blooded and calculated acts of murder to generate mass hysteria via the media.

Initially, the first murder was assumed to be nothing more than some unprovoked attack with overkill. On the evening of 30 October 1966, Cheri Jo Bates, a beautiful 18-year-old student at Riverside City College in California, was brutally murdered. The investigation revealed that the victim had gone to the city college – which was open on Sunday for the students' benefit – to obtain three books for her studies. She checked the books out at 6 p.m. and returned to her car, which was parked in the street outside the library just a short distance away. Cheri Jo attempted to start the vehicle but realized that there was something wrong with the engine. In fact, Zodiac had tampered with it to prevent Cheri Jo from escaping. Zodiac then turned up and seized the teenager, probably at gunpoint, and forced her to accompany him to a dark, secluded spot 200 feet away in the driveway of a house belonging to the nearby school. We'll never know the sheer terror Cheri Jo Bates endured that autumnal evening, but her screams were heard by many in the area. Zodiac stabbed her deeply in the back with a long knife, beat her about the head with a heavy object (probably his gun) and, after several more stab wounds, he callously held her in a vice-like grip as he slit her throat from ear to ear with such ferocity that he almost decapitated the girl. Zodiac later mentioned the Cheri Jo Bates murder in a 1971 letter to the police and added that there were "a hell of a lot more [of his victims] down there [in Southern California]".

On 20 December 1968 a woman was driving through California from Vallejo (just north of San Francisco) to Benica. As she came down Lake Herman Road – a lonely stretch of highway known locally as a "lovers lane" – the woman came across a parked station wagon. Next to the vehicle a body lay on the cold macadam, and another one lay on the ground further down the road. The woman drove into town and called the police, and so began the baffling case of the Zodiac murders.

The police established that the bodies in the road were of two teenage high school sweethearts. David Faraday, 17, had been shot in the head whilst in the station wagon. His girl-friend, 16-year-old Bettilou Jensen, had evidently been running from the gunman but had been shot in the back five times as she fled. Both victims had been shot with a ·22 calibre gun loaded with long-rifle ammunition. Robbery was naturally suspected as a motive initially, but the boy's wallet in his jacket pocket still contained cash. Furthermore, the girl had not been raped or interfered with in any sexual way, so the police were naturally mystified, and assumed the killer had carried out a motiveless double murder. Perhaps the murderer had even been an admirer of the girl who had resented her involvement with Faraday, but even this theory seemed way off the mark, because the killer apparently struck again in the following July.

A man with a gruff, monotone voice telephoned the Vallejo Police Department on 5 July 1969 to report a second double murder, and again the victims were a couple. The anonymous caller said: "I wish to report a double murder. If you will go one mile east on Columbus Parkway to a public park, you will find the kids in a brown car. They have been shot by a nine millimetre Luger."

The man then chillingly added: "I also killed those kids last year. Goodbye!"

Police converged on the scene of the crime as the caller had directed them. In a car at the parking lot of the Blue Rock Springs Golf Course, they found 24-year-old waitress Darlene Ferris – the mother of a young child – dead from gunshot wounds. Next to her in the car was Michael Mageau with blood pouring from a bullet hole in his neck. Mageau had also sustained three other gunshot wounds but was still alive and later made a full recovery. He told the police that shortly after he and Darlene had driven to the parking lot, a car drove up and parked beside them. It then drove away, but returned ten minutes later, again pulling up alongside the couple's car. An intense beam of light suddenly shone into the couple's car, blinding them. Mageau couldn't be sure if the driver of the other car had shone the light into his eyes, but presumed he had. The driver walked up to the couple's car and started to shoot them both. Despite the dazzling light, Mageau still caught a glimpse of the assailant, and said that he was white, around 25 to 30 years of age, stockily built, around five feet eight inches in height, with a round face and wavy light brown hair.

On the first day of the following month, two San Francisco dailies and the Vallejo *Times-Herald* received letters which began: "Dear Editor, This is the murderer of the two teenagers last Christmas at Lake Herman and the girl on the 4th of July . . ." The letter then went on to describe details about the crime, including the guns and type of ammunition used, which made it clear that the writer was the killer and not some crank out for kicks.

The letters were all signed with a curious symbol: a cross superimposed on a circle which looked like the hairs of a gunsight. But someone later discovered that the symbol was actually an ancient astrological sign which represented the Zodiac – an imaginary belt in space which encompasses 13 constellations ranging from Aries to Pisces.

Why did the killer use an astrological symbol? Was he some twisted astrology freak who carried out his crimes when his horoscope was favourable? It was anyone's guess. Stranger still, the killer's letters also contained a weird-looking code made up from pictograms – letters and signs arranged in a complex cypher. The murderer stated in his letter that if the code was broken it would reveal his identity. Military experts were brought into the investigation to crack the code, but failed, so the police wondered if the killer was just teasing them with a random jumble of letters and signs which meant nothing. Just when the code was about to be dismissed, a teacher from Alisal High School in Salinas named Dale Harden finally cracked the killer's cypher. The chilling deciphered message, however, did not reveal the identity of the cold-blooded murderer, but it did throw some light on the sick, warped fantasy world he inhabited. The weird message read:

> *I like to kill people because it is so much fun. It is more fun than killing wild game in the forest, because Man is the most dangerous animal of all. To kill something gives me the most thrilling experience. It is even better than sex. The best part will be when I die. I will be reborn in Paradise, and then all I have killed will become my slaves. I will not give you my name because you will try to slow or stop my collecting of slaves for my afterlife.*

Shortly afterwards, a further letter to the newspapers started off: "Dear Editor, This is Zodiac speaking . . ." and the missive proceeded to accurately detail the murder of Darlene Ferrin and the wounding of Michael Mageau in the parking lot.

The police and the press naturally expected more killings by Zodiac, and on 27 September of that year, a man with the same distinct monotonal voice telephoned the Napa Police Department to report a particularly savage murder. On this occasion, Zodiac had captured two students of Pacific Union College who had been picnicking near Lake Verriesa. Police found the victims' car parked on the shore of the lake. Cecilia Shepherd and Bryan Hartnell were lying bound together in the vehicle, soaked in their own blood. The girl had died from 24 knife wounds. Hartnell had received six stab wounds but was still alive. When the college student had recovered from his injuries he gave a graphic account of the terrifying ordeal he'd undergone. He said he and Cecilia had been accosted by a pudgy-looking man who wore a black hood with eye slits in it. The hood resembled the type worn by medieval executioners. On this hood was the Zodiac's circle and cross symbol painted in white. Through the eye-holes, Hartnell could make out a pair of spectacles with black frames. He could also see wisps of the masked man's hair, which looked light brown. The killer carried a pistol and a knife, and he demanded money from the couple, then said he was an escaped convict. He tied the trembling couple up and then calmly announced: "I'm going to have to stab you people."

Hartnell bravely volunteered to be stabbed in an effort to spare the life of Cecilia. The masked fiend then thrust the long blade of his knife into Hartnell six times. But the nightmare wasn't over yet. He plunged the knife into Cecilia's body and went berserk. The coroner later saw that the 24 knife wounds on the college girl's corpse formed a bloody cross. A fisherman who had been in the area while the frenzied attack was taking place told police he'd heard the girl's terrible screams.

After the enraged butchery, Zodiac had evidently been composed enough to leisurely scrawl his symbol on the door of Hartnell's car with a felt-tip pen.

Detectives traced the telephone that Zodiac had used to notify them of the frenzied stabbing. It was a public call box embarrassingly situated near to the Napa Police

Headquarters. Forensic experts managed to lift three fresh fingerprints from the call box, but were disappointed to discover that the prints matched none held in the police records. This meant that all the detectives could tell the newspapers was that Zodiac didn't have a police record, which was hardly a breakthrough.

A fortnight later, on the evening of 11 October, Zodiac struck again under the cover of a thick fog. He asked 29-year-old taxi driver Paul Lee Stine to drive to 3898 Washington Street in the Nob Hill area of San Francisco, then changed his mind because there was a group of people on the corner of that street. Zodiac asked Stine to drive on for one more block, then he shot him in the back of the head, killing him instantly. This gratuitous snuffing out of yet another innocent person's life was actually witnessed by three teenagers from a window in the upstairs apartment, directly across the fogbound street. The teens trembled as they watched the shadowy figure of Zodiac wiping down the cab and tearing a piece of shirt off his victim. As the murderer coolly strolled away down the tree-lined street into the depths of the dark fog, he was actually observed by two police officers in a patrol car. Alas, the dispatcher had radioed the wrong description to the policemen; the description broadcast to their car radio had described Zodiac as a black man, and the figure seen in the vicinity of the shooting had obviously been a Caucasian. Police soon discovered that Zodiac had made off with the taxi driver's wallet and a strip of fabric torn from the victim's shirt. Ballistics experts also recovered the bullet that had taken Stine's life and noted that it had been fired from the same pistol that had killed Darlene Ferris.

On the following day, the *San Francisco Chronicle* received a letter from the killer which criticized the police for being incompetent:

> *The San Francisco Police could have caught me last night had they searched the park properly instead of holding road races with their motor cycles seeing who could make the most noise. The car drivers should have just parked their cars and sat there quietly waiting for me to come out of cover.*

But the letter ended with a shocking threat. Zodiac wrote: "Schoolchildren make good targets. I think I shall wipe out a school bus one morning some time. Just shoot out the tyres, then pick off the kiddies as they come bouncing out." To rule out the idea that the letter had been penned by a sick hoaxer, Zodiac had also enclosed a fragment of the bloody shirt he'd torn from the murdered taxi driver.

Police escorted school buses throughout Zodiac's territory for weeks but, fortunately, the killer failed to carry out his repugnant threat.

The murder of the taxi driver was the last known Zodiac murder, but the killer continued to give the police a headache for many years to come. On 21 October 1969 the murderer manipulated the media in a most sensational way. He telephoned Oakland police and sincerely stated that he would willingly give himself up if he could be represented by a top-notch lawyer. Zodiac named two particular maverick lawyers he had in mind; Melvin Belli or F. Lee Bailey. The serial murderer then stipulated that he would require a period of air-time on an early morning TV chat-show. Arrangements were made by the television executives who saw the request from Zodiac as a spectacular once-in-a-lifetime ratings winner, and so, at 6.45 a.m., the "Jim Dunbar Show" was broadcast to a record TV audience. Thousands of viewers tuned in to the show, eager to hear the killer speaking live. Almost one hour later, the waiting was over. At 7.41 a.m. a caller came on the line, chatting to lawyer Melvin Belli. The caller had a soft, boyish voice, and he said he was the Zodiac Killer. He explained that he killed because he suffered from blinding headaches, and discussed some of the murders. Police tried to trace the call, but Zodiac kept hanging up and telephoning the studio back from different locations. He called back 15 times, and finally ended his "performance" by agreeing to meet Belli in front of a certain store in Daly City. At long last it looked as if there was a chance of catching the killer and bringing him to justice but, alas, Zodiac failed to keep his appointment with the lawyer.

Two months later, shortly before Christmas, Belli received a letter containing another piece of the murdered taxi driver's shirt. Zodiac wrote: "Dear Melvin, This is Zodiac speaking. I wish you a happy Christmas. One thing I ask of you is this, please help me . . . I am afraid I will lose control and take my ninth and possibly tenth victim." It seems as if Zodiac then retired from hunting his "afterlife slaves" and nothing more was heard from him until 1971, when the killer wrote to the *Los Angeles Times*. The letter read: "If the blue menaces are ever going to catch me, they had better get off their fat butts and do something." The letter was signed in the usual way, with his astro-sign, but also included the number 17 followed by a plus sign.

That seemed to be it. The years dragged by, and many detectives thought that Zodiac had either died or was killing more and writing less. Then in 1974 the San Francisco Police Department received another letter from him. The killer now boasted killing 37 people. A police graphology expert confirmed that the handwriting was Zodiac's. The media thought the latest claim was astounding, but the police – fearing an hysterical outcry from the taxpaying public – played down Zodiac's atrocious claim as a "slight exaggeration".

The last word from the killer seems to have been in 1990, when the *New York Post* received a letter signed by Zodiac. The letter-writer intimated that he was now at large in the Big Apple, and described four unsolved murders in New York and certain details that could have been known only by the killer. The writer's claim of "NYPD 0, Zodiac 9" may be an exaggeration, but some detectives in the city are keeping an open mind in the light of evidence on the Zodiac killings which suggests that the murder toll quoted by the murderer for New York is a fairly accurate figure. Zodiac has claimed to have carried out 37 murders and attempted murders across North America, but confirming this astounding contention is almost impossible. A case in point is the murder of Doreen Gaul and Jim Sharp in Los Angeles on 21 November 1969. It was claimed at the time that a letter from Zodiac was found in the personal belongings of Doreen Gaul, and that the Examiner of Documents for the State of California had even authenticated the letter. A high-ranking police officer also claimed that the Zodiac letter was genuine. Furthermore, forensic investigators commented that there was an "object" placed under the head of Doreen Gaul's body which indicated strong similarities to other Zodiac murders in northern California. There were also allegations that Bruce Davis, a member of the notorious Charles Manson Family, had actually known Doreen Gaul. Does this mean that Zodiac had a connection with Manson? That's a question that has never been answered.

In Los Angeles in 1975 Sonoma County Sheriff Don Striepeke fed all the murder records filed in the state attorney's office into a computer. The computer linked 40 murders to one particular killer because of the modus operandi, the geographical area and the time window. When the sites of these murders were plotted on a map of northern California and Washington State, the results were incredible. In Washington State, the murder sites formed two large rectangles connected by a line. County Sheriff Striepeke researched the strange geometrical shape, and discovered that the same shape had been used as an occult symbol by witches in England during the late Middle Ages. The symbol represented the afterlife (a subject Zodiac was certainly obsessed with), and was painted on the hearth of homes were people had recently passed away to speed their spirit into the hereafter.

Striepeke may have been onto something with his computer-aided analysis of Zodiac's murders, because it later came to light that alongside some of the bodies of girls killed by the occult-minded murderer police were intrigued to find twigs and stones – arranged to form two small rectangles linked by a line.

Atlantis

During World War II, scores of American pilots on submarine duty in the Caribbean reported sightings of artificial underwater structures. Many of these geometrical constructs were seen in the coastal vicinity of Mexico, Yucatan and British Honduras, and seemed to fly in the face of the textbook history of the Americas. Today many more submerged buildings of uncertain origin have been discovered, and they are providing quite a headache for conventional archaeology, because evidence is gradually mounting that hints at a pre-Inca (and possibly pre-Egyptian) civilization, which might have actually had a transatlantic trade route with Europe. Furthermore, it is entirely possible that the shipping lanes of this route had a regular port of call on their journeys: the mid-Atlantic continent of Atlantis.

The primary source of a legendary ancient super-civilization that existed on a mid-Atlantic island 10,000 years before the birth of Christ originated in Plato's books *Critias* and *Timaeus*, written circa 355 BC, when Plato was in his seventies. Among these works, Plato gives a detailed description of the Atlantean metropolis. When describing the dimensions and measurements of the island and its architecture, Plato often refers to the *stade* – which is an archaic measurement of length, equivalent to 606 feet. According to Plato:

> At the centre of the island, near the sea, was a plain, said to be the most beautiful and fertile of all plains, and near the middle of the plain about 50 stade inland a hill of no great size . . . There were two rings of land and three of sea, like cartwheels, with the island at their centre and equidistant from each other . . . In the centre was a shrine sacred to Poseidon and Cleito, surrounded by a golden wall through which entry was forbidden . . . There was a temple to Poseidon himself, a stade in length, 300 feet wide and proportionate in height, though somewhat outlandish in appearance. The outside of it was covered all over with silver, except for the figures on the pediment which were covered in gold . . . Round the temple were statues of the original ten kings and their wives, and many others dedicated by kings and private persons belonging to the city and its dominions . . . The two springs, cold and hot, provided an unlimited supply of water for appropriate purposes, remarkable for its agreeable quality and excellence; and this they made available by surrounding it with suitable buildings and plantations, leading some of it into basins in the open air and some of it into covered hot baths for winter use. Here

separate accommodation was provided for royalty and commoners, and again, for women, for horses and for other beasts of burden . . . The outflow they led into the grove of Poseidon, which (because of the goodness of the soil) was full of trees of marvellous beauty and height, and also channelled it to the outer ring-islands by aqueducts at the bridges. On each of these ring-islands they had built many temples for different gods, and many gardens and areas for exercise, some for men and some for horses . . . Finally, there were dockyards full of triremes and their equipment all in good shape . . . Beyond the three outer harbours there was a wall, beginning at the sea and running right round in a circle, at a uniform distance of 50 stade from the largest ring and harbour and returning in on itself at the mouth of the canal to the sea. The wall was densely built up all round with houses and the canal and the large harbour were crowded with vast numbers of merchant ships from all quarters, from which rose a constant din of shouting and noise day and night.

Where was this civilization sited? According to Plato, Atlantis was located "Beyond the Pillars of Hercules", which means beyond the Straits of Gibraltar (on either side of which the Herculean pillars once stood) and out into the Atlantic Ocean.

Many think that Atlantis was merely a figment of Plato's imagination; a pure myth that the Greek philosopher used as a vehicle for his theories of a utopia. Aristotle flatly rejected Plato's tale, and right up to the Middle Ages a majority of the academics agreed with him, although Aristotelian reasoning on many things, such as metaphysics and astronomy, was faulty, and held up the advancement of empirical science for centuries.

Where did Plato get his information about Atlantis from? He says he heard it from a young man named Critias, who says he heard it from his grandfather who in turn heard it from his father, a friend of Solon, a famous Greek elder statesman, who had learned of the story of Atlantis from the Egyptian priests of Sais. Solon was visiting Sais on the Nile

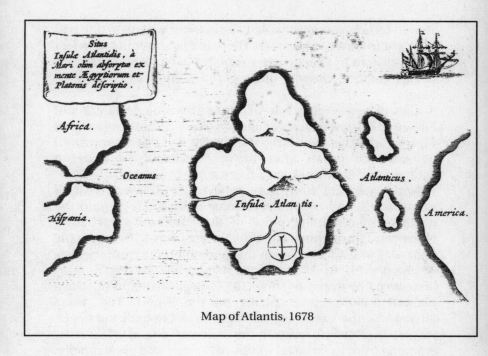

Map of Atlantis, 1678

delta around 600 BC. His work of framing a constitution for Athens and of instituting social and economic reforms was ended, so Solon had decided to devote the remaining years of his life to poetry and the study of history. He was particularly interested in the origins of the Hellenic civilization, so he asked the Egyptian scholars what they knew of his nation's genesis. The scholars of the college of the goddess Neith, the protectress of learning, confided to Solon that there were records in their archives, thousands of years old, which referred to a continent beyond the Pillars of Hercules which sank around 9560 BC. This continent was named Atlantis. The people of this continent – the Atlanteans – prized fellowship and friendship above worldly possessions, and enjoyed an advanced system of socialism that meant no one ever lived in poverty. Like the Incas (who were said to be descendants of the Atlanteans) the people of Atlantis also had a money-free economy and all land was held in common. Virgil's *Georgics* and Tibullus's *Elegies* state that land in ancient times was shared by large communistic-like societies where no one had the right to own a single acre. There is also a mention of a lost social system in which "there were no liars, no sickness, nor old age" in the 5000-year-old *Engidu* and the poem of Uttra of Sumer.

Alas, Plato says that the Atlanteans became decadent and bellicose. They waged a war against the neighbouring areas of Europe and Asia. Not long afterwards, Atlantis disappeared beneath the ocean after being devastated by either a catastrophic earthquake or a meteor.

Some sceptical historians believe the dramatic end of Atlantis is a very convenient epilogue that gets around the problem of obtaining proof of the continent's existence. However, throughout history, there have been many instances of land masses sinking and emerging from the seas of the world. In 1780 Falcon Island in the Pacific was discovered by the Spanish. In 1892 the government of Tonga planted 2000 coconut palms on the island. Two years afterwards, the island dramatically sank beneath the ocean waves. In November 1963 the volcanic island of Surtsey emerged from the coastal waters of Iceland and grew rapidly. After three weeks, the island – which was half a mile across – had risen to 390 feet above sea level. Its lava rapidly solidified and the island now has vegetation. In 1819 the delta of the Indus was shaken by a mighty earthquake which caused most of the local territory to sink. One of the worst cases of a drowned city occurred on 1 November 1755, when a tremendous earthquake struck Lisbon. Every dwelling in the lower part of the city was demolished by the quake, then a gigantic tidal wave swept in from the ocean. Over 60,000 people perished in the catastrophe. The shock from the quake was felt over an area of $1\frac{1}{2}$ million miles, and people all over Europe who were attending masses in their cathedrals that All Soul's Day actually saw the chandeliers dance and sway.

If Atlantis did disappear under the waves, surely there must be some traces of the island on the bed of the Atlantic? Deep-sea soundings of the Atlantic sea bed have been made over the years with sonar and submarine investigation, and there have been some very curious finds. In 1898, 500 miles north of the Azores, an American telegraph company lowered grappling irons onto the sea bed and tried to retrieve the broken ends of the snapped transatlantic cable. Instead, they brought up samples of basaltic lava. A French geologist named Pierre Termier who analyzed the dredged-up lava was flummoxed, as the sample was vitreous instead of crystalline. This meant that the lava had been submerged under water after cooling. As lava disintegrates after 15,000 years, this told Termier that there had been some volcanic activity above sea level near the Azores in the fairly recent past, perhaps around the time of the Atlantis cataclysm.

In other areas on the sea bottom in the vicinity of the Azores, beach sand has been found. It was first discovered by Professor M. Ewing of Columbia University in 1949, at a depth of three miles. The find was just as perplexing as the lava discovery. Beach sand is a product of sea erosion, and non-existent on the bed of the ocean, so its presence indicates that coastal land must have sunk into the Atlantic at some period in the recent past.

Some think that these underwater findings suggest that the Azores are the vestiges of Atlantis, but there is another site in the Atlantic where the legendary continent may have been located: the West Indies. The West Indies is an archipelago that extends in a curved chain for over 1500 miles from the peninsula of Florida to the Venuzuelan coast. The islands are mostly volcanic in origin, but the Bahamas and Antigua are composed largely of coral. In September 1968 a local Bahamian fishing guide known as "Bonefish" Sam brought Dr J. Manson Valentine, an archaeologist and honorary curator of the Museum of Science in Miami, to see an intriguing geometrical structure lying in 23 feet of water off North Bimini. Dr Valentine, who had been searching for traces of lost civilizations in the Bahamas for 15 years, was naturally excited. After investigating the underwater structure, Dr Valentine described his findings in his museum magazine as:

> *An extensive pavement of regular and polygonal flat stones, obviously shaped and accurately aligned to form a convincingly artefactual pattern. These stones had*

evidently lain submerged over a long period of time, for the edges of the biggest ones had become rounded off, giving the blocks the domed appearance of giant loaves of bread or pillows of stone . . . Some were absolutely rectangular and some approaching perfect squares.

The J-shaped "Bimini Road", as it is now called, quickly fired speculation that evidence of a submerged civilization had been uncovered; perhaps the very site of Atlantis had now been found. Strangely enough, the renowned American psychic and prophet Edgar Cayce (1877–1945) went into a trance in 1933 and said that parts of Atlantis would be discovered in the late 1960s. His actual words were: "A portion of the temples may yet be discovered under the slime of ages and sea water near Bimini. Expect it in '68 or '69 – not so far away." The stones of the Bimini Road cannot be dated, but analysis of the fossilized mangrove roots growing over the stones in the road has given a date of around 10,000 to 12,000 years.

In 1975 the explorer Dr David Zink discovered an unusual fragment of worked stone lodged in the Bimini Road; a block of tongue-and-groove masonry. One edge of the man-made fragment is semi-cylindrical and the other is rectangular. The remnant is hard but was evidently never fired, so it cannot be dated by thermoluminescence, and no archaeologist or architect can identify its origin.

Three miles south of the Bimini Road, underwater explorers have found fluted marble columns, which is hard to explain, as marble is not native to the Bahamas.

Around the time of Zink's discovery, Maurice Chatelain, a French space engineer who worked with NASA on the Apollo missions, said he had found a strange reference to the sinking of a continent in an ancient Tibetan scripture. The reference stated that in 9564 BC a very large part of a continent sank into the ocean in what is now the Caribbean and the Gulf of Mexico. Chatelain believes that the writers of the Tibetan script were themselves Atlanteans who had escaped the disaster.

Beneath the waters of the Great Bahama Banks, a large pyramidal building measuring 180 by 140 feet has been located. In the same area, a pilot spotted a wall under 12 fathoms of unusually clear water. Curiously, the wall had an archway going through the middle of it. There was also a recent report of another architectural anomaly a few miles from this wall: a large marble citadel covering five undersea acres with roads leading from it. Unfortunately, diving on the citadel is too hazardous, as Cuban patrol boats regularly visit the waters around it.

Surely if Atlantis did exist in the vicinity of the West Indies, its culture would have rubbed off on the peoples of the eastern coast of Mexico and the North and South Americas? The Aztec capital of Tenochtitlan, which was inhabited by 300,000 people, was situated on an island in a vast lake in the middle of concentric canals. The Aztecs built the capital as a replica of "Aztlan", a land which lay in the east, from which the Aztecs claimed their descent. Tenochtitlan's concentric layout was a copy of the description of Atlantis given by Plato.

The Mayan civilization of Central America left curious accounts of the destruction of an early civilization. Brasseur de Bourbourg, an eminent French ethnographer, deciphered a Mayan document in 1869 which told of the annihilation, millennia before, of two countries on an island that was rocked by a massive earthquake and "suddenly disappeared in the night" along with 64 million people.

The American Indians also have stories about a drowned civilization in their folklore. According to the anthropologists, the Indians came across the Bering Straits from Siberia, but the Indians themselves believe that they came from a homeland in the east which was destroyed in a flood. The Okanogan Indians of British Columbia tell a similar story. They maintain that a continent existed in the middle of the Atlantic long ago called "Samah-tumi-whoo-lah" – which translates as "White man's island". This island – which was destroyed in a terrible war – was said to be ruled by a tall white-skinned ruler named Queen Scomalt.

In the year 1519 Hernando Cortés and his conquistadores landed in Mexico at Vera Cruz. Cortés and his men gazed in awe at Mexico City, the capital of the New World. The Emperor Montezuma II greeted the explorers and promptly surrendered himself and his empire of 5 million people to

Cortés and his 600 soldiers. Cortés was baffled. He was not aware that to the Aztecs and Mayas his arrival signified their Second Coming. Like the Red Indians of North America, the races of Central America were awaiting the return of the White God, known as Quetzacoatl, who was expected to appear soon. To the Incas he was called Viracocha. The Toltecs described the god as fair and ruddy with a beard and long hair who wore a long robe of black linen cut low at the neck with short sleeves – a dress worn by the natives to this very day. To the baffled Cortés, the Emperor explained (through the daughter of an Aztec chieftain, who acted as an interpreter) that the Aztecs had not lived in Mexico long, and that their ancestors had been led by a bearded white man from the east named Quetzacoatl who displayed great wisdom. Before sailing back towards the east, the White God had promised to return to Mexico to govern the land. Cortés could make no sense of the Emperor's story, and gave an account of his journey from Cuba and his mission to secure the pagan lands for King Charles V of Spain. The Emperor replied, "You tell us that you come from where the sun rises, the things you tell us of this great Lord or king who sent you hither to us we believe and take it for certain that he is our natural Lord, especially as you tell us that he was known of us for many days. And therefore you may be certain that we shall obey you and accept you as Lord in place of this great Lord of whom you speak."

Unfortunately, the Emperor could not dissuade Cortés and his gold-crazed conquistadores from proceeding to Tenoctitlan. He was held hostage, but won the affection of his captors. However, the white visitors caused an uprising among the natives, and as Montezuma tried to address them, they showered him with stones, and he died several days later.

Fourteen years later, the same tragedy unfolded in Peru, when Atahualpa, the tyrannical Inca ruler, venerated the Spanish soldier of fortune Don Francisco Pizarro as a descendant of the White God Viracocha. In shining armour, Pizarro and 168 soldiers had been sighted by the natives riding inland from the sea towards the Inca city of Cajamarca. The awe-struck Incas greeted the strange visitors, and at

Cajamarca Atahualpa hailed Pizarro as the divine son of Viracocha. When Pizarro gave a demonstration of his power by firing a cannon, the Incas shuddered, as they recalled the legends which told of Viracocha's control over thunder. In no time, Pizarro's men were plundering their way across the country. Atahualpa saw that the visitors were not gods, but gangsters, and he demanded that the thieves from the west return the goods they had stolen. Instead, Pizarro sent a Bible-carrying priest to the Inca ruler to convert him and his people from sun-worship to Christianity, but the catechism lesson ended abruptly when Atahualpa threw the holy book to the ground. The outraged Spaniards immediately went on the rampage and slaughtered the unarmed natives. Atahualpa was taken captive and held for ransom for nine months, and during this time a huge room was filled with silver and gold and offered to Pizarro for the Inca ruler's release. Pizarro had already planned to kill Atahualpa in order to disrupt and conquer the Inca society. The Spaniard mercenary arranged a mock trial and found Atahualpa guilty of trumped-up charges. Pizarro gave him a choice; he could be burned alive as a heathen, or he could be strangled as a Christian. Atahualpa chose to be strangled. He was baptized Juan de Atahualpa "in honour of St John the Baptist" then tied to a stake and garrotted. Pizarro and his soldiers then laid on a full-scale Catholic funeral for the "converted" ruler. It was then only a matter of time before the "men from the rising sun" sacked the rest of the country.

The strange aspect of these dark episodes in the exploration of the Americas is the way the explorers were assumed to be long-awaited white gods from an eastern land.

If Atlantis really was situated near the West Indies, there is evidence that an earthquake may not have been the demise of the legendary landmass. On the ocean floor of the south-west Atlantic there are twin depressions 23,000 feet deep, near Puerto Rico, which look remarkably like craters. There are similar craters of meteoric origin on the North American mainland at Arizona and Charleston, South Carolina, where an elliptical area extends out into the Atlantic. It has been estimated that the craters near the hypothetical site of Atlantis in the West Indies were created with an explosive force equivalent to the detonation of 30,000 million tonnes of nitroglycerine around 10,000 to 15,000 BC. An explosion of this magnitude could also be produced by 3000 medium-sized hydrogen bombs. Such an apocalyptic explosion would punch a hole in the planet's crust and some theorists think this was how the Gulf of Mexico was formed millions of years before. The celestial object that inflicted such a devastating hammer blow to the Earth is estimated to have been around six miles in diameter, which rates it as an asteroid. An earlier asteroid fall is thought to have wiped out the dinosaurs 65 million years ago, and in modern times, our world has had a number of close shaves with so-called "Earth-grazers" – asteroids that come dangerously close to the planet as they orbit the sun. The asteroid Eros, which has a diameter of ten miles, came within 14 million miles of the Earth in 1931. In February 1936 another asteroid named Adonis came within 1,500,000 miles of the Earth, which is too close for comfort. Incredibly, in 1993 an asteroid designated 1993 KA2 made the closest approach ever made by an asteroid. It passed within 90,000 miles of the Earth, travelling at a speed of 48,000 miles per hour. Although it was only 30 feet in diameter, the asteroid had an estimated mass of 6,000 tons, and had it survived a fiery plunge through Earth's atmosphere, it would have caused the equivalent of an atomic explosion.

Despite all the speculation, the truth about Atlantis still eludes us, yet the legends of the submerged civilization continue to hold a growing fascination over each generation. There are many who think Atlantis is just a fable, but they should remember that prior to the excavations made by the explorer Heinrich Schliemann in the late nineteenth century, Troy was also regarded as fiction.

PART FOUR
Time and Space
●●●●●●●●●●●●●●●●●●●●●●●●●●●●●●●●●●●

Mysteries of Time and Space

In the relatively short span we spend on earth, one thing above all rules our lives: time. Even the richest man in the world lying on his deathbed cannot buy one extra second of time. Time is more precious than gold but cannot be borrowed or bought, although we often talk of someone buying time or living on borrowed time. These are just misleading idioms. As Paul Henri Spaak, the Belgian statesman, once wistfully remarked on the almost cruel ephemerality of fleeting time: "If an hour seems long, I remind myself that it will never return, and it immediately becomes terribly short."

But what is time? Does it really have something to do with the clocks and watches which dictate our lives, or is it all in the mind? We all know that if you're having an unpleasant experience, time drags by, but if you're enjoying yourself, the hours fly; it's as if time is a subjective experience. Neurologists now claim that the brain's complex architecture may be partly responsible for our experience of personal time. If you have a personal computer nowadays, the manufacturer often states how "fast" the PC is by quoting the speed of its processor, which is usually measured in megahertz (MHz). One megahertz is a measure of frequency equal to 1 million cycles per second. Personal computers have a component containing a quartz crystal which vibrates millions of times a second and acts as the heart of a clock for the computer system to work by. Most computers have a processor speed of 200 MHz but, believe it or not, the human brain – the most complex computer known to man – has a much slower frequency of just 18 Hz, or 18 cycles per second. The eminent neurologist J. Hughlings Jackson recently stated that "Time in the form of some minimum duration is required for consciousness."

Many other prominent neurologists concur, and believe that psychological time – our experience of the present – is merely an illusionary side-effect created by the ticking of the brain's electrical 18 Hz clock. This would mean that the ego of the reader only exists in relatively slow measurable pulses of 18 cycles per second. In other words, the ego is discontinuous, like a number of beads spaced out on a thread. Curiously, the Buddhists have long asserted that the ego is a flickering, virtually non-existent illusion of continuity. A good analogy to illustrate this concept of discontinuity is the way we are fooled into believing we are watching a continuous "motion" film in the cinema when we are in fact only looking at 24 still frames being swiftly flashed onto the screen in succession each second. The audience experiences a sense of "now" unfolding each moment in the film's time frame when, in reality, it is just a discontinuous illusion full of blank gaps and static images.

The clock theory of the brain would also explain why certain people suffer convulsions and seizures when they are bombarded with rapid flashes of light from a strobe. Most of the seizures take place when the strobe flashes at a frequency of 15 to 20 Hz. It's as if the flashes are sending high-speed signals down the eye's optic nerve which throws the brain out of synchronization with its 18 Hz rhythm, just like a drummer losing his beat. Despite these intriguing mechanistic theories of consciousness, it is probable that the neurologists are grossly underestimating the complex workings of the psyche and are merely skirting the fringes of the human mindscape.

So much for psychological time. Does time exist outside of our brains in the physical universe?

The Greek philosopher Heraclitus (c.540–c.480 BC) was one of the earliest people to ponder the nature of time, and he observed that "All things flow, nothing stays still; nothing endures but change."

Heraclitus was remarking on the apparent constant "arrow of time" which travels into the future from the past, relentlessly in one direction. Empires rise and crumble, the baby grows into an old person and expires, and the eternal seasons roll on. In the midst of this ever-changing universe, the nostalgic animal homo sapiens longs for the familiar golden days of yesteryear, often yearning to turn back the clock; the receding out-of-reach past, which rouses Shakespeare's Richard II to cry: "O! Call back yesterday, bid time return."

Thanks to the development of photography, films and video technology, we can call back yesterday in limited form. We can revisit a wedding captured years back on video, be enthralled by films starring actors and actresses who have been dead for decades, just as we can listen to tapes and CDs featuring performers who have long gone to their graves. And, of course, leafing through the simple family photograph album never fails to evoke some emotion or memory of days gone by.

But can we somehow circumvent the seemingly cast-iron laws of nature and actually visit the past (or the future, for that matter) in person? This is a seductive notion that has occupied minds for thousands of years. We are now venturing into the territory of the theoretical physicist, because we are posing the age-old question "Is time travel possible?" I say it is.

We are all time travellers, moving into the future at a rate of 60 seconds a minute, although we often think that it is time that is going by. No, time stays, we move on. In each second which goes by as you read these words, the earth is whizzing through space in its orbit around the Sun at a phenomenal speed of 18 miles per second, but no one is aware of this. Nor are most people aware that when they look at the incandescent orange disc of the setting Sun, they are seeing it not as it is "now", but as it was eight minutes ago. The rays which travel from the Sun across 93 million miles of space take eight minutes to reach us here on earth. So we are then looking eight minutes into the past. Please note that you should never look directly at the Sun, or you risk blindness; and you should never look at the solar disc through binoculars or a telescope. The only safe way to observe the sun is to use a telescope as a projector, sending the image onto a white screen held or fixed behind the eyepiece.

The stars in the sky are even further away than the Sun (which is the nearest star to us), and the light from them can take anything from four years to billions of years to reach us. For example, if you go out on a cloudless night and look up at Polaris, the so-called "North Star", your eyes will be seeing it as it was 680 years ago when Edward II was King of England. And, if by some remote chance, there are aliens peering at us through their version of a super-Hubble telescope on some planet orbiting a star 932 light-years away, they will be witnessing the Battle of Hastings. Sadly, if the extraterrestrials take another look at us 900 years on, they will see there are still conflicts going on down here.

So, just by gazing at the stars we can look into the remote past, which illustrates how our perspective on time changes when we look at it from beyond the petty confines of our day-to-day mundane world of clock watching. But looking at stars is hardly physical time travel; isn't there a nuts-and-bolts way of visiting the past down here on Earth? The surprising answer is yes.

Viewers of all ages have been terrified by Dr Who with his grisly gallery of outlandish monsters (and low-budget egg-box sets). The good Doctor and his Tardis were once regarded as pure science fiction but there are many distinguished scientists with impeccable academic credentials who believe that time travel will be a reality one day. Indeed, some boffins think timelords like the Doctor may have already visited history. Before I examine the blueprints for hypothetical time machines, let me mention just one curious historical character of the eighteenth century who may have been a real-life timelord: the mysterious Count of St.-Germain. Various books refer to this enigmatic aristocratic-looking individual as nothing more than some oddball adventurer. In the Century of Enlightenment, the French police suspected him of being a Prussian spy, but the Prussians surmised he was a Russian agent. The English thought he was a Jacobite sympathizer when he was arrested in London in 1745, but whenever he was interrogated, it became clear that the count was not in the pay of anybody, and made many disturbing and seemingly astounding claims. He said he had met Jesus of Nazareth and had been a wedding guest at Cana, where he actually witnessed the water-into-wine miracle. The count added that he had always known that Christ would meet a bad end, and many were outraged by his sacrilegious claims. The count said he had also met Cleopatra, Nefertiti, Henry VIII, Shakespeare and many other historical personages. Stranger still, when quizzed by bemused historians about his meetings with celebrated characters from the past, the Count of St.-Germain always went into amazing detail about his encounters, and could even describe the food, weather and trivialities of the age he had lived in. All of these details would be thoroughly checked by the academics and always found to be true. Another mystery was the count's wealth. He was incredibly rich and had an abundant supply of unusually large gemstones, which he used as currency. Then there is the puzzle of his multi-linguistical talents. He spoke fluent Greek, Spanish, Russian, Italian, Portugese, French, Arabic, Sanskrit, Chinese, English and the language of Christ – Aramaic. The count was also a gifted violinist, pianist, sculptor (in the ancient Greek tradition), painter, and an accomplished chemist. He set up many laboratories during his extensive travels throughout Europe, Russia and India, but his work was always shrouded in secrecy, although many thought he was an alchemist trying to turn base metals into gold.

The great French writer and philosopher Voltaire quizzed the count, initially suspecting him to be a silver-tongued charlatan, but ended up declaring: "He is truly a man who never dies and knows so much."

But the greatest conundrum concerning the Count of St.-Germain is his incredible longevity. According to reliable eyewitness reports and the numerous entries in aristocrats' diaries, the count appeared to be 45 to 50 years of age in 1710, yet he is known to have been active in the French Revolution of 1789. In fact, he was even mentioned in the diary of one condemned Marie Antoinette, who recorded her regret at not taking the advice of the "Comte de St.-Germain, as he had long ago warned of the gigantic conspiracy which would over-throw the order of things". During the Reign of Terror in France, the unfathomable nobleman from nowhere still looked no older than 50. The last reliable documented sighting of him took place in 1821, 111 years after he appeared on the European scene, and the Count still looked like a 50-year-old man. Shortly before he vanished from the Continent, he told a writer named Franz Graeffer: "Tomorrow night I am off; I am much needed in Constantinople, then in England, there to prepare two inventions which you will have in the next century – trains and steamboats."

After his arrival in England, the Count of St.-Germain travelled north, and there were several reports of him collaborating with the engineers and promoters of the early Liverpool to Manchester railway. There were even sightings of the mystifying count in Lancashire and Cheshire around 1829.

The only document that can be attributed to the count is now kept in the library at Troyes. It contains strange, apparently symbolic diagrams and a baffling text. One paragraph reads: "We moved through space at a speed that can be compared with nothing but itself. Within a fraction of a second the plains below us were out of sight, and the earth had become a faint nebula. I was carried up, and I travelled through the empyrean for an incalculable time at an immeasurable height. Heavenly bodies revolved, and worlds vanished below me."

The Count of St.-Germain's lifespan seems incredible to us today, when the average expectation of life is 70. How much more phenomenal it must have seemed in the eighteenth century when reaching 35 was an achievement. The count's true identity will probably never be known, but I have a sneaking suspicion that he was a traveller in the realm of time, and may have really met Jesus and Henry VIII. If he was a timelord, what sort of technology would have allowed his trek through history?

At the moment, there are two spheres of modern science which might allow a limited form of time travel: subatomic physics and cosmology. The world of subatomic particles is a topsy-turvy one which would have delighted Lewis Carroll. In the surreal "inner space" universe of positrons, quarks and electrons, a ray of light consists of photons which paradoxically act as particles and waves. There are also elementary particles called muons which are incredibly short-lived and unstable. After 2·2 microseconds the muon decays into an electron, neutrino and anti-neutrino. However, if the muon is pushed towards the speed of light in a particle accelerator, its lifetime is stretched a little. Travelling at 0.99 per cent of light's speed, the muon's life is extended from a couple of microseconds to 155 microseconds. This strange effect is known in scientific circles as time dilation, and was predicted by Einstein's Special Theory of Relativity (published in 1905). Time dilation not only stretches the lifetime of a particle; it can also extend the lifetime of a human, although the energy output and technology to achieve this would present engineering difficulties at this moment in time. To illustrate the weird world of time dilation, consider the following example, which was foreseen by Einstein before space travel was a reality. Picture identical twins named Jack and Joe, both aged 25. Joe stays on Earth and Jack embarks on a five-year tour of outer space in a rocket that travels close to the speed of light.

When Jack returns to his home planet, he is five years older, but Joe is 75 years old, because 50 years have elapsed on Earth since Jack set out on his relativistic journey. People accustomed to relying on "common sense" down here on Earth are usually puzzled at this twin brother paradox, but it is totally in accordance with relativity. Atomic clocks have been carried on Concorde, and at the end of their journey, the clocks have been compared with synchronized high-precision timepieces left on the ground. The results are always the same; the clocks moving on the supersonic Concorde jet ticked more slowly compared to their stationary counterparts on the ground.

Building a rocket that travels near the speed of light is not exactly a realistic option to propel a person into another time. In fact, time dilation can only send the traveller into the future. To travel into the past you would obviously need to go backwards through time, and this would appear a trifle trickier to achieve. The universe we are familiar with is made up of "tardyons" – particles that travel slower than the speed of light. But for some time now, scientists have been speculating upon the existence of an intriguing particle they have dubbed the "tachyon" – a subatomic particle that travels faster than light. The tachyon only exists in theory at the moment, but there is mounting evidence which suggests that it is at large in the universe. Tachyons, because of their incredible velocities, travel backwards in time, and seem to fly in the face of terrestrial common sense. An encounter with a spacecraft made of tachyons would play havoc with our sense of reality. We would see it in our vicinity first, then the spacecraft's slower light image would catch up some time later, so that we would perceive the tachyon ship as moving backwards in time, and could subsequently witness its launch! This would not be some weird optical illusion, but the effect of tachyonic dynamics as predicted by the Theory of Relativity.

Should scientists of the future discover a way to convert the hull of a spaceship or time machine into tachyons, the door to the past will be open and the long-held dream of returning to yesterday will become a reality. Unfortunately, the military and intelligence forces of any country would surely regard a time machine as a threat to national and global security. And sadly, they'd have a point. Imagine some future Hitler in the 22nd century abusing time travel to alter the past, perhaps to massacre his adversaries' ancestors. For all we know, these assassins from the future could already be at work in history, carrying out murders which would seem motiveless to us yet have far-reaching influences in the politics of the future. Would this chilling possibility explain why certain people (who are always alone) have been struck down by an incredible energy force which has literally reduced them to ashes? I am referring to the hundreds of recorded deaths from so-called spontaneous human combustion, where victims have been charred to death – sometimes within seconds – often leaving their clothes and surroundings unscorched. Cremating a human body requires a considerable amount of heat. In the crematorium a temperature of 2500–3000 degrees Fahrenheit is required for up to four hours. But a majority of the people who die from spontaneous combustion are incinerated to powder in minutes or seconds, and the fierce burning is usually so localized that a victim can be seated on a chair which remains untouched by the heat; one victim's nylon tights were not even singed. Then there is the sinister disturbance in the earth's magnetic field which precipitates the lethal self-contained inferno. Each day, observatories from all over the world record readings of the Earth's magnetic field. Researchers in spontaneous human combustion have discovered that in many areas where people have turned into human incendiary bombs, "something" has disturbed the magnetic field of the earth in those regions, making it more intense. The Sun's solar activity was initially blamed, but the real source of the disturbance remains elusive and seemingly impossible to pin down. It's as if something "comes through" from out of the blue to strike down the unsuspecting and apparently well targeted victim with an unimaginable burst of powerful yet containable energy. Could that energy be the beam of some deadly tachyonic laser-device of the future, aimed through a tiny aperture in the space-time fabric? Is this just all paranoia – or could someone up the timeline be targeting you soon?

Getting back to the physics of time travel; most physicists have now accepted that black holes are a reality and exist in our own galaxy. A black hole is created when a massive object, such as a star, collapses in on itself, resulting in a highly compressed sphere of super-condensed matter. The gravity is also condensed in the collapsed star, and is concentrated to such an extent that even light cannot escape from it; hence it is known as a black hole. Einstein taught us that space and time are inseparable, so a hole in space is a hole in time, and a whole new generation of theorists now believe that black holes are gateways to the past and future. However, a static black hole is to be avoided. Amateur time travellers entering black holes that do not spin would be simply crushed out of existence at the central point of the black hole – a nightmarish point of super-condensed time and space called a singularity, where the laws of physics break down. A rotating black hole is more hospitable and offers an incredible option: travel into the remote past and future of the universe. These amazing possibilities are not pie in the sky; all the equations have been worked out and put to the test in computer simulations; all we need is a rotating black hole, but finding one near enough in the interstellar neighbourhood is a daunting problem. Locating a black hole is fairly easy, as they are usually pulling apart other stars, and as the stellar material goes down the event horizon plughole at an incredible velocity massive emissions of X-rays are generated which we can pick up on Earth. There are many suspicious-looking sites in the sky which look like black holes, but all of these objects are simply too remote to be of any practical use to the enthusiastic time traveller.

This predicament has cornered some scientists into considering alternative forms of time-tampering. One respected American scientist named Frank Tipler has published several ideas for time machines in reputable journals such as the *Physical Review* and *Annals of Physics.* Tipler's design for a time machine involves a lot of abstruse mathematics, and the dynamics of rotating cylinders. All of the work centres on twisting time and space with high-speed rotation devices but, as far as we know, no one has tried out Tipler's machines. The technology does exist to make some headway with Tipler's designs, however. NASA technicians are currently developing high-speed dynamo flywheels to power satellites and manned spacecraft. These flywheels are the size of a bicycle wheel and capable of 90,000 revolutions per minute. The outer rim of the wheel travels at more than 7000 miles per hour, generating kilowatts of electricity to power up the space stations of the future. Some wheels are now on the drawing board which will be magnetically suspended on frictionless, superconducting axles. The speeds of these flywheels will be even more phenomenal, and it will be interesting to see if they produce any time distortion as predicted by Tipler.

Of course, we have been concentrating only on man-made time travel. Could it be that time occasionally malfunctions all by herself through some poorly understood phenomenon? Also, could the fabric of space-time down here on Earth have weak spots or holes which could provide us with an opportunity to explore another era? With a magnification of 30 million, the electron microscope taught us that nothing in the universe has a smooth surface. The apparent flat level smoothness of a pane of glass or the veneered top of a coffee table is in reality pitted and pockmarked with grooves and chasms. Could the same be true of the space-time fabric? If the space-time continuum does have weak spots and holes in it, it could explain some of the following timewarp cases.

In the summer of 1992 a successful entrepreneur and experienced pilot named Mr Davies took off from a private airfield on the outskirts of Chester. Mr Davies was at the controls of a Cessna and was headed for Liverpool's Speke airport. As the Cessna was passing over the Stamford Bridge area, Mr Davies noticed something quite strange. Thousands of feet below there were no signs of the M53 or M56 motorways. Nor was there any sign of a single A or B road. Intrigued and somewhat alarmed at the apparent missing roads, Mr Davies descended in his plane to take a closer look at the now unfamiliar territory. What he saw made his heart somersault: a tight formation of men were marching down a road towards a long rectangular squat building. Mr Davies located a pair of 10 x 50 binoculars and trained them on the marching figures. They were Roman soldiers, and the building they were walking towards looked like some sort of Roman villa. At this point, a strange low mist seemed to materialize and enshrouded the landscape below. When it cleared, there was the A548 motorway and Mr Davies saw to his relief that everything had returned to normal. He flew over the M56 and decided to circle back to see if he could get a glimpse of the soldiers again, but they were nowhere to be seen. Mr Davies subsequently made extensive inquiries to ascertain if the soldiers had been extras in some film. But there were no films about Romans being shot anywhere in Cheshire, or anywhere in Britain for that matter. Mr Davies gradually realized that he had somehow ventured into the airspace of Cheshire during the Roman occupation of over a thousand years ago. Mr Davies has since heard that several other pilots have experienced strange time-displacements in the skies over Cheshire. One highly respected helicopter pilot with a military background lost radio communication during his "episode", but has never gone into detail over just what exactly happened to him. He did state that his greatest fear was being stranded in the past. Perhaps this was the fate of Flying Officer Brian Holding. On 7 March 1922 Holding took off from the airfield at Chester on what was intended to be a short flight over the border to an airstrip in Wales. On the return journey from Wales, Holding's plane was spotted by scores of witnesses droning through the skies back towards Chester. That plane and its experienced pilot never reached the airfield and was never seen again. A massive search for the wreckage of the missing plane was launched but not a trace of the craft was ever found. Stranger still, weeks before Holding flew into limbo, peculiar lights were seen flying in formation over North Wales.

Without a doubt, one of the most intriguing timewarp incidents of recent years unfolded in the autumn of 1984 at a small terraced house known as Meadow Cottage in the village of Dodleston near Chester. A schoolteacher named Ken Webster was working on his BBC "B" personal computer at the cottage late one night and accidentally left it on. When he returned to the computer some time later, Webster was surprised to see that a poem of some sort had been typed out on the VDU screen. At first, Webster suspected someone was pulling his leg, but hoax was soon ruled out when further messages came through. There was no modem connected to the computer (which had only 32K memory), and even the floppy disk in the machine's drive was checked, but there were no suspicious files hidden on it. Webster's home also became the focus of poltergeist activity. The cooker and heavy furniture were hurled about by the invisible force, and cups and cans of food were stacked into towers and arranged side by side. Strange messages were also scratched on the floor and wall in an elegant calligraphy, signed by one "Tomas".

The eerie messages continued, most of them written in a "quirky mock Tudor" style. Webster tried to communicate with the mysterious writer via his computer keyboard and received several startling replies. There were six people communicating with him from somewhere (or somewhen) back in the seventeenth century. But how could people from the Elizabethan period contact a teacher in the twentieth century by computer? That was never answered. The main communicator identified himself as Tomas Harden, and the following message, which occupied three screens of the computer, was analyzed by experts in archaic language and even the staff of the *Oxford English Dictionary*, who could not detect a hoaxer at work. The message from Mr Harden runs:

Myne goodly friend, I muste needs say, how cometh this, that there are manye thyngs for whiche I hath no rekenyng. Me thinketh it, that if thou cannot telle thee for what art in myne home, then I can namoor helpe yow than if myne witts had gone. I hath no kinfolk to fynd, myne wif was wreched with thy pestilence and the Lord didst take here soule and her unbore son (1517). Myne farme 'tis humble but it hath a pretty parcel o land, it hath redstoon footyngs and cleen rushes on myne beeten floor. This season I hath much to do, I hath to sow myne barly for myne ale, 'tis this that is myne craft and for whiche I am beste atte I fancy. Also I hath to go to Nantwhiche to myne cowthe freend Richard Wishal whois farme be so greet as to turn a four yeer rotacion o fallow. I do envye him he hath much there, but nought that delits me moor than his cheese it cannot be equalled by any other for pleasantness of taste and wholesomness of digestion. I shall als calle atte Nantwyche Market 'tis not so greet as Cestre market by thy crios but 'tis of som desport. I shal need to go to Cestre this season to get myne soes, myne goodly freend Tomas Aldersay, a tailor by craft, makes them sometymes, I als mayketh soes but non of myne swyne are reedy 'tis far costly unlest I need kil one. Do you knoweth the country of Cestre the Water Gate is a plas that bringeth manye traders 'tis a shame the port doth shrynk I can record greet shipps now they grow small by each tyde, but Cestre port is still greeter than that o Leverpoole I am oft to the east wall of Cestre. Cow Lane, 'tis not so tyresome than that by the crois that it when myne fowl or swyne doth not trip up myne poore body I hear telle that thou art a teache in Hawardine doth yow meeneth Haodine cloth, thou stil earn thy greetly sum of twenty pounds per yeer I recorde myne unfavourable dean Henry Mann, who is likened to a fissh "If any boy shal appear naturally avers to learning aft fair trial he shalt be expelled else wher lest lik a drone he should devour the bees honey." Ney I cannot make merry on holy day for feer of myne lif myne freen was once a floytinge on a holy day did hath hus ears pinned to thy wood bloc methinks when thou sayeth Dodleston yow meeneth Dudlestun. Myne Queen is of cource Katherine Parr.

The Society for Psychical Research (SPR) were invited to investigate, and accepted the invitation. The SPR is a highly professional and unbiased investigative body of scholars and scientists who look into alleged paranormal incidents. The SPR was founded in 1882 and has investigated thousands of hauntings and mediums with strict scientific method. Many mediums were debunked by the SPR and a lot of hauntings were also discredited, but the SPR investigation into Ken Webster's seemingly haunted computer resulted in an electrifying development. The SPR investigators left ten secret questions on the computer screen, out of sight of Mr Webster, and although the questions were not answered directly messages came through on the screen referring to the questions, which naturally fazed the SPR people. This ruled out any deception, and an SPR investigator urged the sinister communicator to reply to the questions. A chilling reply came back. The communicator would give an answer to the SPR investigator – if he was willing to lose his soul. The SPR man backed off.

The BBC micro was later stripped and experts scrutinized its printed circuit boards, its monitor, disk drive, keyboard, every inch of the machine, but there were no hidden radio transceivers and no modem. In those days, the Internet in Britain was just a programmer's pipe dream.

The SPR people were completely baffled and withdrew from the cottage without even making a report. The chief investigator never got back to Webster and became uncontactable for years. Ken Webster became frustrated at the ham-fisted inquiry and wrote a book about his bizarre experience called *The Vertical Plane*.

In April 1986 Tomas Harden said he was going to "leave the area" and after a few more messages, the seventeeth-century computer hacker ceased communication.

On the morning of 7 December 1939 dozens of citizens of Owensville, Indiana, looked down in puzzlement at the huge three-word sentence painted in enormous letters on the sidewalk outside of a public grade school. Someone had daubed the perplexing message: "Remember Pearl Harbor!" in white paint. A policeman who had been summoned to the baffling graffito shook his head and muttered, "Crazy kids. Where is Pearl Harbor anyway?" No one in the town seemed to know – until exactly two years later, on 7 December 1941. On that date 350 Japanese carrier-launched warplanes attacked the US Pacific Fleet at Pearl Harbor, Hawaii. The Japanese killed 2330 military personnel and wounded 1145 in the surprise attack, as well as destroying 247 aircraft, sinking three battleships, and eleven warships. Who gave the United States an advanced warning of this attack two years before it occurred? It was obviously someone with a devious sense of humour, because although the sinister graffiti artist apparently had foreknowledge of the military assault, he or she may have withheld vital details such as the date of the attack, which, if it had been given, would have spared the lives of almost two and a half thousand American soldiers.

The next timewarp incident seems to indicate that occasionally, for reasons our science has yet to explain, different time periods widely separated by a span amounting to a millennium can sometimes overlap.

The Vikings were Scandinavian sea-warriors of the eighth to tenth century AD who raided and settled on the coasts of Britain and western Europe. They also sailed as far as Constantinople, Africa and Greenland, and were the first real discoverers of America. The first main attack on Britain occurred in the reign of Alfred the Great, who was the King of Wessex, in AD 885. But something else happened that year which has never been satisfactorily explained. Shortly before the invasion of England, the Vikings sent about a dozen ships to survey the coast, and on one of these ships there was a Norse map-maker named Olaf, who made very accurate maps of England's eastern coast. When Olaf's ship was crossing the North Sea one evening, one of the Norse warriors on board shouted out and pointed to the gigantic thing in the waters about a mile ahead.

It was a dark shape on enormous legs, and it was blowing

out a jet of yellow flame into the air. Olaf was spellbound. He thought it was some sea monster, and told the Viking crew to keep on rowing, but the men were naturally afraid. When the ship was about half a mile away from the monster, Olaf made a sketch of what he could see by the light of the full moon: an enormous black body wider than five Viking longships placed end to end, and taller than any castle he'd seen. The body was supported by six or more legs, and above the body, the monster seemed to have four necks with small horned heads at the end. From one of these heads, the fierce jet of flame spurted out. Olaf warned the crew that the monster in the waters was obviously a dragon. As brave as the Vikings were, they were very superstitious, and all the ships turned around and the Norsemen made the voyage home with an incredible tale to tell.

As Olaf looked back at the monster through the mists of the North Sea, he saw the flame flicker out, and the dragon seemed to disappear. Olaf assumed that the monster had now submerged beneath the waves.

In the 1970s historians discovered Olaf's sketch of the dragon he'd encountered in the North Sea, and were shocked to see that the monster looked exactly like an offshore oil rig. An offshore drilling rig was supported by many legs, and had a jet of flame continually burning at the end of a tall chimney. The four necks Olaf counted would probably have been the cranes and derricks with their pulleys and winches. It was as if Olaf had seen a phantom of the future; an oil rig that was 1000 years away in the future North Sea. Stranger still, it doesn't seem to have been a one-way timeslip, because in 1988 six workers on an oil rig in the North Sea saw a line of phantom Viking ships sailing by in the moonlight one summer's night. As the men watched, the ghostly convoy of ships faded away.

If the fabric of space-time can occasionally malfunction or "warp", could it be detrimental to anyone within the immediate vicinity of the distortion? This hypothesis would certainly go a long way to explain the following strange incident, which was reported in the *Times* of London in the nineteenth century.

In the early hours of the morning on 9 December 1873 Thomas B. Cumpston was sleeping soundly in bed with his wife in their room at the Victoria Hotel, Bristol, when Mr Cumpston had the urge to go to the toilet. He gently pulled back the blankets so as not to disturb his spouse, and placed his foot on the carpet – but it wasn't there. In fact, the floor wasn't there. There was nothing but a black swirling vortex, and Mr Cumpston sank into it as if it were quicksand. He cried out and turned to grab the blankets, and heard the curious echo of his scream reverberate below in the twirling shadowy spiral. He also heard the screams of other people, but his only concern was to stop himself being sucked down into the bizarre whirlpool. Mrs Cumpston was startled out of her slumbers by her husband's cries, and she peered over the edge of the mattress, expecting to see him on the floor. Instead, she was astounded and filled with terror at the sight of Mr Cumpston clinging onto the edge of the mattress with a maelstrom of darkness and screams twisting below him. Mrs Cumpston instinctively grabbed at her husband's elbow and summoned an inner strength she never knew she possessed. She hauled him out of the black vortex and he scrambled onto the mattress, trembling and speechless. The Cumpstons were so terror-stricken that they climbed out of a window rather than risk crossing the floor to leave via the door. The couple ran barefooted to a police station and stammered out their incredible tale to a highly sceptical desk sergeant who presumed they had been drinking. The sergeant dispatched a constable to investigate, and he found the floor of the Cumpstons' hotel room quite solid and normal. The hotel manager was also interviewed by police, and he could not throw any light on the alleged weird phenomenon the Cumpstons had experienced.

Perhaps if Thomas Cumpston had fallen into the space-time whirlpool, he would have been consigned to the files marked "vanished without a trace", which contain many bizarre disappearing acts. For example, in July 1924 Flight Lieutenant W. T. Day and Pilot Officer D. R. Stewart flew from a British military airfield in Mesopotamia for a routine reconnaissance flight over Arab territory. When the men failed to return, a search was launched. Hundreds of square miles of desert were combed until Day and Stewart's plane was finally found, intact and with more than enough fuel to make the return journey home. However, there was no sign of Day and Stewart; just two unsettling indications which suggested that the men had met an uncanny fate. The two tracks of the men's footprints in the sand stretched just 40 yards from the plane, then came to an abrupt end – as if the men had vanished in their tracks. Day and Stewart were never seen again, and no sun-bleached corpses were ever found, despite an intensive search of the area. What was their fate? Did they, as the tracks indicate, walk into some other dimension?

The aforementioned timewarp cases seem to indicate that all time is "eternally present", so to speak; that all of the historical periods of the past, present and future are contained within each other like Russian dolls. As you read this book right now, perhaps beyond the wafer-thin dimension of the present, a ravenous Tyrannosaurus Rex of the Jurassic era is galumphing through your home. Until we learn how to manipulate time, we will go through this life as if our heads were facing back to front; we only know where we have been and where we are, but can never know where we are going.

The Lincoln and Kennedy Coincidences

Does history repeat itself? This certainly seems to be the case when we look at the following series of uncanny coincidences which link two of America's most popular presidents: Abraham Lincoln and John F. Kennedy.

Lincoln was elected to Congress in 1846; Kennedy was elected 100 years later, almost to the day in fact. After their deaths from assassination, both of these presidents were succeeded by Southerners with the surname Johnson. Lincoln was succeeded by Andrew Johnson, who was born in 1808, and Kennedy was succeeded by Lyndon Johnson, who was born in 1908. Both Johnsons have 13 letters in their names and both of them served in the US Senate.

Timeslip on TV

On the morning of Saturday, 1 June 1974, housewife Lesley Castleton of Humberside was watching a film when it was suddenly interrupted by a newsflash. A sombre-faced newscaster came on and announced that there had been a massive explosion at the chemical plant at Flixborough. He said that huge black clouds were billowing over the scene of devastation, and that 29 people had died in the explosion. The Saturday morning film then continued. When the film had ended Mrs Castleton mentioned the Flixborough disaster to her neighbours and friends, but they said they hadn't heard anything of the tragedy on the radio or TV. Later that day, at 4.20 in the afternoon, a giant fireball engulfed the chemical plant at Flixborough and the deafening explosion shook the area for miles. Twenty-nine people at the plant died, and the tragic accident was soon being reported in TV and radio bulletins. All the friends and neighbours of Lesley Castleton were truly baffled, because they had been told of the chemical plant disaster six hours before it had actually happened. The strange premonition incident has never been explained.

Mary Lincoln and Jackie Kennedy both had children who died while their husbands were in the White House.

Both Lincoln and Kennedy studied law.

John Wilkes Booth and Lee Harvey Oswald both had 15 letters in their name, and were both Southerners, were both in their twenties and, of course, both assassins were shot before they could stand trial. Kennedy had a secretary named Miss Lincoln, and Lincoln had a secretary named John Kennedy.

John Wilkes Booth shot Lincoln in a theatre and ran to a warehouse, and Oswald shot Kennedy from a warehouse and ran to a theatre. Stranger still, the car Kennedy was travelling in when he was shot was a Ford Lincoln. Lincoln was shot in Ford's Theatre.

Both assassinations took place on a Friday, and the two presidents were shot in the back of the head while their wives were at their side.

Kennedy and Lincoln were both historic civil rights campaigners who were heavily criticized while in office but were glorified after they died.

On the day of the assassinations Kennedy and Lincoln made strange prophetic statements. Hours before Lincoln was shot, he said to his personal guard, "If somebody wants to take my life, there is nothing I can do prevent it." And hours before Kennedy went to Dallas in 1963, he said to his wife Jackie, "If somebody wants to shoot me from a window with a rifle, nobody can stop it, so why worry about it?"

And finally, both presidents were said to have been victims of a conspiracy. When Lincoln was shot, the telegraph lines out of Washington DC remained silent for three hours on the orders of a high-ranking official who has never been identified. It is thought this information blackout was arranged to give John Wilkes Booth – who was fleeing from the scene of the crime – a head start.

The Ship that Sailed into Limbo

On 11 March 1841 the Atlantic steamship *President* sailed from New York to Liverpool. She was something of a prestige ship, being one of the biggest and most reliable vessels of her day. Her powerful engines, constructed by Fawcett-Preston of Liverpool, had 81-inch cylinders with seven-and-a-half feet stroke, and were considered as a novel design in those days. And so, as the steamer cut through the Atlantic, none of the passengers or crew felt anxious about the crossing.

One of the passengers bound for Liverpool on the *President* was Tyrone Power, an actor who was famous on both sides of the Atlantic. He was the grandfather of his Hollywood namesake Tyrone Power who died in 1958. The celebrated Mr Power had just completed a successful tour of the United States and was returning to England.

In the early hours of the morning on 13 March 1841, there

was a heavy succession of knocks on the door of a mansion in Blackheath, London. The large impressive house belonged to a wealthy theatre manager named Benjamin Webster. Mr Webster's butler went to the door in his pyjamas and dressing gown and asked who was calling at such an unearthly hour.

A well-spoken voice replied, "Mr Webster! Mr Webster! I am drowned in the rain!"

The butler thought he recognized the voice. It sounded like Tyrone Power, a close friend of Mr Webster. The butler wasn't sure what to do, so he went up to Mr Webster's bedroom and shook his master by the shoulders to rouse him.

Mr Webster woke up, and in an irritated tone said, "Good Lord, what's the matter?"

The butler said, "Someone is knocking at the hall door. He is calling for you, sir."

"At this damned hour? Who is it?" Mr Webster asked, glancing at his bedside clock. It was almost 4 a.m.

"It sounds like Mr Power's voice, sir. He keeps calling for you, and says that he is drowned in the rain," the butler answered with a worried look.

Benjamin Webster immediately got out of his four-poster bed, put on a heavy coat, and ran downstairs with the butler. The bolts of the heavy mahogany door were drawn back as the butler nervously rattled the key in the lock and turned it. Old Mr Webster pulled the heavy door wide open and stared out in the heavy rain and the darkness, expecting to see Mr Power.

There was nobody there. Webster popped his head out of the doorway and looked right and left, but there was nobody to be seen in the gas-lit street. So Webster closed the door and asked his butler to go through the details of the eerie incident again. Benjamin Webster felt very uneasy over the ghostly night-caller, because he knew that Tyrone Power had boarded the *President* on 11 March and couldn't possibly be in England yet. Mr Webster left the butler in the hallway and returned to the bedroom, plagued with anxiety.

On 31 March the *President* and another Liverpool-bound ship, named the *Britannia*, were overdue, and an article appeared in the *Times* highlighting this fact. Benjamin Webster read the article, and thought about the mysterious knocking at the door in the wee small hours. He hoped that the *President* had not met with disaster.

Another week elapsed and there still wasn't any sign of the two overdue vessels. Relatives of the crew and passengers of the missing ships naturally started to worry. There was a reassuring rumour that the steamship *Orpheus*, which had left New York for Liverpool two days after the *President*, had caught up with then passed the *President*, which had merely had a minor mechanical breakdown.

But on 2 April the *Orpheus* steamed into Liverpool docks, and her captain said he definitely had not sighted the missing ship during his journey. Hours after the arrival of the *Orpheus*, a ship called the *Virginia* sailed into Liverpool from New York, and her captain was asked if he had set eyes on the overdue vessel. He said he hadn't; he had only seen the *Orpheus* in the distance.

Suddenly, on the day after the *Orpheus* and *Virginia* had docked at Liverpool, the missing steamer *Brittania* arrived in the Mersey and docked at Liverpool. Her captain explained that the ship had suffered a little damage due to the storms, hence the delay. The *Brittania*'s captain was also quizzed about the whereabouts of the *President*, but he hadn't seen the missing ship, and had assumed she had already docked at Liverpool.

On 7 April the *Times* published a full list of the *President*'s passengers. There were 121 people on board the missing steamship, including the son of the Duke of Richmond, Lord Fitzroy Lennox. The *Times* also mentioned that the famous thespian Tyrone Power was a passenger. On the same day, the Liverpool *Albion* newspaper printed its theory about the *President*'s disappearance. The article maintained that the ship had probably burnt too much fuel fighting the Atlantic storms and was therefore making the remainder of the trans-atlantic journey by sail.

On 13 April there was good news at last about the missing steamer. A report reached London that a special night train had just pulled into Birmingham station from Liverpool. A specially appointed messenger on the train declared that the *President* had docked at Liverpool at last in a severely weather-battered state. But when the authorities in London made inquiries at Birmingham and Liverpool, they learned that the whole story was a cruel hoax, and the *President* was still missing.

Several relatives of the people on the missing steamer broke down and sobbed when they realized that a cruel joker had built up their hopes and demolished them.

When the *President* was three weeks overdue, several Irish ships coming into Liverpool brought some interesting news with them. The crews of the Irish ships swore they had all seen an enormous steamer standing off, waiting for water, in the vicinity of the Victoria Channel. But because of the early morning haze, none of the witnesses was able to clearly identify the mystery steamship; but what other ship could it be?

The words of the Irish sailors spread like wildfire through Liverpool docks within the hour, and that morning the flag of consignee was hastily hoisted at the signal station. Lloyd's of London were informed, and messages were promptly sent to Tyrone Power's wife and the Duke of Richmond. The news reached the royal ears of Queen Victoria, and on the following day the *Times* reported that the Queen and Prince Albert expressed the highest satisfaction at the gratifying communication.

But the Irishmen had been mistaken. The steamer they had sighted came down the Mersey. She was the steamer named *Falmouth*. She was not the *President*.

Around this time, a Cork newspaper reported that a bottle had been picked out of the sea which contained a scrap of paper. Written upon this paper were the words: "The President is sinking. God help us all." And it was signed by Tyrone Power.

Many dismissed the newspaper report as yet another time-wasting hoax. The last rumour about the missing craft came from a Portuguese ship. The captain of the foreign ship said he had passed a large steamer that fitted the description of the *President* on 24 May. The steamer seemed disabled, and was drifting in the Atlantic with no sign of life, but no one followed the story up.

Some relatives of the passengers on the lost ship never gave up hope, while others who had husbands or wives among the missing passengers remarried and rebuilt their lives. For decades, the seafaring communities on both sides of the Atlantic debated the steamship's strange disappearance. Some thought the steamer had gone under in a storm, while others were convinced that the ship's fate had something to do with the supernatural. If she had gone down in the Atlantic storms of 12 and 13 March, why had the ships following the steamship encountered no floating wreckage? After all, the ship was almost completely a wooden ship. To this day, the fate of the steamship *President* remains one of the great mysteries of the sea; it was as if she had sailed into limbo . . .

Haunted by His Future Wife

At a house in the suburbs of North Vancouver in June 1996 a young couple named Troy and Stacey were watching television one night. A little after 11 p.m. the couple's Aberdeen Terrier – Judy – came in whining and looked at Stacey. The dog wanted to go on its nightly round, and Troy said it was Stacey's turn to take the dog out. Stacey put on her sandals, grabbed her coat, and then put the leash on Judy. She walked out and did a circuit around the familiar roads of the neighbourhood for about 15 minutes. When she returned to her house, she tiptoed through the garden and went to spy on Troy through the living-room window to see if he was having a cigarette, as Troy had quit smoking for almost a week, as Stacey was convinced he had stashed away a packet of his usual Marlboro Lites. However, when Stacey peeped through the window, she was absolutely stunned by what – or who – she saw. For there was a red-haired young woman of about 25, sitting on the sofa, wearing nothing but a revealing négligé, black lacey underwear and a bra. The stranger was dipping a spoon into a small tub of ice cream as she watched the TV, seemingly unaware of Stacey.

Stacey's heart skipped a beat. She knew it couldn't be Troy's sister, because she'd met all his family. Who, then, was the girl on the sofa? She certainly intended to find out, and Stacey stormed to the front door and hammered on the knocker. After almost a minute, Troy came down wearing nothing but a towel around his waist and said, "Hey, I was in the shower. Don't tell me; you forgot your key again."

Stacey pushed her boyfriend aside and let go of the leash. She went into the living room saying "What's going on?"

But there was no red-haired girl there. Just the TV set blaring out the MTV channel to an empty living-room.

"What's up?" Troy said, watching his girlfriend pulling the curtains back, as if she was looking for someone.

Stacey was naturally confused, and she told Troy about the girl she'd seen in their living room. Troy shook his head and laughed nervously. He said, "You've been looking through next door's window. That girl next door, Brittany, she's got red hair."

Stacey said, "I looked through this window. This one! And the girl next door has brown hair and she's only 15. She was nothing like the girl I saw; her hair was red, and she looked about 25 at least."

Troy sat Stacey down and hugged her. He said, "Unless it was a ghost."

"Oh get serious, Troy; don't be talking about things like that at this time of night." Then Stacey said, "It was really weird. She looked so real. She was eating ice cream."

On the following day, Troy went for a job interview at a waterfront pub. At 3.40 p.m. that afternoon Stacey returned from college and went into the house. She made herself a coffee, then heard the gate outside clang shut. She assumed it was Troy returning from his interview. But when Stacey looked out the window, she was astounded to see that it was the mysterious red-haired woman she'd seen sitting on her sofa last night. The woman was walking down the path towards the house. Stacey readied herself in anticipation. She thought, "That scheming lowlife of a boyfriend has been seeing someone else. I knew it."

Stacey waited tensely for the girl to knock, but was surprised to hear a key rattle in the lock. Stacey heard the girl open the door, and her footsteps clunked up the stairs. Stacey put down her coffee and went up the stairs to confront her rival. But the rooms upstairs were empty. Then something even more bizarre happened. Stacey walked into the empty box room where Troy stored all of his CDs and videos. The room had been transformed – into a nursery. A baby was crying in a cot in the corner of the room. Stacey felt dizzy with the shock. Something told her that the child was Troy's.

The door opened downstairs. It was Troy coming back from his interview. He shouted, "Stacey? I got the job! I start Monday!"

Stacey came down the stairs and seemed to be in shock. She muttered, "Whose is that baby upstairs? What the hell is going on here?"

A perplexed Troy followed her upstairs. He was really worried about his partner, and thought she was having a breakdown. When he looked into the box room, all he could see was his stacks of CDs and videos. Stacey put her hands to her face and said, "Troy, I think I should see a shrink or something. I think I might be going mad. I saw a baby in a cot in here. And I saw that red-haired girl again; she came into the house."

A week later, Stacey dreaded coming home from college. She came into the house, which was empty, as Troy was working the early shift at the bar. Stacey went upstairs to the bathroom and looked in the mirror at the small spot on her cheek. As she inspected her reflection, she noticed something pass the bathroom doorway behind her in the mirror. Someone had passed by on the landing outside. It had looked like a fleeting glimpse of . . . the red-haired girl. Then, as Stacey recovered from that fright, she heard a distinct voice come from the bedroom. Someone in an English accent said, "Hello there, Lauren. Mummy's come to change your nappy."

And Stacey then heard a baby babbling. She went into each room and found it empty. Stacey went downstairs and phoned the bar where Troy was working. She begged him to come home at once, and told him about the spooky goings-on at the house. Troy said his shift ended in half an hour, and he came straight home. At around six o'clock, Troy was sitting on the sofa with his troubled girlfriend, fearing for her sanity. He really loved Stacey, and was very concerned about the state of her mind. Then he too heard something that defied explanation.

A radio came on upstairs, but Troy knew there was no radio upstairs. A rock song boomed out at full volume, then the voice of a girl with an English accent said, "Turn that down,

Troy." Troy and Stacey looked at one another in utter disbelief. The song sounded just like a number by the rock band Aerosmith, but Troy, who was familiar with the group, had never heard the song before, yet he had most of the albums and the singles released by the band. Suddenly, the sounds faded away. Troy went upstairs with Stacey, but there was no one about, and certainly no radio to be seen anywhere.

But the biggest shock came in the following week. Early one Sunday morning, Stacey came downstairs and smelt a strange sweet aroma. It was the scent of flowers, and the smell seemed to originate from the lounge. Stacey went in and almost had an heart attack when she saw what was in there. It was an open coffin on a stand, and wreaths and other floral tributes and bouquets were all over the room. Stacey's body was in that coffin.

Stacey ran screaming up the stairs, startling the dog. She threw herself at Troy and told him what she had seen downstairs. He began to tremble and said it had just been a bad dream. But he too could smell flowers when he went downstairs, but found the lounge empty.

A fortnight later Stacey was tragically killed in a car crash while visiting her cousin in Mission City. Before the funeral her body was brought home and she was laid in her coffin in the lounge, where heartbroken friends and relatives laid their wreaths and floral tributes.

In November 1997 Troy met a 25-year-old English woman who was working in Vancouver as part of a student exchange programme. She had red hair. The girl is currently living with Troy, and was instrumental in helping him to get over the loss of Stacey. In early January 1998 Troy's new girlfriend discovered she was pregnant, and the couple plan to call the baby Lauren if it's a girl. Troy has already cleared out his box room and converted it into a nursery, just as Stacey had foreseen a year before. Another thing: Troy shuddered when he heard Aerosmith bring out a single entitled "Pink"; Troy recalled that he had heard the song years before, blaring out from a radio upstairs. It was as if Troy and Stacey had been seeing and hearing sneak previews of Troy's future life with another girl.

What Mr Butler Saw

The following true story took place in North Wales in the 1920s. It was mentioned briefly in the old *Daily Mirror*, investigated by several psychic investigators, and even attracted the attention of Sir Arthur Conan Doyle, the man who created Sherlock Holmes.

In the long hot sultry summer of 1921 a postcard photographer from Banbury, England, named Roger Butler was assigned to take photographs of the seaside villages of Wales. Mr Butler enjoyed his occupation and was generously paid to do what would seem to be a dream job to many males: taking pictures of bikini-clad women on the sunny beaches of picturesque seaside resorts.

During an infernal July in 1921 Roger visited Caernarfon, Bangor and then Llanfairfechan, where he was to stay for a couple of days before going to Llandudno. But at Llanfairfechan Roger had a whale of a time. A beautiful Welsh girl named Joan posed on the beach for one of his photographs. Roger said, "Do you realize I'll make you a star overnight? You'll be on hundreds of postcards."

Joan blushed. She was only just 20, and Roger was 44, but Joan kept following him around on his photo shoots, holding his photographic plates while Roger set up his camera tripod. Roger tried to dissuade the girl from getting involved with him, as his roving occupation meant he could never settle down. He was always on the road. But Joan wouldn't have it, and continued to tag along.

Roger booked into a little hotel in Llanfairfechan. It wasn't exactly five-star but it was comfortable enough and quite an old building. One evening he was lying on his bed in the hotel, thinking of Joan, and how she was so innocent and infatuated with him. He had just developed the plates in his portable darkroom, which was just a red light, several trays, and three bottles of developing and fixing chemicals. To get rid of the acrid smell of the chemicals, Roger had opened the window, and he listened to the distant rush of the sea as he looked at the photographs of Joan. Suddenly, he saw a light out the corner of his right eye. Roger saw that there was a small hole in his bedroom wall, and the light from the room next door was shining into his room.

"This is bloody marvellous – holes in the wall," Roger muttered to himself, and he looked at the hole and saw that the wall was just a plasterboard partition. He knew it wasn't the thing to do, but burning curiosity got the better of Roger – and he put his eye to the hole and peeped through it. He could see a bed, and could hear voices murmuring. Roger could see that the hole was inches from the bottom of the bed, facing the bed-rail. A naked woman suddenly sat on the bed. She had long black shiny hair. The woman was sitting on the mattress of the bed, looking up at someone and smiling. She wore only a pearl necklace, and the woman – who was incredibly beautiful – playfully bit at the pearls and said, "You'd say anything but your prayers. A white wedding?"

A low voice in the room next door shouted back, "Yes! When your husband kicks the bucket, we'll be married up in Harrowgate. Until then, you little temptress, we will live in sin."

The woman then accidentally pulled the necklace and it snapped, sending pearls everywhere. She laughed at the mishap, then laid lengthwise on the top of the bed, revealing all of her pale, untanned body. The woman lay there, making suggestive gestures to her partner, who Roger could not yet see. A naked, overweight man with a bulging stomach suddenly got onto the bed and started to make love to the woman. The man looked as if he was about 50, and the woman looked about 25 to 30 years of age. Roger felt like a real Peeping Tom, and started to perspire with nerves as he watched the couple giggle and swap places. Suddenly, there was a succession of gentle raps on his door. Roger bolted away from the hole and jumped onto his bed, where he pretended to look at the photographic plates. "Who is it?" he asked.

"Me, Joan," said a girl's voice.

Roger sighed, "Come in." He stood up to confront his unwanted admirer and said, "What is it, Joan?" Roger thought about the sensual action next door that he was missing.

Joan came in and looked stunning. She said, "What are you doing, Roger? I was a bit bored so I thought I'd come up and see you. Was I interrupting anything?"

"No, I was just looking at the snapshots I took today," said

Roger, inwardly seething. He said to Joan, "Take a seat," and went to grab a bottle of wine from a tray that had been left there courtesy of the hotel management.

"No, it's quite all right," said Joan, awkwardly. She frowned and glanced about.

"Pardon?" Roger said, about to insert the corkscrew into the wine bottle.

"Couldn't we go to the pub?" Joan asked him, timidly.

"Er, right, but I'll have to change and shave first. I can't go like this," Roger said, and he now had an excuse to enjoy his peepshow again. Roger opened the door and said, "Look, go to the pub and wait for me, here's some money. I shan't be long. It'll take me about 20 minutes to get ready."

Joan turned red with embarrassment and coyly accepted the ten-shilling note Roger had kindly offered her. She walked out the room smiling ear to ear.

"And don't run off with any dashing gentlemen," Roger said, and he closed the door after winking at his young admirer. He waited for a few moments, then peeped through the hole in the wall. The naked couple next door were still making love. Roger saw the large obese man haul himself off the bed and walk away. It was such a hot night, and he and his young lover were exhausted and sweating heavily.

"Come back, Howard. Please come here. It isn't fair," the woman moaned.

"No, it's too damn hot, Christine, and I've had my fun," said Howard. Suddenly there was a knock on the door of the room next door. Howard said, "Who is it?"

"It's me, you fornicator!" said a man with a Welsh accent.

"Oh, Howard, it's Philip!" said Christine, and she warned Howard not to open the door.

"If we don't answer him he'll never go away," said Howard, and he unlocked the door as Christine screamed for him not to.

Roger was gripped with fascination at the scene unfolding next door. He heard a loud thumping noise and a dull thud. Then he heard someone moaning. Christine screeched and said, "Howard! Don't, Philip." Then suddenly Christine was thrown by someone onto her bed. Her face and breasts were spattered with blood. Howard's blood.

"You've killed him," Christine sobbed and looked at the floor.

A man wearing a trilby and a brown coat seized Christine by the throat and started to strangle the life out of her.

Roger shuddered as he saw Christine's eyes open wide with terror. Her tongue dangled out of her mouth and she made a horrible choking sound as the man tightened his grip. The strangler said, "Thou shalt not commit adultery!" over and over as he throttled the naked woman.

Roger summoned up his courage and ran out of his room. He rushed along the landing and pounded on the door of the room next door.

"Who is it?" said a woman's voice.

"Open up! Police!" Roger shouted and booted the bottom of the door.

The door opened and an old woman answered, "Police? What do you want, constable?"

Roger ran past the woman and stormed her room, expecting to encounter the strangler. But the room bore no resemblance to the room Roger had peeped into. There was no one there. Roger was completely baffled, and he simply said, "So sorry" to the woman as he walked out, scratching his head. He went back into his room and saw the hole. He put his eye up to it, but this time he saw nothing, because it was blocked with a plug of hard plaster.

Half an hour later, Roger went to the pub near the hotel and met Joan. She asked him what was wrong, and Roger said, "Oh nothing, really." How could he tell her he'd been spying at a naked couple? So he decided to be somewhat economical with the truth and said, "I heard a woman screaming blue murder before, in the room next to mine at the hotel. When I went next door to investigate, I saw to my surprise that there was no one in that room but an old woman. Very peculiar indeed."

Joan coughed and spluttered as she sipped her lemonade.

"What's the matter?" Roger asked, "Went down the wrong way?"

Joan put the lemonade down and said, "Did you say the room next to yours?"

Roger nodded as he ordered another drink.

Joan said, "Room 12?"

"That's right room 12 – why?" Roger asked.

"Roger," Joan replied, "my Aunt Christine was murdered in that room ten years back."

Roger said, "Your Aunt . . . Christine?" That had been the name he'd heard. Roger said, "How dreadful. Who killed her?"

"Her husband – my Uncle Philip. She was having an affair with this man from another town. Uncle Philip broke his skull and killed him, and he strangled Aunt Christine. He was hanged for murder."

Roger downed his drink and a cold chill ran through his body. The photographer realized that he had been spying on the ghostly victims of a double murder! He refused to return to that hotel and slept with Joan in his car all night. Joan told him that other people had heard the sound of a woman screaming in room 12. That's why Joan wouldn't have a drink with Roger in his room; Joan had always thought the hotel was spooky.

The Lost Family

The following true story has to rank as one of the strangest tales on record. It actually happened in Manchester, England, in the late 1970s, but for legal and ethical reasons the people named and certain details in the account have been changed. The story was briefly mentioned about ten years ago in the *Lancet* medical journal, and has had little publicity since.

In 1978 a 45-year-old man named Steve Jones returned home to his family in Newton Heath, Manchester, after a hectic day at his office in the city. His dog, a Great Dane named Leo greeted him in the driveway of his house, and then Mr Jones's seven-year-old son Damon came out of the house with a bundle of drawings he'd done for his dad in school. Damon proudly showed the sketches to his father, and Mr Jones patted him on the head and said they were great. Father and son – and the family dog – then entered the house, where Mrs Jones was watching the TV.

Barbara was heavily pregnant, and her eldest daughter, 15-

year-old Emma, told her father that her mum had been having contractions. Mr Jones panicked and told her to get in the car straight away, but his wife said Emma was talking nonsense; she had only had a slight cramp in her leg; that was all.

The family had later settled down to tea when suddenly Mrs Jones stood up and with a shocked expression said to her husband: "Steve. I think it's time. Oh God."

Steve jumped up, almost knocking the table over, seized his wife, and manically guided her out of the living room. He was taking her straight to the maternity hospital. It was a real nightmare; the contractions were getting worse by the minute; the baby wasn't supposed to be due for almost a month.

Steve Jones ushered his wife into the car and gently fastened the seat belt. Emma went to get into the car too, but her father told her to look after Damon and the house. He then sped off up the dual carriageway. Mr Jones kept saying, "Hang on, love! Hang on; you're gonna be all right."

At a roundabout, the couple's car hit a lorry which zoomed out right in front of the Jones's car. The impact sent the car rolling end-over on its roof for about 60 yards, and as it came to rest, a taxi also hit the car and spun it round.

Mr Jones screamed; not for fear of losing his own life, but because he saw that his heavily pregnant wife seemed lifeless. Blood trickled from the woman's forehead, and she looked as if her neck was broken. The last thing Steve Jones saw before he blacked out was a couple of upside-down faces peering into the smashed-up car.

Steve Jones regained consciousness a day later in the neurological department of the local hospital, where he had undergone emergency brain surgery to remove impacted skull fragments.

The surgeon shone a light into the patient's eyes and asked him who he was.

"My name is Steve Jones," said the patient, in a groggy voice. Then his thoughts turned to his wife and her unborn child. Steve said: "Where's my wife? Where's Barbara?"

The surgeon told him everything was fine, and advised him to rest. Outside in the corridor sat Bob Jones, Steve's older brother. As the surgeon came out of the ward, Bob confronted him and the nurse and said: "How is he?"

The surgeon said: "He was asking how his wife was."

Bob looked puzzled, and said: "But he isn't married. As far as I know he isn't even going with anyone named Barbara."

And the mystery of the missing wife deepened as Steven gradually started to recover. Bob listened at the foot of his bed as his brother told him of the events leading up to the crash at the roundabout.

Bob thought that his brother was just confused with the head injuries, and he finally had to tell him he was disoriented. Bob said: "Steve. You're a bachelor, mate. You've got no family."

Steven sat up and seemed aghast at his brother's assertion. He said: "What's going on, Bob? Are you trying to tell me I don't have a family? Why are you saying this? Is it a way of telling me that Barbara's dead? She didn't survive the crash, did she?"

Bob sighed and looked down at his hands, then said: "You're a bit confused. Don't worry mate."

Steve got out of bed and said: "That's it, I'm signing myself out."

Bob had to wrestle with him to get his irate brother back into bed. A nurse heard the shouting and came running in with an orderly.

Steve asked for a phone to be brought to his bedside. One was wheeled in and plugged in by his bed.

"You'll see who's confused," Steve said, and he dialled his home number. He pictured Emma reaching for the phone. She'd prove he wasn't imagining things. "Come on, Emma, answer the phone," Steve muttered. The nurses and Bob looked on with sympathetic expressions. Steven gripped the receiver tightly, but the phone just kept on ringing at the other end – and no one answered it. "They must be at school; what time is it?" Steven asked.

"It's Saturday, mate," Bob said, and shook his head with despair.

Steven said: "Look, please believe me. I have – or I had – a wife, a daughter named Emma, and a seven-year-old son named Damon. Please send someone to fetch them. Call

Emma's school, please. Better still, I'll phone one of the neighbours." And the patient put the receiver down, then lifted it and dialled again. Almost immediately, a woman answered. It was his neighbour, an elderly woman named Mrs Steele.

"Hello?" Mrs Steele said.

"Mrs Steele? It's me. Steve Jones," said the patient excitedly. At last he was making progress to convince the doubters.

"Oh, how are you, Steve? I read about the crash in the newspaper. I called the hospital the other day but they said you were critical," Mrs Steele said.

Steve interposed excitedly and said: "Mrs Steele, could you just confirm something? I know this is going to sound nuts, but could you tell me that I have a family?"

There was a pause, then the bemused old lady said. "Of course you have a family."

Steve shouted out, "Yes! I told them but they wouldn't believe me. Please tell me how many there are in my family."

Mrs Steele said: "Well, there's you, of course; then there's Bob, and – "

Steve's heart jumped. He said: "No, Mrs Steele, not my family; not my brothers and parents. My own family. Y'know – Damon and Emma."

There was a long silence, then Mrs Steele said: "I thought you didn't have a family, Steve."

Steven said: "Yes, you do know I have a wife and kids. You gave Damon some toffees the other day, remember?"

Mrs Steele said: "I'm sorry, Steve, but you're not making much sense. Damon? Who's Damon?"

Steve swore and said: "What are you all playing at, eh? Is this supposed to be some joke?"

Mrs Steele said: "Erm, someone's at the door. I'd, er, better go. Hope you get better soon."

And she hung up.

"No, hang on!" Steven said, and he dialled again, but got an engaged tone. Mrs Steele had left the phone off the hook.

The surgeon came into the room and he quizzed Mr Jones about his non-existent family, and assured him that his memory would soon return. But Steve Jones said that he was not suffering from amnesia, and demanded to be allowed to return home so that he could prove his claims.

The surgeon said that would be out of the question for at least a fortnight. Mr Jones pleaded to be released from the neurological department, but the surgeon said that was impossible. However, he did allow the patient to keep the phone at his bedside to make him feel better.

At 6 p.m. that night, something quite bizarre happened. A young girl came into the room and gently stroked Steve Jones's face.

He awoke to her touch and saw to his great surprise that it was his daughter Emma, holding a big bouquet of flowers.

"Emma! Oh I thought I'd imagined you! Where's your mum?" Steve asked, and sat up, so reassured at the sight of the girl. Emma hugged him and kissed him then said: "What's that big bandage on your head for, Dad? Does your head hurt?"

"Never mind me, love. Where's your mum?" Steve asked, and clutched his daughter's hands tightly.

"She's in hospital. She's had the baby, hasn't she?" Emma said, matter-of-factly.

"But I thought she was – I'm so confused," Mr Jones said, with a tear in his eye.

"You know she's in hospital," Emma said. The girl then got up and went to the foot of the bed to study the progress chart on a clipboard.

"Was it a boy or a girl?" Steven asked. He was immensely relieved that the nightmare was over. Perhaps he'd dreamt the whole episode about his brother and the nurses doubting that his family existed.

Emma said: "Oh, stop acting soft, Dad. You were at the birth, weren't you?"

Steve returned a blank stare.

"You passed out during the caesarean and hit your head on the bed," Emma said, and she added, "It was really embarrassing."

The door opened slightly, and a voice said: "Emma Jones? Here a moment, please."

Emma said: "What?" and she walked out of the ward.

"No, don't go, Emma. Emma! Wait!" Her father got out of

bed and hobbled after her. He opened the door of the room and saw that the long corridor outside was empty. Steve was deeply shocked and became unsteady on his feet. He leaned against the wall then slid down it. A nurse entered the corridor and shouted, "Mr Jones!"

As the nurse came hurrying to his aid, Steve blacked out again.

At 10 p.m. that night Mr Jones regained consciousness. The surgeon was shining a penlight into his eye. The surgeon said: "What's your name?"

Steve said: "Steve Jones. And I know I'm in the neuro-ward. She came here today. I wasn't imagining it."

In a nonchalant voice the neurosurgeon said: "Who came, Mr Jones?"

"Emma did," said Steve, and he angrily pushed the penlight from his face and sat upright in the bed. He said: "Look! Did I imagine them?"

He pointed to the bouquet of flowers lying on the bedside cabinet.

"Your brother left them, didn't he?" a nurse said.

"No, he didn't!" yelled Steve. "Ask him if you want. Emma brought them in."

The nurse shrugged, but then she noticed the card with the flowers. Upon this little card was the message: "Get well, Dad. Love from Mum, Emma and Damon."

When Steve was later discharged, he went home with his brother Bob and a cousin, and he found the house in Newton Heath exactly as he remembered. But there were no traces of his family. Emma's bedroom was empty, as was Damon's room. In his own bedroom there was no evidence whatsoever to prove that his wife had ever been there. No make-up, no wardrobe crammed with her clothes, nothing. And in the garden, there was no sign of the huge kennel Mr Jones and his brother had made for Leo the dog. A telephone inquiry to the vicar who had married Steve and Barbara Jones was treated as a crank call. Steve stormed into a house where Barbara's parents were supposed to live, but the old couple who lived there said that they knew of no Barbara. Nor had the schools Steve Jones visited heard of Damon or Emma Jones. Even the vet who had treated Leo had no recollection of the Great Dane.

Not surprisingly Mr Jones underwent psychiatric observation, and later moved from the Manchester area because it held too many memories for him; memories of a happy family which had apparently been erased from reality.

If we can discount amnesia and brain injury, how can we explain Mr Jones's traumatic experience? How can we explain the bouquet left by Emma with the handwritten note? Could the answer lie in the nature of the universe? Perhaps Mr Jones was transferred after the crash from some parallel world which runs alongside our one. In this world, perhaps Mr Jones did have the family he spoke of. For all we know, there may now be some other version of you, the reader, in this parallel world, perhaps living some entirely different life.

Mysteries of the *Titanic*

At 20 minutes to midnight on 14 April 1912, the White Star luxury liner *Titanic* gently brushed past an iceberg in the calm dark waters of the North Atlantic. Of the 2224 people on board the Liverpool-registered liner, only a handful felt the vessel jolt as it encountered the iceberg, but from that moment on the 66,000-tonne ship was doomed; and within a few hours over 1500 people on board would be dead.

But long before the *Titanic* left the slipways of the Harland Wolff shipbuilders in 1912 there were many eerie premonitions that apparently predicted the White Star liner's tragic fate . . .

In the year 1898 a magnificent floating palace set sail from Southampton on her maiden voyage to New York. She was the 70,000-tonne luxury liner *Titan,* and she carried almost 2500 people, including several millionaires. However, the *Titan* had only 24 lifeboats, which was less than half the number needed to save everyone on board. No one thought it mattered anyway; after all, the *Titan* had been proclaimed "unsinkable". However, through some freak chance, she struck an iceberg 300 miles off the coast of Newfoundland, then sank two and a half miles to the seabed, leaving over 1500 people to drown.

The *Titan* sea disaster only happened on paper. It only took place in a novel called *Futility*, written by a struggling novelist called Morgan Robertson – 14 years before the *Titanic* was built. Like the fictional *Titan*, the *Titanic* was also making her maiden voyage from Southampton to New York, and, like her fictional counterpart, she had also been called "unsinkable", and had carried only the inadequate number of 20 lifeboats. Even the number of people on board her was almost the same as the number of passengers on the ship in Robertsons's book. And most chillingly of all the *Titanic*, like the *Titan*, slid below the waters of the Atlantic 373 miles off the coast of Newfoundland after hitting an iceberg . . . and on board, one passenger on the doomed liner had been reading the prophetic book by Morgan Robertson which had foretold the *Titanic*'s doom.

There were other premonitions regarding the *Titanic*, even further back in time . . .

In 1850 there lived an eccentric old Englishman named Joseph Mercer in the Anfield district of Liverpool. Mercer was regarded as a psychic, and had amazing eyesight. He was said to be able to see ships entering Liverpool Bay, long before lookouts with telescopes could spot them. It is recorded that Mercer once told his grandson that one day in the distant future a gigantic iron ship with four funnels would anchor in the Mersey. Mercer said the makers of this immense vessel would blaspheme against the Almighty, and that God would sink their creation in the middle of the ocean with a terrible loss of life. Had Mercer been referring to the *Titanic*? For decades, scores of people swore that the *Titanic* visited Liverpool, England, on her way to Southampton from the Belfast shipyard. It was said that her Captain, Edward Smith, who lived in the Waterloo district of Liverpool, had come to the port to pick up the president and chairman from the Cunard White Star Line offices, which were situated near the Pier Head. It was alleged that a masonic ship-christening ceremony took place on board the vessel in the Mersey. This is a real possibility because, curiously, the *Titanic* was not launched in the traditional way by having a bottle of champagne cracked against her hull.

Perhaps the blasphemy Joseph Mercer referred to in his

prophecy was the claim made by the *Titanic*'s makers that "God himself could not sink the liner".

But some think that other supernatural forces were responsible for the loss of the super-liner . . .

In the 1880s archaeologists removed the sarcophagus of an ancient Egyptian princess from her death chamber near Cairo. The inscription on the walls of the death chamber warned that anyone who disturbed the resting place of Princess Amen-Otu would be cursed to death. The two men who later discovered the sarcophagus died suddenly from malaria-like symptoms. It was subsequently established that the mummified girl in the mummy case was indeed Amen-Otu, a clairvoyant high priestess who had lived in Thebes around 1000 BC.

Every owner of the Egyptian coffin and its mummy either died in mysterious circumstances or lost a loved one. By 1890 the coffin case was bought by the British Museum, but even the guards at the museum, who did not know about the supernatural reputation of the sarcophagus, were soon having paranormal experiences. Late one evening one guard at the museum came face to face with a hideous phantom which seemed to come out of the mummy case containing the remains of the Egyptian princess. The guard resigned on the following day, and his colleagues also reported seeing the terrifying apparition near the sarcophagus.

In 1912 the British Museum was approached by a wealthy American collector who wanted to buy an Egyptian mummy. The museum decided to sell the mummy of Princess Amen-Otu to the collector, so the corpse was packaged in a wooden crate and transported to Southampton, where it was stored in the hold of the *Titanic*. One of the stevedores who packed the coffin into the cargo hold later died from heart failure, although he was only 21.

Did the cursed mummy of Amen-Otu jinx the *Titanic*?

In the summer of 1910 a young woman named Mary Murray visited the caravan of a Blackpool fortune teller. Miss Murray asked the old gypsy woman what lay in store in the future, and the fortune teller examined Miss Murray's palm with a very concerned expression which soon turned into a look of terror. Understandably, the girl became nervous and asked the gypsy what she could see.

The old woman let go of the girl's hand, and seemed almost ready to faint. She gave Mary Murray her money back and said, "Stay away from boats, dear. Do not travel abroad. You will have three narrow escapes; three brushes with death at sea. Such loss of life, oh, babies in the water."

Two years later, Mary Murray had to board the ill-fated *Titanic* liner to visit a relative in America. She survived the sinking by being allowed into one of the lifeboats. Just as the gypsy had forecast two years previously, there was an appalling loss of life, and many babies drowned along with their mothers.

Then, in 1915, Mary Murray was on board another Liverpool-registered liner, visiting a relative. The liner was the *Lusitania*, which was torpedoed by a German submarine off the coast of Ireland. Once again, the death toll was staggeringly high: 1198 men, women and children perished when she sank. However, Mary Murray was one of the lucky survivors.

For the next 15 years, Mary Murray avoided travelling on ships but in 1927 she had to board a ship called the *Celtic*. She told a few of the passengers to expect trouble because of her past record, but they all laughed and said it had been pure coincidence. A few hours later the ship she was travelling on was accidentally rammed by a ship called the *Anaconda*. Many passengers on the *Celtic* drowned, but Mary Murray was once again spared, and ended up in a lifeboat.

Our penultimate mystery concerning the *Titanic* is very strange. In 1978 the radio officer of the *QE2* received a mysterious Morse code message. The message had been broadcast on a radio wavelength that was no longer in use, and was coded in an archaic fashion which belonged to the Edwardian age. The antiquated message in Morse said: "CQD, CQD – We are sinking fast. Passengers are being put into boats." The radio officer retuned his transmitter to the Morse frequency and in Morse he tapped out: "Identify yourself".

There was a slight pause. Only howls of atmospheric radio interference could be heard, then a reply came back which sent a shiver up the radio officer's spine. The reply said: "Titanic".

The captain of the *QE2* was informed and decided some hoaxer was at work, but someone pointed out that the liner was passing the very spot in the North Atlantic where the *Titanic* went down in 1912.

Under the orders of the curious captain, the radio officer of the *QE2* tried to contact the sender of the Morse code distress message again, but a reply never came. A cold silence descended on the bridge; it was as if through some freak of nature two liners from different eras had come into brief radio contact across time itself.

One final mystery concerning the *Titanic*: many of the survivors huddled in lifeboats swore that they saw a strange light shining from a nearby ship which refused to come to their aid. The light from this unidentified vessel was described as a directional beam similar to a searchlight. It might be wide of the mark, but is it possible that the source of the mysterious illumination could have been the searchlight of a German submarine? In 1912 the German Navy had perfected the U-boat and by 1915 one of these submersibles had torpedoed the *Lusitania*. It is an historical fact that U-boats were patrolling the waters of the North Atlantic at the time, on reconnaissance missions. Perhaps a U-boat torpedoed the *Titanic* as part of some covert military agenda. Or perhaps the Germans wanted to teach Britain that their new state-of-the-art liner was not "unsinkable" at all – and what better way to carry out the torpedo attack than under the cover of night, masked by a large iceberg? The U-boat theory would perhaps throw some light on the muffled explosions heard below decks as the ship was going down. Perhaps those were further torpedoes ramming into the hull to finish the liner off. After the attack, one can imagine the captain of the German submarine surfacing for a while to take a look at the survivors. Was this the "ship" the survivors cried out for help to before it seemed to vanish?

Two Visions of Death

On several occasions in British history prominent individuals have been disposed of for religious and political reasons. In December 1170 Thomas à Becket, the Archbishop of Canterbury was assassinated by Hugh de Merville, William de Tracy, Reginald Fitzurse and Richard le Breton, four of Henry II's knights. Becket was callously slayed because of his opposition to Henry's attempts to control the clergy.

Assassinations of British prime ministers have been exceptionally scarce since the days of Walpole, and in almost three centuries of British politics only one chief minister of government has been killed by an assassin. His name was Spencer Perceval, and the man who took his life was a Liverpudlian named John Bellingham.

Spencer Perceval was born in 1762, the second son of the second Earl of Egmont. He was educated at Harrow and Trinity College, Cambridge, where he graduated as Master of Arts in 1781. In 1783 Perceval's mother, the Baroness Arden, suddenly died, and left her fortune to her eldest son. Young Perceval struggled on, and studied hard to learn law at Lincoln's Inn. In 1786 he was called to the Bar, and soon obtained a reputation as a diligent and brief-hungry barrister. He also displayed a talent for voicing his strong political views, and in 1796 he entered parliament as the member for Northampton and became an ardent supporter of the Tory prime minister William Pitt. When Henry Addington succeeded Pitt as premier in 1801, he persuaded Perceval to join the new government as Attorney General. Perceval worked hard at his new job, and when Pitt formed his second administration in 1804 Perceval still kept his position. In 1807 the Duke of Portland became prime minister in the House of Lords, and Spencer Perceval was made the chancellor of the exchequer, and in those times that meant that he was also the leader of the House of Commons. In 1809 King George III, who thought so highly of the new leader of the Commons, calling him "The most straightforward man I have ever known", asked him to become prime minister, and Perceval accepted.

In the spring of 1812 a 42-year-old bankrupt Liverpool insurance-broker and exporter named John Bellingham entered a gunsmith's shop in the Strand, London, and bought two pistols and ammunition for four guineas. Bellingham then left the gunsmith's and headed for the wide-open spaces of Primrose Hill for a bit of shooting practice, before returning to his lodgings in New Millman Street.

Bellingham was a bitter and disillusioned man. He had once been in the lucrative business of exporting timber to Russia, but had lost everything when a business contact went bankrupt. Unable to pay the resulting mammoth debts, Bellingham was thrown into prison. Upon his release he visited Russia and complained to the authorities there with such vigour that they imprisoned him. Bellingham repeatedly wrote to the British ambassador to intervene on his behalf and secure his release, but the ensuing tangle of British and Russian red tape achieved nothing, and Bellingham remained in the cold Russian prison cell for months.

When he was finally released, Bellingham returned to England and began a feverish campaign to get his case reviewed and to receive compensation. He wrote countless indignant letters to his MP and even informed the Prince Regent of his unjust incarceration. But all the protests came to nothing, and no redress was given. On one occasion, Bellingham stormed into Whitehall and demanded action, but he met a wall of unsympathetic officialdom. At the top of his voice he told one Whitehall official that he was going to take legal action against the government because of the neglect it had shown, and the official roared back, "Go to the Devil!"

So John Bellingham decided to vent his anger at British bureaucracy by shooting the prime minister, preferably in the midst of the House of Commons and in the presence of all its members. But first Bellingham would have to do a spot of reconnoitring at the scene of the intended crime, so he made it his daily habit to visit the Commons, where he lurked about the central lobby, observing the route the prime minister took when entering the chamber. He also became a frequent visitor to the Commons coffee room.

And now for a supernatural twist to this tale . . .

On the night of 3 May that year a Mr John Williams, who was a banker of Redruth in Cornwall, had a vivid dream in which he found himself standing in the lobby of the House of Commons. In this dream he saw a small man dressed in a blue coat and white waistcoat enter the lobby. Moments later, another man in a snuff-coloured coat with yellow metal buttons suddenly drew a small pistol and fired it at the man in blue. The dream was so realistic that the dreamer could actually discern the ball from the pistol striking the left side of the victim's chest, where it left a little neat spot.

Shocked at the incident, the dreamer turned to a group of people in the lobby and asked them who had been shot, and someone replied that the victim was the prime minister, Spencer Perceval. The group of bystanders then charged at the murderer to apprehend him.

At this point in the dream Mr Williams awakened and gave an account of the strange dream to his wife. She assured him that it was only a bad dream and Mr Williams went back to sleep. Almost immediately, the same dream replayed in his mind, and Mr Williams woke up feeling quite uneasy, and told his wife that he had just experienced the same dream about the assassination of Perceval. Mrs Williams assured him that it was only a nightmare and nothing more. Mr Williams turned over and later went back to sleep for a third time, and the same dream of assassination returned to haunt him.

On the following day Mr Williams began to think about the significance of the recurring dream, and wondered if he ought to travel to London to warn Mr Perceval. Later at work he related the events of the bad dream to several business acquaintances and asked them for advice. His friends told him that he would be ridiculed as a madman if he were to go to London on the strength of a mere dream, so Mr Williams decided not to go to the capital, but all the same he scanned the *Times* newspaper each day to see if there had been any shooting incidents at Westminster.

On the afternoon of Monday, 11 May, Spencer Perceval left 10 Downing Street and, seeing it was a pleasant sunny day, he dismissed his carriage and decided to walk to the House. At around 5.15 p.m. Perceval entered the lobby of the House, and a few seconds later Bellingham drew his pistol from his right-hand breeches pocket. He stepped out from behind a pillar, raised his pistol, aimed at Perceval and, in full view of all the constituents, he fired. The ball blasted a small neat hole in the left side of the Prime Minister's chest. Perceval cried, "Murder!" and staggered three paces, fell on his side, then hit the floor face-down. Mr Goodiff, an officer of the House, attacked the assassin and grabbed his arm. He asked Bellingham if he shot the prime minister, and the Lancashire businessman replied, "I am the unhappy man who has shot Mr Perceval. My name is John Bellingham. I know what I have done. It was a private injury, a denial of justice on the part of the government."

Bellingham was instantly recognized by Sir Banastre Tarleton and Mr Gascoyne, two Liverpool MPs who were in the Lobby at the time. Gascoyne also sprung upon Bellingham and twisted his arm while someone removed the smoking pistol from his hand. The assassin was then body-searched, and the second pistol was found on him.

Meanwhile, Perceval was carried into the nearby office of the Speaker's secretary and laid on a sofa. When Dr Lynn of Great Smith Street arrived ten minutes later, he found he could do nothing; Spencer Perceval was dead.

All the doors of the House were locked and Bellingham was taken along several private passages to the prison rooms in the upper storeys of the Commons, where he was interrogated by the Cabinet council for over seven hours.

Perceval's body was taken to his wife and five children, who were devastated by the killing.

News of the murder travelled quickly across the nation, and there were many in the upper echelons of British society who believed that the assassination was but the starting shot of the long-awaited British Revolution. The paranoid aristocrats remembered the revolution across the English Channel in France that had taken place a little over two decades ago and shuddered. The social unrest among the poverty-stricken lower classes because of the introduction of machines into the workplace seemed ready to explode any day, and the riotous activities of the Luddites were becoming more organized. To make matters worse, the country's economy was at an all-time low because of the astronomical costs of the Napoleonic war. But one individual who learned of the assassination was more dumbfounded than shocked. He was John Williams of Cornwall, the man who had mysteriously foreseen the shooting in a recurring dream. Williams immediately travelled to London and purchased a coloured etching of the prime minister's murder. He was astounded when he examined the printed picture, because every detail depicted was identical to the details he had witnessed in his dream, from the colours of the coats and the exact position of the gunshot wound in the chest, to the facial features of the petite Perceval and tall, aquiline-nosed Bellingham.

Bellingham was later hanged for assassinating the prime minister, and John Williams never had any further sneak previews of future events in his dreams. Why or how the Cornish banker caught a glimpse into the future on that summer night will probably never be known.

One hundred and sixty-eight years after the Perceval assassination, another prominent figure was assassinated, but this time a Liverpudlian man was not the assassin, but the victim of one, and this killing was also said to have been foreseen.

On 8 September 1980 an American psychic named Alex Tanous was being interviewed by Lee Spiegel for NBC Radio's "Unexplained Phenomena" show. The interview was going out live and was being held in the office of the American Society for Psychical Research, which is located on West 73rd Street in New York City.

Spiegel asked Tanous to prove his alleged powers of second sight by making a prediction, preferably one that would be of particular interest to the radio station's audience, who belonged to the 18 to 35 age group. Tanous paused for a moment, as if concentrating, then said, "A very famous rock star will have an untimely death, and this can happen from this moment on. I say 'untimely' because there is something strange about this death, but it will affect the consciousness of many people because of his fame. The star will be foreign-born but living in the United States."

After uttering this prediction Tanous glanced through the

windows of his office at the building opposite – a superior high-rise known as the Dakota Apartments.

Three months later, on the night of 8 December, a limousine pulled up outside the Dakota Apartments at 10.50 p.m., and Yoko Ono left the vehicle. Her husband John Lennon followed her a few moments later, clutching several reels of tape from a recording session he'd been working on. As John walked under the archway leading to the Dakota building, he heard a voice behind him call out, "Mister Lennon".

John turned to see tubby 25-year-old Mark Chapman, crouched in a combat stance, a mere 20 feet away with a ·38 Undercover Special handgun pointing at him. A heartbeat later, Chapman pumped four hollow-point bullets into one of Liverpool's most famous and adored sons. The songwriter who had urged the world's leaders to "Give Peace a Chance" staggered up the steps of the building's entrance and fell flat on his face. Minutes later John Lennon was placed on the back seat of a police car which rushed him to the nearest hospital with its roof-lights flashing and siren screaming. As the police car jumped the traffic lights on Broadway, police officer James Moran, who had been a keen Beatles fan in his youth, leaned back and talked to John Lennon in a vain attempt to keep him conscious. Moran was deeply shocked at the shooting, but to his dying idol he managed to say, "Are you John Lennon?"

With his life rapidly ebbing away, John faintly replied, "Yes".

And that was the last word John Lennon uttered. He was the 701st person to be gunned down in New York City that year.

Chapman is currently serving a "20 years to life" sentence at Attica State Prison in northern New York State. He is kept in solitary confinement to prevent any of the prison's other 2000 inmates from attacking him. He may be eligible for parole around the year 2001.

Chapman's motive for killing the ex-Beatle is still unclear. The official theory was that he was simply a psychotic Lennon fanatic trying to make a name for himself, but there is something more sinister about the killing. Chapman was dismissed as a "lone nut" – the same expression that was used to describe Lee Harvey Oswald 17 years earlier in Dallas. In fact the murder of John Lennon has several striking parallels with that of John F. Kennedy. When Lennon's body was taken to the morgue, the gunshot wounds in the cadaver were so close together that one pathologist remarked, "Good shot group" – which is a firing-range term used by the police and the military to describe skilled marksmanship. Yet Chapman was said to be a novice with firearms. But the grouping of the gunshot wounds in Lennon's body was so tight that pathologists at the morgue got mixed up trying to count them as they conducted their post mortem.

The assassin's choice of weapon – the Undercover Special, known on the street as a "Saturday Night Special" – is an extremely reliable gun. It is deadly accurate and never jams or misfires, yet it is small and sleek enough to fit into the back pocket of your jeans. In May 1972 would-be assassin Arthur Bremner used one to blast Alabama Governor George C. Wallace. The bullet that impacted into the politician's spine left him wheelchair-bound for life.

Besides the mystery of Chapman's expert choice of weapon and his inexplicable marksmanship, there is the fuzzy account of the killer's journey from his home in Honolulu to New York that just doesn't stand up to the most cursory examination. According to the official version of events, Mark Chapman persuaded his wife to take out a loan of two and a half thousand dollars from her employer's credit union, and without her knowledge he used this sum to finance the assassination. He bought his well chosen gun and dumdum bullets, and flew overnight from Honolulu to New York on a United Airlines plane. But the distinguished British barrister Fenton Bresler, who researched the Lennon murder for eight years, unearthed a plethora of sinister missing links. Firstly, he discovered that United Airlines had no direct flights from Honolulu to New York. One actually has to fly by way of Chicago. Chapman did not mention this. Further investigations made by Bresler convinced the barrister that the killer spent three unaccounted-for days in Chicago.

Bresler got in touch with the New York County district attorney's office and told them about the three "missing"

John Lennon and the Number 9

Throughout his life the late John Lennon believed that the number 9 affected his destiny. He was born on 9 October, as was his son Sean. In his youth Lennon would leave his Liverpool home at 9 Newcastle Road and get the 72 bus; and he noticed that the bus's two numbers, 7 and 2 added up to 9. Brian Epstein first attended a Beatles performance at the cavern on the 9 November 1961, and he clinched a record contract for the group on the 9 May 1962. The first Beatle record "Love Me Do" was numbered 4949 on Parlophone, and John first met Yoko Ono on 9 November 1966. The couple later moved into an apartment on New York's 72nd Street, and again John noticed that the two numbers of the street, 7 and 2, added up to 9. Of course, John Lennon deliberately wrote songs with nine in the title, like "One After 909", "Revolution Number 9" and "Number 9 Dream", but the number 9, which has been regarded as mystical for thousands of years, continued to feature heavily in the life of the Beatle – up to his death and beyond. Lennon was gunned down on 8 December 1980, but because of the 5-hour time difference, it was actually 9 December in Liverpool when John died. Shortly afterwards, the body of John Lennon was taken to Roosevelt Hospital – on 9th Avenue.

days, but they denied that the facts had any substance. Bresler believes that the days in question – from 2 to 5 December – were covered up by the authorities. During that period, he claims, Chapman was being "programmed" to kill by the CIA with brainwashing drugs and repeated hypnotic suggestion. Is Bresler right? Was there a top-level conspiracy to assassinate John Lennon? Let us examine some less-publicized facts about the late ex-Beatle.

The FBI and the CIA had files on Lennon dating back to the 1960s that detail the star's participation in anti-war demos. There are two reports in one dossier on Lennon for May 1972 with the heading "Revolutionary Activities". The FBI and CIA apparently saw Lennon as a cult-like leader who had the latent ability to overthrow the established government of the United States; a political subversive who could easily produce a stirring song along the lines of "Power to the People" to incite millions of Americans to demonstrate against the reactionary policies of the newly elected president Ronald Reagan. As early as 1972 Lennon knew he was under constant surveillance. He said at the time to reporters, "I'd open the door. There'd be guys on the other side of the street. I'd get into my car, and they'd be following me in a car. Not hiding. They wanted me to see that I was being followed."

By September 1973 Lennon's telephone was bugged, a fact to which even the Justice Department later admitted. In December 1975 Lennon said, "We knew we were being wiretapped. There was a helluva lot of guys coming in to fix the phones."

In the light of these cloak-and-dagger details, Bresler's conspiracy theory seems less outlandish.

Furthermore, the week John Lennon was shot he was due to fly to San Francisco to participate in a rally for Japanese-American workers on strike. He was so enthusiastic to get to the demonstration that he had already bought the airline tickets.

In November 1992 Mark Chapman broke his silence over the Lennon murder when he agreed to be interviewed by American television reporter Barbara Walters in Attica State Prison. Chapman dismissed the commonly held belief that he had killed John Lennon to become famous. He also told Walters that he was horrified by the amount of fanmail he regularly received from people wanting his autograph.

"That tells you something is truly sick in our society," Chapman told Walters in a broken voice.

To the Rescue, a Century Too Late

On the western suburbs of Nantwich, England, near to the banks of the Shropshire Union Canal, an intriguing timewarp incident was reported in 1959. One foggy evening in the December of that year a 29-year-old man from Wrexham named Alan Hughes was visiting his cousins. Alan left the house of one cousin near Acton, and walked almost a mile to the home of his other cousin, George Kinsey, who lived on a farmstead on the western periphery of Nantwich. He had never visited George before and, because of the fog, he gradually lost his bearings. He met an old man who helpfully directed him to follow a lane which would lead him to his destination.

Night fell fast during the journey down the quiet lane, and Alan Hughes was only too glad to see a rosy halo of light in the distance. At first he thought it was the lights of his cousin's house, but soon realized that the source of light was a fire. Alan thought the worst and prayed that it wasn't his cousin's house that was ablaze. The Wrexham man ran off towards the crackling fire, and as he drew near to it he could smell the pungent fumes drifting from the blaze.

A solitary silhouette stood dangerously near to the blazing house. As Alan got closer he saw that it was a woman with a shawl on, and she turned and screamed to him, "My baby is in there! Please save him!"

Alan halted for a moment to regain his breath and coughed as the acidic smoke wafted towards him, but the woman screeched at him again.

"Please! Save my baby! He's upstairs!" she hysterically cried, then backed away from the squat granite dwelling. The building was secluded, and looked like a farmhouse or lodge of some sort.

Alan looked at the thick smoke pouring from the doorway, then held his breath and rushed in. He fought through the billowing smoky blackness until he tripped over what seemed to be a step. He felt his way up the staircase, but the heat and suffocating smoke drove him back out into the open. When he emerged, the woman was nowhere to be seen, and Alan felt dizzy from the smoke inhalation. He fell to his knees, unable to expel the asphyxiating sooty smoke from his lungs, then passed out.

When Alan awoke, he found himself in a field. The fog had evaporated and by the light of a waning moon on the eastern horizon Alan could see that there were no buildings or any landmarks visible. He felt a bit groggy, but his lungs were fine. He searched the field, determined to find the burnt house but, like the fog, it had apparently vanished into thin air. By the time Alan finally found his cousin's house, the time was 3 a.m., and his cousin's home bore no resemblance whatsoever to the house that had been on fire.

However, on the following day in the local inn Alan and his cousin were enjoying a drink as they discussed the strange incident of the previous night, when the old landlady leaned over to them. She said she had been listening to their conversation, then told the men that over a hundred years ago a cottage had been razed by a fire which killed the baby son of a farmer. The farmer had been seeing his mistress at the time of the blaze and many thought that he had started the fire to rid himself of his wife because he claimed her newborn son wasn't his baby. The farmer's wife attempted to save her baby boy from the flames but was driven back by the heat and smoke, and the baby perished. The landlady told Alan and his cousin that, over the years, several people had seen the phantom fire while crossing the field where the cottage had once stood.

The Mirage of Mass Murder

This is a real uncanny story which was reported in several Irish newspapers in the early 1980s.

One blistering sunny afternoon in May 1981 two American children and their Irish grandfather were enjoying the summer weather on the coast of Cork, near a stretch of coastline known as the Old Head of Kinsale. The kids were seven-year-old Aarron Fitzpatrick and his six-year-old sister Siobhan. As their grandfather relaxed back into his deck chair to soak up the sun as he snoozed, the kids ran along the beach, throwing a frisbee to each other.

At ten-past two that afternoon, Aarron and Siobhan almost pushed their sleeping grandfather out of his deck chair as they excitedly tried to wake him.

"What in God's name?" the old Irishman cried out, and his grandchildren pointed out to the strange spectacle that was unfolding in the waters off the coast.

About a mile or so out, an enormous liner resembling the

Titanic was listing heavily to starboard, sinking nose-first. A long plume of black smoke was rising from the stricken vessel, and there was a strange din coming from the direction of the sinking liner. With a mounting sense of horror, Aarron and Siobhan's granddad realized that the clamour was the screams of a thousand or more people he could just about see as dots in the water near the rapidly sinking ship.

Little Siobhan said, "What's wrong with that boat, Granddad?"

Then suddenly, within the blinking of an eye, there was no sinking ship there any more, just a flock of seagulls, skimming across the waves. The screams also ceased abruptly. Even though the temperature was in the seventies, the Irishman felt a cold chill in his bones. He recalled the date: 7 May. On that very date in 1915 the Cunard liner *Lusitania* had been torpedoed by a German submarine in that very same stretch of water. She had been on her way to Liverpool from New York when she was hit and 1198 people perished in the disaster, which was branded as an act of mass murder. As the grandfather left the beach, little Siobhan asked what had become of the ship.

"Oh it's long gone down," her grandfather replied.

The *Lusitania* had gone to a watery grave 66 years before.

What they had all just witnessed was some ghostly replay – a tragic mirage from another era.

Ten Mysterious Disappearances

1. The Mother Who Vanished

In 1889 a mother and daughter from London were returning from a holiday in India. They stopped off at Paris to see the city's exhibition, and booked a room at a prestigious hotel. They signed their names in the register and were taken up to their room, which was numbered 342. Room 342 was a luxurious apartment with heavy plum-coloured curtains, exquisitely designed velvet rose-patterned wallpaper, and lavish furniture. Within minutes of her arrival in the apartment, the mother fell ill and started to feel dizzy. She was put to bed and the hotel doctor was brought up to her room. After examining the woman, the doctor summoned the hotel manager, and after he had arrived the doctor started to argue with him in French. The manager suddenly turned to the ill woman's daughter and said, "Your mother is seriously ill, mademoiselle. The only medicine that can help her is at a doctor's surgery on the other side of Paris. I cannot leave her for a moment so you must go at once and fetch the medicine."

The girl nodded and was escorted to a carriage which took her to the doctor's address. She had to wait there for almost 40 minutes while the medicine was made up, and by the time she returned to the hotel, almost two hours had elapsed. The girl stopped the manager in the hotel foyer and earnestly asked him, "How is Mother?"

The manager returned a blank expression. "I have never set eyes on your mother, mademoiselle."

"You have. We signed in this morning in front of you. Don't you remember?" said the girl with a puzzled look.

"You came here alone," replied the manager, and he went over to the reception desk and brought over the hotel register. He pointed to her signature, and the girl could see that her mother's name was not there. The manager even allowed the confused girl to flick through the register's pages to search for her mother's signature, but she couldn't find it. In desperation she tugged the manager's arm and took him up to the room she and her mother had booked – room 342. Upon opening the door of that apartment, the girl was startled to see that the room bore no resemblance to the room her mother had booked. No plum-coloured curtains or rose-patterned wallpaper. No exuberant furniture or plush carpets either. The girl suspected that the room number on the door had been switched, but the hotel manager allowed the paranoid girl to inspect every room on that floor – but none of the other apartments looked anything like room 342. The girl ran downstairs and called for the hotel doctor. The physician who had treated her mother two hours before came to see her, but he also denied that he had ever met the girl or her mother.

When the girl returned to England, she told the authorities she believed her mother had been kidnapped, but they didn't believe her incredible story, and the girl later suffered from a severe mental breakdown and was committed to a lunatic asylum.

There are a few theories that have been proposed as an answer to the mysterious disappearance. Some thought that the missing mother had picked up a highly contagious disease in India which could have forced the Parisian authorities to close down the hotel. If this was the case, perhaps the hotel manager and doctor conspired to dispose of the infected woman; but how would they have been able to decorate and refurbish a whole apartment in under two hours? Therein lies a mystery that has never been solved.

2. Disappearances in the Outback

In 1847 the explorer Ludwig Leichardt and his party – equipped with fifty bullocks, twenty mules and seven horses – set out into the central desert of the Australian Outback. Every person and animal later vanished during the expedition, seemingly into thin air. Despite repeated large-scale searches covering hundreds of square miles, not a trace of the expedition was ever found. The almost supernatural disappearance of Ludwig Leichardt became one of Australia's greatest unsolved mysteries. In January 1975 it looked as if the Leichardt puzzle would at last be solved when Zac Mathias, a wildlife ranger, drove into Darwin with photographs of strange Aboriginal cave drawings of a pipe-smoking man on a pony who looked unmistakably caucasian. The photograph also showed cave pictures depicting a white man walking alongside and a third white man being carried by a group of Aborigines. Peter Spillet, the President of the Northern Territory Historical Society, told the press that "the paintings will give us the first positive clue to the disappearance of Ludwig Leichardt and his party". Spillet then planned an expedition to the caves which was to be led by Zac Mathias, the man who had taken the intriguing snapshots, but shortly afterwards the photographer himself mysteriously vanished while in the Outback and he too was never seen again.

3. The Hanging Rock Mystery

On Wednesday, 14 February 1900, a party of schoolgirls and teachers left Appleyard College in the village of Woodend, near Melbourne, Australia, and rode out in a hired coach to a local beauty spot four and a half miles away known as Hanging Rock. The Rock, which is of volcanic origin and several million years old, rises majestically over 500 feet from the otherwise flat plain. The party was comprised of 19 girls, the majority of them in their teens, who were accompanied by two teachers, Mademoiselle Diane de Poitiers, who taught dancing and French, and the college mathematics teacher, a Scottish middle-aged spinster named Greta McCraw. The other adult in the party was Benjamin Hussey, a coachmaster from the local livery stables.

The party arrived at Hanging Rock shortly before noon on that infernally hot day and settled down under the shade of the trees and boulders for a picnic lunch. Then something strange happened. Two watches – those belonging to Mr Hussey and Miss McCraw – suddenly stopped dead. The watches were wound sufficiently, yet had stopped ticking for some reason. Minutes later they began to work again.

Meanwhile, on the other side of Hanging Rock, another group of picnickers were encamped. It was made up of a retired Indian Army colonel named Fitzhubert, his wife, their nephew Michael Fitzhubert, and their groom Albert Crundall. Around 3 p.m. three of the college girls – Irma Leopold, Marion Quade and Miranda Grayson (who were all aged 17) asked Mlle Diane de Poitiers if they could explore the rock. The French teacher said they could go ahead of the party, as long as they took the utmost care in avoiding the Rock's poisonous snakes, spiders and hazardous crags and caves. The three girls excitedly set out up the Rock, followed by a fourth college girl named Edith Horton, who was only 14. By 3.30 p.m. the four girls had crossed a stream and were lost to sight. Michael Fitzhubert and Albert Crundall were idly sitting at this stream, ogling the girls as they lifted their skirts to cross the waters. Albert stood up and let out a wolf-whistle, while his friend Michael got to his feet and began to follow the girls, but gave up after walking just a few yards in their direction. The girls were soon disappearing behind a line of trees.

By 4.30 p.m. Mr Hussey had decided to assemble the girls together when he and the French teacher noticed that Miss McCraw was nowhere to be seen. This was a real puzzler, as no one had seen her leave the party. Mr Hussey speculated that Miss McCraw had followed the four girls up the rock. When one hour had elapsed, Mr Hussey and Mlle de Poitiers decided to search for the four missing girls and the maths teacher. Mr Hussey noticed a trail of broken bracken and recently disturbed scrub which led to the southern face of Hanging Rock. At around 5.30 p.m. one of the missing girls – Edith Horton – came screaming out of the bush on the south-west side of the Rock. She was hysterical and was unable to tell Mr Hussey and her French teacher what had become of the three other girls and the maths teacher. Night soon fell, and the three missing girls and Miss McCraw could still not be found, so Mr Hussey, Mlle de Poitiers and the remainder of the party returned to Appleyard College. Hussey made a statement to a Police Constable Bumpher, and the following day the search for the teacher and the girls resumed. Young Edith Horton was examined by a doctor and had only minor scrapes and scratches on her body from running through the bush. The girl was evidently suffering from mild concussion, and she made an intriguing remark to Constable Bumpher. She said that as she had been running down Hanging Rock to Mr Hussey, she had noticed Miss McCraw walking in the opposite direction, and what's more, she had noticed that the spinster had not been wearing a skirt – only her drawers. The police quizzed the prime suspect in the bizarre case: Michael Fitzhubert from the other party that had been camping on the Rock. Michael strenuously denied he had anything to do with the girls" disappearance, and the police were "persuaded" to drop this line of inquiry by the powerful Fitzhubert family.

An Aboriginal tracker with a bloodhound was brought to Hanging Rock to trace the four missing people, but the dog became terrified of something halfway up the rock and refused to go further. Days later, one of the girls – Irma Leopold – was found unconscious on the Rock. She was badly bruised, and her corset was missing, although it was later established that the girl had not been sexually assaulted.

When Irma regained consciousness, she could remember nothing of her mysterious ordeal. And that is where this tantalizing story ends. Miranda Grayson, Marion Quade and Miss Greta McCraw were never found. There is one strange epilogue to this tale. Around noon on that Valentine's Day when the watches of Mr Hussey and Miss McCraw stopped dead, an unusual pink-coloured cloud was seen directly over Hanging Rock; could this hint at some extra-terrestrial explanation of the enigmatic group disappearances? We will probably never know.

4. The Disappearance of a Diplomat

In November 1809 Benjamin Bathurst, Britain's envoy to Vienna, was making his way back to England with important dispatches. The itinerary he took through Europe had to be carefully planned, as almost every country on the Continent was infested with Napoleon's French troops. At Berlin Bathurst and his Swiss servant acquired false passports, then headed for Hamburg, a city that had retained its independence. Halfway through the perilous journey, Bathurst decided a change of horses was necessary, and so the coach stopped at the small rural town of Perleberg, and Bathurst and his servant disembarked and entered an inn for refreshments. Around nine o'clock that evening, the diplomat and his servant left the inn and headed for the coach. Bathurst walked around the coach, apparently to look at the horses, but never emerged from the other side. The servant followed him a moment later, but could not find a trace of the vanished diplomat. In desperation, the servant paid a visit to Captain Klitzing, the town governor, and told him of his master's baffling disappearance. Captain Klitzing organized a thorough, extensive search of the town and also had the nearby river dragged, but to no avail. Benjamin Bathurst was never seen or heard from again.

5. The Army that Disappeared into Thin Air

In December 1937 China and Japan had been at war for a duration of six months, and the Chinese were suffering the worst casualties in the struggle. Shanghai fell, and in spite of the protests from the powerless League of Nations, the

Japanese advanced on Nanking, the capital of the city. South of Nanking, Chinese commander Colonel Li Fu Sien decided to make a last-ditch stand in the low hills. An urgent request brought forth over 3000 reinforcements, and Colonel Li Fu Sien disposed of the troops in a two-mile-long line, close to the strategically important bridge across the Yangtze River. The troops were equipped with heavy artillery and were prepared for the life-and-death struggle that lay ahead. Colonel Li Fu Sien had a close rapport with his men, but military protocol forced him to retreat two miles behind the lines to headquarters. At the following dawn the colonel was awakened by his aide, who told him that all contact had been lost with the army, and that there were rumours that the troops had been overrun by the Japanese forces during the night. Colonel Li Fu Sien could not accept what he was told, and he and an escort visited the front lines themselves to get to the bottom of the mystery. To their utter amazement, the positions at the front lines were deserted. Every gun was still in position but the soldiers were nowhere to be seen. Hours later an isolated group of 100 soldiers was found still encamped near to the bridge. They were apparently unaware of the thousands of soldiers who had vanished on either side of the line, and the sentries on the bridge swore that no one had passed them in the night.

The Chinese had no time to ponder on the incredible mass disappearances, as the Japanese army was soon advancing across the river. Forty-eight hours later Nanking fell and there followed one of the most horrifying massacres of all time. The atrocities were so shocking that three Japanese commanders and many of their soldiers were recalled to Japan to be punished for their part in what was to be known by future historians as "the rape of Nanking".

After the war, many people in China talked in hushed voices about the army that disappeared in the night. The general consensus is that the disappearances were the work of some demon.

6. The Farmer who Walked into Limbo

A farmer from Gallatin, Tennessee, named David Lang was walking across a 40-acre field one sunny afternoon on 23

September 1880 when he spotted his brother-in-law with Judge August Peck (a friend of the Lang family) approaching in a buggy down a lane that ran adjacent to the field. Farmer Lang waved to his brother-in-law and the judge – then vanished instantly before their eyes. Lang's wife screamed in the distance, as she saw her husband dematerialize. Her children, eleven-year-old Sarah and eight-year-old George, had also witnessed Lang's amazing instant disappearance, and they looked at their mother in a confused manner, then glanced back to the spot where their father had been strolling a few seconds before. The children raced across the field to the spot where their father had vanished, expecting to see a hole in the ground, but they found that the earth hadn't been disturbed at all. Within minutes the alarm was raised and almost every member of the community turned up and joined in a search for the farmer. The search party combed the vicinity until nightfall but they found no clue to Lang's disappearance.

The following year Lang's children visited the spot where their father had inexplicably vanished, and were amazed to find a circular patch of overgrown grass, 24 feet in diameter, which the cattle had left ungrazed.

"Father, are you around?" Sarah enquired, because she felt a strange presence at the spot.

Her brother George also felt as if someone or something indefinable was close by, and he too assumed it was his lost father.

About ten minutes later the children were walking away with their heads bowed, when they heard their father's faint voice shouting for help.

Sarah and George stopped in their tracks. The faint voice was coming from the circle of overgrown grass. The children raced non-stop to the farmhouse and brought their mother to the ungrazed spot. Mrs Lang shouted for her husband and strained her ears listening for a reply. A distant-sounding voice seemed to call her name. Alas, the voice soon became too feeble, and David Lang never made a reappearance, even though his wife bought the parcel of land he had vanished on, and lived in eternal hope of him coming back from limbo.

7. The Cripple who Vanished on a Busy Street

Owen Parfitt, of Shepton Mallett, England, was a 70-year-old man who had led a chequered career as a soldier in Africa and America. Later in his life he decided to become a tailor, and it was during this final occupation in his life that he suffered a major stroke which rendered him a wheelchair-bound paraplegic.

On a fine afternoon in July 1768 Parfitt was sitting in his invalid chair in the doorway of his cottage, whiling away the humdrum hours of his existence by observing the daily bustle of life in the small English town. Parfitt's sister, Susannah Snook, who looked after him, came out of the cottage and saw that her brother's chair was empty. Owen was nowhere to be seen. Only his coat remained, drooped over the chair.

Susannah was baffled and very concerned, because only 15 minutes earlier she herself had sat her crippled brother in the chair before going off to make his bed. Owen's paralysis was so extensive that Susannah had to spoon-feed him, so she wondered how he had been able to leave his chair. Haymakers opposite the cottage at the time of Mr Parfitt's disappearance said they never saw him leave his chair. However, some of the workers claimed they had heard a peculiar high-pitched whistle the very hour when Parfitt vanished.

A widespread search was mounted, but Parfitt couldn't be found, and was never seen again. There were many in Shepton Mallet who claimed that the Devil had been passing through the town on that hot July afternoon and had "collected" the old reprobate Parfitt because of the sinful life he had once led.

8. The Stockholm Ferry Disappearances

In 1975 a bizarre mystery of vanishing passengers unfolded on the 9000-ton Helsinki to Stockholm ferry. However, not until May 1977 were the public and press aware of the strange case. In May 1977 the ferry had docked at Stockholm at the end of its 12-hour night crossing with 700 passengers and 250 vehicles on board. Everyone disembarked from the ferry and all of the vehicles drove off onto the mainland – all but one. There was one lorry whose owner had not appeared to drive it away. Police soon established that this missing owner was Juho Heino, a Finnish road hauler. The ferry was searched from nose to stern, but Mr Heino could not be found. After further enquiries the police learnt that the Finnish lorry driver had not been seen since he had gone into his cabin at midnight. Mr Heino's business was flourishing and his family life was happy. His doctor said that he had no health worries and told police how Mr Heino had been looking forward to the trip because he was transporting furniture to his married daughter.

Police were concerned about Mr Heino's disappearance because he had been the seventh person to vanish without a trace on that same Helsinki to Stockholm ferry in the previous two years. Three of the missing had been Swedes, four had been Finns, and not a single body had been recovered or washed up anywhere. In all seven disappearances suicide had been ruled out as a cause, so the police in Sweden speculated that the seven missing ferry passengers had perhaps been murdered and disposed of for some sinister reason.

One inspector involved in the investigation remarked to the press, "We must assume that a crime of some kind has been committed. If we can get to the bottom of Mr Heino's disappearance we may find an explanation for the other six."

But the police reached a dead end, even after detectives had spent weeks on board the ferry during its Helsinki-Stockholm run. Even today the Swedish police files on the Stockholm ferry disappearances are still classed as "unsolved".

9. "Gone in the Blink of an Eye"

James Worson was a well known and much-liked resident of Leamington Spa, an English health resort eight miles south of Coventry which is renowned nationally for its salubrious saline springs. Worson was a shoemaker by trade and a hypochondriacal health fanatic. He was also something of an extrovert and an attention seeker who continually boasted about his physical prowess in his local pub. One day in June 1873 James Worson was enjoying a lunchtime pint of ale in his pub when he overheard two young men debating how far a man could run in one day, and their line of talk incited the cobbler to boast that he could run to Coventry and back without stopping. Worson's friends, a sign-painter named Hammerson Burns and a linen draper named Barnham Wise, overheard the cobbler's claim, and wagered that he could not complete the non-stop run to Coventry and back. Worson turned red with anger because his friends had challenged him in front of the impressionable young men, so he accepted the wager.

Half an hour later the linen draper and sign-painter and a third man named George Turpin got onto a cart, ready to follow Worson on his 16-mile jog to Coventry and back. Worson ran ahead about a hundred yards, and the cart carrying the three observers trundled after him. About 20 minutes into the run, Worson's friends shouted words of encouragement to the shoemaker, because they realized he did have good stamina after all. It was a hot afternoon, but Worson wasn't flagging yet, and his arms were like pumping pistons as he ran down the tree-shaded country road. Then, suddenly, James Worson appeared to stumble over something, and he tripped, cried out – then suddenly he wasn't there anymore.

The three official observers and the driver of the cart refused to believe their eyes at first. They left the cart and went to the spot where Worson had vanished. Hammerson Burns examined the spot in the road where his friend had disappeared and seemed in shock. He muttered to Barnham Wise and the cart driver, "Gone in the blink of an eye."

Mr Wise looked about and shouted, "Okay, Worson, tell us how you did that trick and we'll call off the wager."

But there was no reply, and none ever came, because James Worson was never seen or heard from again.

10. The Three Missing Lighthouse Keepers

On 21 December 1900 Joseph Moore sailed to Eilean Mor, a tiny island in the Flannan Islands which lies 20 miles west of the Scottish island of Lewis. Eilean Mor is the smallest of the Flannan Isles and has long had a reputation for being haunted, so when Mr Moore had noticed that the 140,000-candlepower light of the island's lighthouse was out, he had felt a shiver down his spine. Now he and two men had to find out why the lighthouse was in darkness. He sounded the foghorn of his supply vessel three times but it failed to elicit a response. No one came from the lighthouse to the jetty, so Mr Moore and the two men advanced slowly to the eerily silhouetted building towering against the stormy evening sky. The entrance gate and main door to the lighthouse were closed, but unlocked. Moore and his men shouted the lighthouse keepers' names as they entered the building and climbed the winding staircase of the turret. There was no sign of life anywhere in the lighthouse, just a baffling scenario. All the wicks of the lanterns had been cleaned and trimmed, but there was no sign of the three lighthouse keepers Thomas Marshall, James Ducat and Donald McArthur. Everything in the lighthouse was in neat order, but there was one curious clue; two of the three sets of oilskins and seaboots belonging to the keepers were missing.

James Moore inspected the logbook of the abandoned lighthouse for further clues to the disappearances, and he came upon the book's final perplexing entry, which read: "December 15: 1 p.m. Storm ended. Sea calm. God is over all."

The fate of the three lighthouse keepers is still a complete mystery. It was said that long ago the hermit St Flannan (who the isles are named after) had a terrifying religious vision on Eilean Mor in which he saw God. The reclusive saint was left insane by his vision. Could the dark history of Eilean Mor have had something to do with the disappearance of the lighthouse men?

Ghostly Planets

According to the orthodox textbooks of astronomy, Venus, the nearest planet to Earth, does not have a moon circling about it. This is entirely true. Venus is continuously under the surveillance of the world's most powerful optical and radio telescopes, and it has also been visited by several space probes, so astronomers and astrophysicists are more than certain that there is no Venusian moon. Yet this was not the case over three centuries ago. On 11 November 1645 Franciscus Fontana, the Italian astronomer who was the first to see and map markings on Mars, turned his telescope to Venus during excellent viewing conditions and saw that the planet had a small crescent moon next to it. Another Italian astronomer, Giovanni Cassini, who discovered four Saturnian moons and the planet's ring division, also saw the Venusian satellite on 28 August 1686 at the Paris Observatory. Cassini was naturally intrigued by the hitherto unseen moon and he scrutinized it through his 34-foot telescope until it was lost in the light of dawn. The next sighting of the enigmatic satellite occurred one morning just before sunrise on 23 October 1740 when James Short, a mathematician and Fellow of the Royal Society, pointed his reflecting telescope at Venus. To the right of the planet Short was very surprised to see a small light which he at first took to be an unusually bright star. However, upon examining the star at a greater magnification, Short was astounded to see that the pinpoint of bright light was either a small planet or a large moon in very close proximity to Venus. The unidentified planetary object showed the same phase as Venus, and Short estimated that the body's diameter was approximately a third of the diameter of Venus. Short excitedly looked for the new moon at the same time on the following morning, but it had vanished. Short surmised that the moon had possibly passed behind Venus, and so he kept watch on the planet for months, but he never saw the mysterious object again.

In 1761 Johann Lambert, the German mathematician and scientist, rediscovered the transient Venusian satellite. The superior optics of Lambert's telescope enabled him to calculate the orbit of the Venusian moon, and he deduced that it took eleven days and five hours to circle Venus at a distance of around 259,000 miles. Frederick the Great of Prussia proposed that the newly discovered satellite of Earth's sister should be named after the French philosopher and mathematician Jean d'Alembert, but the latter kindly declined the offer. Other names were put forward by the monarchs of Europe but, before the moon could be given a name, it went missing in March 1764 and has not been seen since.

How can we explain the appearances of the Venusian moon? All the astronomers who sighted it were professional observers, so we can rule out the satellite being a double image of Venus. In fact, at one point when Venus was obscured entirely by cloud, the image of the satellite persisted, which would not have been the case if the moon had been a false image of Venus.

Could the answer lie in the paranormal? Could it be that under certain conditions a window to the remote past was somehow opened which allowed the astronomers to glimpse the ghostly image of a planet which once circled Venus thousands of years ago? Perhaps the next time the Venusian satellite appears the high-powered Hubble Space Telescope will be trained upon it.

The planet Mars has also presented the astronomers of Earth with a fair share of mysteries. On 16 January 1950 there was a huge explosion on Mars that created a massive cloud 900 miles in diameter which extended over 50 miles above the planet's surface. The cloud was yellow in colour, and the Japanese astronomer Sadao Saeki, who had the best view of the Martian blast, speculated the explosion was the result of a huge volcanic explosion. The strange cataclysm on the Red Planet took place as the Atomic Energy Commission in America was debating whether to build a hydrogen bomb, and the press picked up on public anxiety about the proposed super-weapon and drew a parallel with the devastating explosion on Mars, hinting that perhaps the Martians had just wiped themselves out with their own H-bomb.

The great explosion of 1950 is just one of a series of puzzles from Mars. In 1877 the world-renowned Italian astronomer Giovanni Schiaparelli announced that he had discovered an intricate latticework of straight lines covering the Martian surface. Schiaparelli was not the first to notice these lines, or "canali" (Italian for channels or canals) as he called them; others had seen them too, decades before, but Schiaparelli was the first to draw detailed maps of the dark geometric lines.

In 1894 Schiaparelli's theories about the Martian canals fired the imagination of a former American diplomat who had a keen interest in astronomy. His name was Percival

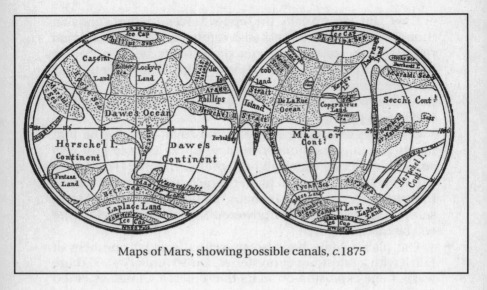

Maps of Mars, showing possible canals, c.1875

Lowell, founder of the Lowell Observatory at Flagstaff, Arizona. In October 1894, Mars was rapidly moving into its most favourable position for observation, and Lowell was ready to focus on it with his new telescope. Seconds after the planet was fixed in the eyepiece, Lowell sighed with amazement as he recognized the latticework of canals Schiaparelli had mentioned. Some of these networks consisted of radiating interconnected lines shaped like a spider's web. Lowell gradually inferred that the criss-crossed lines were irrigation canals which transported water from the polar caps to the arid lands of the Red Planet. Such a feat of engineering surpassed the marvel of the Suez Canal of Earth. The Martians, it seemed to Lowell, were a technically superior but doomed race trying their utmost to save their dying waterless world. Lowell wrote several newspaper articles about the canal networks which proved very popular with public. After the articles, Lowell penned three highly successful books on the Martian civilization, and his controversial views were backed up by radio pioneers Marconi and Tesla, who both believed that they had received coded signals from Mars. However, in the 1960s NASA sent its series of Mariner probes to Mars, and the pictures they beamed back of the planet revealed it had a cratered moon-like surface. There was no trace of the canal network that Lowell, Schiaparelli and others had seen. It was therefore reasoned that no canals had ever existed on Mars; they had been an optical illusion caused by eyestrain. That was the official explanation of NASA; but then, in 1971, a great dust storm cleared on Mars, and two prominent American astronomers, Peter Boyce and Jim Westfall, took a look at the Red Planet with one of the most sophisticated telescopes in the world, at Cerrotollollo in Chile. For three entire hours Peter Boyce saw the Lowellian canal system stretching from the pointed tip of Syrtis Major – a dark triangular marking on Mars. Boyce's colleague Jim Westfall, who was viewing Mars through a separate telescope, was also dumbfounded to see the Martian canals. As the two professional astronomers studied the fantastically constructed canals on the planet Mars in complete awe, the lines faded away. The astronomers were left with the impression that they had just witnessed a mirage of some sort; perhaps a ghostly echo from the past when Mars had a civilization?

PART FIVE

Hauntings

• •

The Cock Lane Ghost

Cock Lane is a short curved thoroughfare in the City of London on the periphery of Smithfield, where a gilded statue of a naked cherubic boy juts from a wall to indicate where the flames of the Great Fire finally petered out in 1666. In the middle of the eighteenth century, Cock Lane was a respectable locality that consisted of tradesmen's shops, private houses, a charity school, and a tavern named the Wheat Sheaf. What is now Number 20 was once the home of Richard Parsons, who drew a wage as the officiating clerk at the local church of St Sepulchre, Snow Hill. Parsons had a wife and two young daughters, the eldest of these being Elizabeth, who was 11 when the strange episode of the Cock Lane Ghost began.

Encumbered with mounting debts because of his incessant heavy drinking in the Wheat Sheaf, Richard Parsons had no choice but to take in lodgers. In October 1759 a well-mannered couple from Norfolk looking for lodgings approached Parsons. They were William and Fanny Kent, and they explained that they were only looking for a temporary place to stay until their newly purchased house in Clerkenwell was ready for them. Parsons took them in after William Kent paid him advance rent. Within a few days the landlord and lodger were on sufficiently congenial terms for Williams to lend Parsons 12 guineas, to be repaid at a guinea per month. Williams regarded Parsons as a trustworthy man, and he let the landlord in on his dark secret; he and Mrs Kent were not married at all. Fanny was in fact the sister of his deceased wife Elizabeth, who had tragically died during childbirth two years previously. A month after Elizabeth's death, her child also died, and the trauma of the two dreadful events brought William and Fanny – who had been looking after her sister – very close indeed. The law at that time in history forbade marriage between bereaved brothers and sisters-in-law, so the couple had opted to live in sin. Now they had come to London to start a new life together. Mr Kent went on to tell Parsons that he and "Mrs Kent" had recently proved their mutual love and trust by making wills in each other's favour. If Fanny died, she would bequeath £100 to

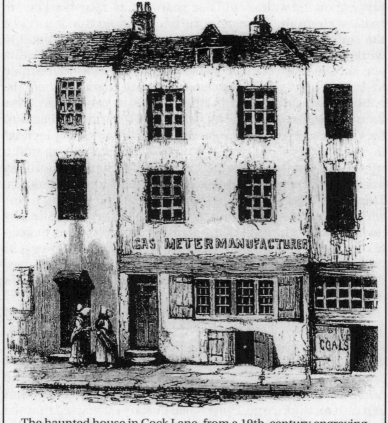

The haunted house in Cock Lane, from a 19th-century engraving

him, and half a crown to each of her two brothers. If he should expire, he would leave his sweetheart a vague "considerable fortune" – the amount of which was never specified.

The Kents soon settled in at the house in Cock Lane, and Fanny Kent gradually struck up a friendship with Parson's young daughter, Elizabeth. One night in the autumn of that year Fanny's maid, Esther Carlisle, a red-haired girl nicknamed "Carrots", was away on leave, and Fanny was so uneasy about sleeping alone that she asked Elizabeth to share her four-poster bed for a few nights. During the couple of nights the pair slept together, they were both startled from their sleep by an eerie noise that sounded as if someone was rapping on the wainscot of the bedroom. Elizabeth asked her mother about the strange noise, and was told that it was just the sound of the cobbler next door who was in the habit of working into the early hours of the morning. This explanation was subsequently rebutted when the rapping sound resumed in Fanny Kent's bedroom on a Sunday night – when the cobbler was absent from the premises next door. This naturally alarmed Elizabeth, Fanny and Mr and Mrs Parsons; they quickly surmised there was a ghost at work. Why it chose to knock on the wall was a puzzle. What was the phantom trying to communicate? The neurotic Fanny morbidly interpreted the knocks as a warning of her impending death. The eerie sounds continued night after night, playing havoc with the nerves and sleeping patterns of everyone in the household. Around this time Richard Parsons failed to keep his agreement to pay back one guinea a month to Mr Kent, so the lodger put the matter into the hands of his attorney, and Parsons retaliated by telling everyone that Mr Kent's marriage had been a bogus affair.

In January of the following year the Kents finally moved into what they had long regarded as their "little dream house" at Bartlet Court, Clerkenwell, but soon after they settled down in their new home Fanny, who was six months pregnant, became very ill. A Dr Cooper examined Fanny and noted the symptoms of fever, prostration, and the telltale signs of a rash on the face and hands. He quickly diagnosed that she was suffering from "a confluent smallpox of a very virulent nature".

William Kent immediately hired Dr James Jones, a highly-regarded apothecary from Grafton Street, but Jones could do nothing to save her, and so, on 2 February 1760, Fanny Kent passed away in a delirious state. The hypocritical Richard Parsons saw the woman's death as a punishment from God for her sins. The sanctimonious inebriate also had a theory about the ghost which was still tapping on the wainscot of his house; he believed the supernatural entity was the restless spirit of Fanny's dead sister Elizabeth. Furthermore, a week before Fanny's death, he had been terrified by a visual sighting of the ghost at the Cock Lane house, and he knew he had not been imagining things, because James Franzen, the landlord of the Wheat Sheaf (who had been bringing a tankard of beer to Parsons late at night), had also witnessed what was described as a highly luminous figure of a shrouded woman with no hands. The radiant spectre had flitted across the hallway and darted up the stairs at an incredible speed. Parsons and Franzen had both noted that the shining vision was sufficiently luminous to light up the face of the clock on the charity school across the street.

Distraught with grief, William Kent ordered a decent "lined and covered" coffin for Fanny Lynes. Fearing prosecution because of the sham marriage, Kent instructed the undertaker to leave the nameplate on the coffin lid blank. As her family seethed over the questionable stipulations of her will, Fanny was laid to rest in the twelfth-century vaults of St John's Church in Clerkenwell.

Back at 20 Cock Lane, the rappings continued. Two new lodgers, Joyce Weatheral and Catherine Friend, heard the poltergeist and fled the house. Richard Parsons tried to persuade the lodgers to stay, but the women sought accommodation elsewhere. Parsons realized that the spook would soon leave him broke if he didn't get it exorcized, so he called for the services of the Reverend John Moore, the curate at Smithfield's St Bartholomew the Great. The curate was a follower of John Wesley, the Methodist founder who had allegedly communicated with a "knocking spirit" by rapping once for yes and twice for no. Moore discussed the nature of the noisy ghost with Parsons, who now believed that the rapping spook was the spirit of the recently departed Fanny

Lynes. The curate was gullible enough to be convinced of the alcoholic landlord's theory, and when he held a seance in young Elizabeth's bedroom where the ghost was currently performing he asked the entity questions that had been posed by Richard Parsons. The result of the lengthy interrogation was the following chilling statement, made by the poltergeist via the rap-code: "I am the ghost of Frances Lynes, who lived in fornification with Mr Kent, whose first wife was my own sister. He poisoned me by putting red arsenic in my glass of purl which I drank while recovering from the smallpox. One hour before I died, I told Carrots what he had done."

The sensational accusation from beyond the grave impelled Parsons and Moore to do some practical detective work. They obtained Fanny's will and read of the suspicious proviso it contained. Parsons made the case against William Kent look grimmer by inventing another piece of damning evidence; he told the curate that Fanny's other sister from Pall Mall had informed him that she had called at the house at Clerkenwell on the day before Fanny's death, and her sister had been rapidly improving from her sickness. Moore was horrified at this revelation. Parsons then published a paper accusing William Kent of poisoning his pseudo-wife for her money.

Kent, who had been setting himself up as a stockbroker in the City as he recovered from his bereavement, read of the continuing Cock Lane saga in a series of melodramatic articles in the *Public Ledger*. He was absolutely appalled by the vicious allegations from a drunk who still owed him 11 guineas. Kent visited Revd Moore at his church in West Smithfield and almost broke down as he denied the "cruel untruths perpetuated by the blackguard Parsons".

Moore was swayed by Kent's gentle manner and bearing, but told him that he was convinced there was a real spirit or possibly a demon at work at Cock Lane. The curate convinced Kent to come to the haunted house to sit in on a seance so he could experience the phenomenon himself. Kent soon regretted confronting the ghost. The knocks accused him of murdering Fanny with arsenic. "Should I be hanged, then?" asked Kent, with tears streaming from his eyes. The curate had asked Kent to pose that question out loud.

The answer was a single knock, the code for "yes".

"Thou art a lying spirit," Kent cried. "Thou art not the ghost of my Fanny. She would never have said such a thing!"

By now, the story of the Cock Lane ghost had all London talking. Thanks to street gossip and the *Public Ledger*'s astonishing articles, the supernatural affair had become a matter of enormous public interest, and crowds flocked to Cock Lane to congregate around Number 20 to witness the comings and goings of clergymen and reporters. One spectator of the mania was the chronicler Horace Walpole, who wrote to a friend in Italy:

> *I am ashamed to tell you that we are again dipped into an egregious scene of folly. The reigning fashion is a ghost – a ghost that would not pass muster in the paltriest convent in the Apennines. It only knocks and scratches: does not pretend to appear or to speak. The clergy give it their benediction; and all the world, whether believers or infidels, go to hear it. All the taverns and ale houses in the neighbourhood make fortunes.*

Walpole's curiosity grew as the supernatural occurrences at Cock Lane developed. More clergymen visited the haunted premises, accompanied by William Legge, the Earl of Dartmouth. Walpole decided to call in at the house himself with the Duke of York, Lord Hertford, and two peeresses.

William Legge had Elizabeth Parsons – who seemed to be the focus of the poltergeist activity – moved to another house to see what would happen. The knocking ghost went with her. This indicated that Elizabeth, and not the Cock Lane premises, was the catalyst in the ghostly goings-on. The girl was watched closely as the rapping sounds echoed around the room of her temporary dwelling, but no fraud could be detected. Elizabeth's hands and feet were held tightly and scrutinized at close quarters, and it could plainly be seen that she was not generating the strange noises.

The proceedings in the Cock Lane "trial" had now taken on the air of a kangaroo court. The maidservant "Carrots" Carlisle had been traced and brought before the rapping spectre. She admitted she had been in the service of the Kents for the last four days of Fanny's life, but fiercely denied that her mistress had told her she had been poisoned. The ghost said she was lying, and Carlisle shouted, "Then I am sure, Madam, you may be ashamed of yourself, for I never hurt you in my life!"

The doctor and apothecary who had attended Fanny 50 hours before she passed away denied that William Kent could have poisoned her. Both men maintained that Fanny had drunk only their preparations. But the clergymen argued that a lot could have been done within the 50 hours when the medical men were not present.

Meanwhile, Elizabeth Parsons began to have epileptic fits after claiming to have seen the Cock Lane ghost, which she described as a bright shrouded figure with no hands. This description tallied well with the accounts given by her father and James Franzen, who had also allegedly had encounters with the ghost. Elizabeth's fits seemed to accompany her expressed concern for the fate of her father, for she feared that the authorities would brand him a charlatan and throw him into prison.

Moore became totally convinced of Kent's guilt, and he urged the Lord Mayor, Sir Samuel Fludyer, to arrest Kent for suspected murder. The Lord Mayor refused Moore's request, and he also rejected Kent's plea to arrest Richard Parsons for fraud and malicious defamation. Instead, the mayor insisted on an unbiased independent investigation into the affair at the house of the Revd Stephen Aldrich, vicar of St John's Church at Clerkenwell. Aldrich formed a committee with Lord Dartmouth. They selected Dr John Douglas (the future Bishop of Salisbury), a seasoned ghost-hunter who had exposed a number of frauds, Mrs Oakes, a hospital matron, Dr George Macaulay, a distinguished physician, two gentlemen, and the writer Dr Samuel Johnson, a man who had long been fascinated by ghosts and the spirit world. Johnson had once confided to his biographer James Boswell that he was absolutely horrified at the idea of total oblivion after death.

The "Committee of Gentlemen" as the press of the day called them, gathered at Aldrich's house at Clerkenwell on the evening of 1 February 1762. Several justices of the peace also arrived to act as independent observers. Elizabeth Parsons was undressed, examined and put to bed by Mrs Oakes. The bed was the only piece of furniture in the room. At ten o'clock the investigators came up to the bedroom and waited there for almost an hour, but there were no rappings or any metaphysical manifestations. Dr Johnson noted that Elizabeth Parsons seemed restless, and when he inquired why this was so, the girl said that she could feel the spirit tickling her back like a little mouse.

At a previous seance the spirit had signified by knocking that it would manifest itself in the vault under St John's Church, where the coffin of Fanny Lynes lay, so the committee went downstairs and prepared to make the trip to the vault. Minutes later, the ghost started to scratch the bedroom walls upstairs. The committee rushed up to the room to hear the last scraping sounds. Elizabeth was ordered to lift her hands from beneath the bedclothes for all to see. One of the men addressed the ghost, requesting it to make its presence known by a single knock. An uneasy silence followed, but the ghost did not answer.

Thirty minutes later, the committee entered the eerie vault of St John's Church and, again, the spirit was addressed and reminded of its promise to signal its presence by rapping on Fanny's coffin. The men waited in the cold but no answer came. Suspecting that they had been the victims of an infantile hoax perpetrated by the young Elizabeth Parsons, the learned gentlemen returned to Aldrich's home and interrogated the girl for hours, but she would not admit that she had been fooling them. Shortly before 3 a.m. Elizabeth was allowed to go home with her indignant father, who rejected all the allegations that his daughter had manufactured the Cock Lane ghost for fun and attention. Mr Parsons also maintained that the spirit had not performed at the vault because the coffin of Fanny Lynes had been robbed of its corpse by some curious ghoul. This claim was later disproved when William Kent permitted the sexton at St John's Church to remove the lid on Fanny's coffin. The shroud was lifted from the corpse, and the heartbroken Kent almost fainted as he looked upon Fanny's body. He simply said, "Yes. That is her," and the lid was replaced.

Elizabeth was given one final chance to prove her innocence at the house of a gentleman named Missiter in Convent Garden. If she should fail to verify her innocence there would be dire consequences; she and her father and mother would be sent to Newgate. Elizabeth was naturally afraid of what would befall the family if the spirit did not communicate, so, at an opportune moment, she took a wooden board (used for standing the kettle on) from the kitchen, concealed it in her night-dress, and later scratched upon it to simulate the poltergeist sounds. But two maids spotted the board beneath the blankets and alerted her father. He showed it to the investigators and explained that his daughter had been frightened by the non-appearance of the ghost and of the terrible consequences with which the family would be threatened, so she had amateurishly tried to fake the sounds of the ghost herself. Mr Parsons then added that all the previous visitations of the Cock Lane ghost had been genuine, and that he would willingly swear upon the Bible to prove that he had seen an apparition of the spirit in the company of James Franzen, the landlord of the Wheat Sheaf. But the tide was turning in Kent's favour. He published a pamphlet entitled "The Mystery Revealed" which contained a powerful account of his innocence, and how he had been defamed by Richard Parsons, the drunken debtor who still owed him a large sum of money. By the summer of that year proceedings were begun against the Cock Lane hoaxers at the Court of King's Bench, Guildhall. Appearing before Lord Mansfield, the Revd John Moore and Mr and Mrs Parsons were charged with conspiring to take away the life of William Kent by charging him with the murder of Frances Lynes. The trial lasted for a day, and the accused were found guilty. Lord Mansfield decided against pronouncing sentence until he had discussed the extraordinary case with other judges. It was decided that William Kent was entitled to more than the vindication of his good name. In the name of justice he merited substantial damages for the slanderous statements that had been made against him for over six months. Revd Moore was ordered to pay Kent £300, and later had to foot the bill for court costs. The curate was so shaken by the ordeal that he died soon afterwards. Eight months passed, and the

Parsons had still not paid a penny in compensation to Mr Kent, so Mr Parsons was sentenced to two years in Newgate and required to stand in the pillory three times. Mrs Parsons was imprisoned at the Bridewell for six months' hard labour.

For some reason the crowd of bystanders who watched Parsons in the pillory did not jeer at him or pelt him with pieces of stinking fish or rotten eggs. Many were moved by the sight of the pilloried man, and passed around the hat for a collection. When Parsons was released from Newgate in February 1765 he was given the proceeds from the two-year collection and started his life anew. Elizabeth Parsons still maintained that the ghost had been real, but was too terrified to talk about the affair in detail. She later married, but not at St Sepulchre's. She seems to have spent her last days in obscurity, far from Smithfield. Richard Parsons gave a speech upon his return to the Wheat Sheaf ale house. He said it was true that he had had his differences with William Kent, but he was, drunkenness apart, a well-liked and good-natured man of previous good character who had made nothing from the Cock Lane affair. He also drew attention to the fact that hundreds of people – including Horace Walpole, the Duke of York, and Lord Hertford – had heard the knockings from the wainscot of his daughter's bedroom, and that all of these people had vouched that the sounds had come a good distance from Elizabeth's bed.

Did Elizabeth Parsons fake the Cock Lane ghost, or was she the centre of a genuine poltergeist case? Parapsychologists today have noted that, for some unknown reason, prepubescent girls are often the focal point of poltergeist outbreaks. Perhaps the entity at Cock Lane was genuine, but interpreted wrongly by Mr Parsons and Revd Moore; after all, the mysterious scratchings were first heard when Francis Lynes was alive, so why were the noises later attributed to her? Unless the original noises were made by another ghost; perhaps the spirit of William Kent's first wife, Elizabeth? If this was the case, was Elizabeth warning her sister of an untimely death – at the hands of Kent? There is a twist in the tale of the Cock Lane ghost that points the finger of suspicion to Kent.

In 1850 J. W. Archer, an illustrator, got permission to open the coffin of Francis Lynes so he could sketch her remains for a book by Charles McKay entitled *Memoirs of Extraordinary Popular Delusions*, which contained an account of the Cock Lane ghost. By the light of the sexton boy's lantern, Archer watched as the coffin lid was unscrewed and removed. The body within was perfectly preserved, and Archer beheld the face of a beautiful woman with an aquiline nose. The cheeks of her face showed no scarring from the smallpox that was said to have killed her. Archer remarked that such preservation in bodies was usually evidence of arsenic poisoning. But no proper inquest was held; forensic science in the middle of the nineteenth century was virtually non-existent.

The Penny Lane Poltergeist

When the Beatles immortalized Liverpool's Penny Lane in their world-famous song, they didn't mention the poltergeist who lives at No. 44 . . .

In 1930 a family living in Penny Lane were startled out of their sleep one night by loud noises and thudding footsteps emanating from No. 44, the unoccupied house next door to them.

The source of the nocturnal racket was sought, but to no avail, and every night the eerie sound of a restless, insomni-acal walker prevented them from sleeping. In the end the tormented neighbours decided to move to another house to escape the nightly cacophony, and another unsuspecting family moved in to take their place.

The new neighbours of the noisy Penny Lane ghost had no knowledge of the previous family's predicament, and they soon settled down into their new home. Then, one night in 1945, the sounds of a heavy tread and an unearthly voice were heard.

The family knew the sounds were coming from the shop next door at No. 44, but couldn't fathom out who was making all the noise, as the shop had been left uninhabited since being damaged by bombs during the Blitz. Many more noisy, nerve-shattering nights followed, and the new residents quickly realized that something strange was going on in the empty shop next door.

After a long hiatus, the poltergeist came out of retirement and, in January 1971, gave an unprecedented performance. At the time of the comeback No. 44 was the "Xerolith" printing shop, owned by Ken Shackman and John Hampton. One winter evening, when Messrs Shackman and Hampton had left the shop's premises, the loud sounds of some-one pacing the floor of the empty shop grew to such intensity that neighbours complained to the police and the shop's owners.

The police investigated the matter with the usual scepti-cism they show when they look into such matters, and drew a blank, but Shackman and Hampton remained open-minded about the ghost in their shop, and they decided to research the history of No. 44.

They shuddered when they unearthed the accounts of the previous families who had left the houses on each side of No. 44 after reporting the same walking and shuffling noises.

After a journalist from the *Liverpool Echo* wrote a number of articles on the ghost's activities Shackman and Hampton were inundated with letters and phone-calls from former Penny Lane residents who had actually heard the noisy spectre. One woman who had lived in a manor house near the haunted printing shop as a child wrote about a supernatural entity she encountered just after World War I.

The woman wrote to say she heard the sound of feet walking heavily on stone steps while in her bedroom one night with her four sisters. Shortly afterwards the figure of a young woman materialized in front of her. The phantom girl just stood there for a few minutes, calmly combing her long locks of blonde hair before vanishing.

Eager to get to the bottom of the mystery once and for all, Shackman and Hampton resorted to a thorough search of the printing shop, and had the floorboards taken up, then the walls checked, the furniture examined, and the roof inspected. When the search failed to throw any light on the matter, the owners of the printing shop equipped themselves with a tape recorder and sat up all night in the house next door.

It was to be a night to remember. The tape rolled and the two brave men waited anxiously for the ghost to walk. They didn't have to wait long.

Banging and shuffling started echoing through the room, then pandemonium let loose and the walls began to vibrate. At the end of the vigil the amateur ghost-hunters rewound the tape and listened. The tape had actually recorded the sounds of the unseen walker – conclusive proof that the phenomena were not of a psychological origin.

Shackman and Hampton and the neighbours of No. 44 noticed that the ghost was most active on Friday, Saturday and Monday nights, but why the ghost worked overtime on these particular nights of the week is anybody's guess.

In time the ghostly noises became fainter and fainter, until the nights at the printing shop were filled with an uneasy silence.

Nowadays, No. 44 is a pottery shop, and at the present time the new residents have not reported any nightly disturbances, but strange sounds have apparently been heard in the shop next door . . .

The Penny Lane Poltergeist might make a comeback yet.

The Berkeley Square Entity

Long before Mayfair's Berkeley Square was synonymous with nightingales (thanks to Eric Maschwitz's song), the place was invariably associated with a rather nasty ghost that was alleged to inhabit No. 50, a four-storey townhouse that dated back to the 1740s. It was once the London home of prime minister George Canning (1770–1827), but it seems very unlikely that the well-documented supernatural occurrences there are anything to do with his spirit, as Canning died at Chiswick.

No one seems to know just what haunted No. 50, because few who encountered it lived to tell the tale, and those who did survive were always left insane by the supernatural confrontation. All we can do is piece together the fragments of anecdotes and accounts that concern the Berkeley Square entity.

In 1840 the 20-year-old dandy and notorious rake Sir Robert Warboys heard the eerie rumours about the Berkeley Square "Thing" in a Holborn tavern one night, and laughingly dismissed the tales as "unadulterated poppycock". Sir Robert's friends disagreed with him, and dared him to spend a night in the haunted second-floor room in Berkeley Square. Warboys raised his flagon of ale in the air and announced: "I wholeheartedly accept your preposterous harebrained challenge!"

That same night Sir Robert visited the haunted premises to arrange an all-night vigil with the landlord. The landlord tried to talk Sir Robert out of the dare, but the young man refused to listen, and demanded to be put up for the night in the haunted room. The landlord finally gave in to Sir Robert's demands, but stipulated two conditions: if the young man saw anything "unearthly" he was to pull a cord that would ring a bell in the landlord's room below; secondly, Sir Robert would have to be armed with a pistol throughout the vigil. The young libertine thought the conditions were absurd, but agreed to them just to get the landlord out of his hair.

The landlord handed Warboys a pistol and left as a clock in the room chimed the hour of midnight. Sir Robert sat at a table in the candlelit room and waited for the "Thing" to put in an appearance.

Forty-five minutes after midnight, the landlord was startled out of his sleep by the violent jangling of the bell. A single gunshot in the room above echoed through the house. The landlord raced upstairs and found Sir Robert sitting on the floor in the corner of the room with a smoking pistol in his hand. The young man had evidently died from traumatic shock, for his eyes were bulged, and his lips were curled from his clenched teeth. The landlord followed the line of sight from the dead man's terrible gaze and traced it to a single bullet hole in the opposite wall. He quickly deduced that Warboys had fired at the "Thing", to no avail.

Three years after Warboys's death, Edward Blunden and

Robert Martin, two sailors from Portsmouth, wandered into Berkeley Square in a drunken state and noticed the "To Let" sign at No. 50. They had squandered most of their wages on drink and couldn't afford lodgings, so they broke in. Finding the lower floors too damp, the sailors staggered upstairs and finally settled down on the floor of the infamous room. It proved to be a serious mistake. Blunden told his friend he felt nervous in the room, and felt a "presence", but Martin told his shipmate he'd been at sea too long, and was soon snoring.

A little over an hour later, the door of the room burst open, and the enormous shadowy figure of a man floated towards the sailors. Martin woke up and found himself unable to move. He was paralyzed with fear. Blunden tried to get to his feet, but the entity seized him by the throat with its cold, misty-looking hands and started to choke him.

Martin suddenly gained enough courage to enable him to spring to his feet. He tried to confront the apparition, but was so horrified by its deformed face and body that he found himself fleeing from the house. He encountered a policeman in the square outside and told him of the vapoury assailant that was throttling his friend. The bemused policeman followed the distressed sailor into No. 50 and when the two men entered the room up on the second floor there was no sign of Blunden. They searched the entire house, and found the missing sailor's body in the basement. His neck had been broken and his face was contorted in a terror-stricken grimace.

Documentary evidence for the aforementioned incidents is very scant, but the eminent psychical researcher Harry Price unearthed a great deal of data on the Berkeley Square bogeyman while investigating the case in the 1920s. Price scoured periodicals and newspapers from the mid eighteenth century onwards for a reference to the ghost of Berkeley Square, and discovered that in the 1790s a gang of counterfeiters and coin-clippers had used the house as their headquarters. Price speculated that the criminals had invented the ghost to disguise the true nature of the bumps in the night: the printing presses churning out bank notes. But the theory could not explain how the ghost was heard decades after the counterfeit gang had been detected and thrown into prison. Price discovered more intriguing references to the ghost. In 1840 several neighbours of 50 Berkeley Square heard a medley of strange sounds emanating from the haunted house: bumps on the stairs, dragging noises as if heavy objects were being moved around, jangling of signal bells below the stairs, and the tramping of footsteps. Price read that one of the braver neighbours who had grown weary of the noisy spectre obtained a key and dashed into the house one night during the creepy cacophony. There was no one in the house. Down in the kitchen, the signal bells were still bouncing on their curled springs.

Price found another thought-provoking account of the ghost in *Notes and Queries*, a magazine published during the 1870s. An article in the publication by the writer W. E. Howlett stated:

> *The mystery of Berkeley Square still remains a mystery. The story of the haunted house in Mayfair can be recapitulated in a few words; the house contains at least one room of which the atmosphere is supernaturally fatal to body and mind. A girl saw, heard and felt such horror in it that she went mad, and never recovered sanity enough to tell how or why.*
>
> *A gentleman, a disbeliever in ghosts, dared to sleep in No. 50 and was found a corpse in the middle of the floor after frantically ringing for help in vain. Rumour suggests other cases of the same kind, all ending in death, madness, or both as a result of sleeping, or trying to sleep in that room. The very party walls of the house, when touched, are found saturated with electric horror. It is uninhabited save by an elderly man and his wife who act as caretakers; but even these have no access to the room. This is kept locked, the key being in the hands of a mysterious and seemingly nameless person who comes to the house once every six months, locks up the elderly couple in the basement, and then unlocks the room and occupies himself in it for hours.*

Price continued to research the history of No. 50, and learned that the house had been empty for remarkably long periods, yet the address was one of the most desirable ones in London, so why had the house been left vacant for so long? Had the rumours scared off prospective occupants, or had the ghost itself frightened them away? Price could not answer this question, nor could he draw any firm conclusions to the whole case. His final surmise was that a particularly nasty poltergeist had been active in the 1840s, but doubted that the "Thing" was still at large. But there have been many ghostly encounters at No. 50 in recent times. In January 1937 Mrs Mary Balfour, an octogenarian lady of a stately Scottish family, moved into a flat in Charles Street, which lies adjacent to Berkeley Square. One night Mrs Balfour's maid summoned her to come to the kitchen situated at the rear of the flat. The maid was staring intently through the window at the rear of a house diagonally opposite. It was the rear of Berkeley Square. The maid drew Mrs Balfour's attention to one of the rear windows of No. 50, where a man stood dressed in a silver-coloured coat and breeches. He wore a periwig and had a drawn, morose, ashen face. The two women thought he had been to some New Year fancy dress party, because his clothes were centuries out of date. The man moved away from the window, and Mrs Balfour and her maid were later shocked to learn from a doctor that they had sighted one of the ghosts of 50 Berkeley Square. The doctor told them that it was currently unoccupied, but workmen in the building two months back had seen the phantom of a little girl in a kilt on the stairs.

Stories of the haunted house continue to circulate today in Mayfair. Late at night, faces are said to peep out from the upper windows of No. 50, which is now occupied by a firm of antiquarian book sellers. Will the "Thing" ever make a comeback? Only time will tell.

The Ancient Ones

The following very old legend is mentioned all over the world by different nations and tribes in one form or another; many mystics and students of the Occult say it is the true history of mankind. According to the legend, a long time ago, long before the flood, long before humans walked upon the Earth, intelligent godlike beings came across our world and fought among themselves over the ownership of the planet. This ancient legend says that there was a war in the heavens over the possession of Earth, and that a brilliant scientist-like figure named Lucifer was defeated by a group of super-intelligent beings known as the Elohim. The rebellious Lucifer and his followers took refuge beneath the planet in caves and caverns, and the Elohim took possession of the Earth, which they called Eden, and all other extraterrestrial beings were warned off from the planet's vicinity. The mystics say that there are ancient texts in Tibet which tell of how the gods destroyed horrific dragons and monsters that lived in the land and the seas; could these monsters have been the dinosaurs, which were mysteriously wiped out 65 million years ago?

What became of Lucifer and his cohorts? According to the legends, they are still beneath the earth in a type of sleep, but their physical bodies have long decayed, and only their evil spirits exist now. The folklore experts of the world mention these underground spirits, and call them the Ancient Ones. It is said that they are lying dormant, just waiting for a source of energy to revitalize them, and they are also said to be the very essence of evil, with a tremendous drive to kill those who disturb them.

In 1996, during massive excavations across the Berkshire countryside for the planned Newbury bypass, a bulldozer overturned for no apparent reason and its driver was seriously injured. Green activists were immediately suspected of sabotaging the vehicle, but investigators saw that no human agency had been involved in the incident. There were two groups of four dents in the panels of the bulldozer as if something with titanic strength had seized the bulldozer with its hands and pushed it over.

That same night a squad of 12 security guards who were patrolling the cyclone fences and enormous barbed-wire barriers of the excavation zone heard a frantic cry for help on their radios. The call came from a guard in an overturned portakabin. The guard, named Steve, said something was attacking him, and the message from his radio receiver seemed garbled with interference. When the guards arrived at the scene, they saw that the enormous 46-foot-long mobile living-quarters unit had been turned on its side. Something had uprooted the enormous portakabin and had apparently bashed its walls in. A ladder was brought to the scene and three guards climbed it to gain access to the door of the tipped-over cabin, which was now on the top of the living quarters. Inside, they found Steve in agony with a broken collarbone and a sprained arm. He seemed terrified, and clutched his torch in the darkness. He rambled on about a huge misty object with long arms that rose out of one of the excavated pits and chased him. The guards told Steve to be quiet and carefully lifted him out the overturned portakabin. Then something unbelievable happened. As the guards were descending the ladder with Steve, one of the eight other security guards pointed to a huge hole and shouted: "Look! What is it?"

Reports differ about what exactly happened next, but it is said that a vapour rose from the hole and materialized into a strange elongated figure with long arms which hovered threateningly towards the security men. Five Alsatians were unleashed and ordered to attack the vaporous entity. Three of the dogs dropped dead in their tracks, and the other two yelped and ran off. The guards fled when they saw the menacing thing drifting in their direction, and noticed that there was suddenly a lot of interference on their radios and mobile phones. The nebulous object was heard to buzz and crackle as if it was made up from electrical energy. Two guards who were near to the apparition said it had two twinkling spots of yellow light which looked like a pair of eyes. It is alleged that a governmental committee sanctioned a team of ghost busters and even a Church of England vicar to identify and hopefully exorcize the ghost, but the cleric and the paranormal researchers both agreed that the thing that had scared the wits out of the security guards was not a ghost – but a powerful spirit of something that had never lived as a human. Research uncovered that even the Saxons had regarded the place where the thing had been seen as a taboo area for some reason. The vicar was of the opinion that the entity was extremely ancient, and advised the committee to fill in the pit where the thing was seen to emerge from. The pit was filled in with earth that had been excavated from the spot and, as yet, there have been no further sightings of the mighty apparition. Was the vaporous being a manifestation of one of the fabled Ancient Ones who took refuge under the earth with Lucifer?

The Camera Never Lies

The following strange story is a well documented incident which took place in the late nineteenth century in San Francisco.

In July 1900 Eliza Marwood, the 56-year-old wife of wealthy silver merchant Charles Marwood, passed away at her palatial home in the exclusive Nob Hill district of San Francisco. In the front parlour of her house she was laid to rest in an open coffin, covered in roses. Thick white drapes on the windows, put up as a traditional mark of respect, allowed very little light into the parlour. Mr Marwood summoned a competent photographer named Anthony Parkes to take a tasteful series of photographs of the wake, but when the cameraman arrived he said the thick curtains on the windows were not letting in sufficient light to allow him to take a photograph of the subject in the normal manner. A flash would have made the corpse seem even paler.

"Then what do you propose?" asked Mr Marwood. He certainly had no intention of opening the curtains; that would be highly disrespectful.

Mr Parkes said: "I will have to take a long exposure. A series of exposures, in fact, if you wish to have several plates made."

"Very well, do what you must," said Mr Marwood, and the photographer said he would need the utmost privacy with no interruptions. The husband of the deceased woman therefore left the parlour and told the rest of the family and grieving relatives not to enter the parlour for an hour.

Mr Parkes was a little unnerved by the task. It was the first time he had photographed a corpse, although many families who regarded the camera as a novelty were now having loved ones who had passed away photographed for posterity.

Parkes set up his camera on the tripod and after focusing

and opening the aperture to its full extent to allow as much light into the camera obscura as possible, he opened the shutter, uncapped the lens, and stepped out of the parlour for a while. He calculated he would give the first exposure just three minutes, but didn't fancy hanging around the corpse in the silent parlour for even that short span of time.

"Has a problem arisen?" Mr Marwood asked the cameraman, who emerged from the parlour with a slight look of anxiety.

"No, sir," Mr Parkes replied, "merely came out to minimize any vibration to the camera while it takes the scene in." And the photographer occasionally studied his pocket watch until the allotted time had passed. Mr Parkes took two more exposures of the corpse that day, then returned to his darkroom in the attic of his house. By the red lamp which hung from a crossbeam in the attic, the photographer began his familiar routine to develop the glass plates. He held the plate by the edges beween his fingers and moved it about in the tray of developer fluid. Slowly, the ghostly image of Mrs Marwood started to materialize on the plate. What Mr Parkes saw on that plate almost made him drop it with fright.

Mrs Marwood's eyes were open wide, and staring with an angry but sinister look, straight into the camera lens.

And yet Mr Parkes had known that the eyes of the corpse had of course been closed while it was lying in the parlour.

Although he was very nervous in the quiet darkroom with that weird picture, Mr Parkes put the plate in the stop tray to prevent over-development, then treated it with fixing fluid to stabilize the image.

With trepidation and a pounding heart, the photographer went about developing the next tray. This picture was even more disturbing, for it showed a curious blur. It was a blur seemingly caused by the corpse moving its head during the long exposure. Mr Parkes knew this was impossible. The only explanation he could think of was that a small child had hidden in the parlour during the exposures, and had moved the coffin – but that wouldn't explain how the eyes were staring with such a lifelike gaze.

The third plate was finally developed, and it showed what

resembled a long finely transparent veil hanging vertically over the open coffin, and the end of this strange cobweb-like mass seeming to taper into Mrs Marwood's mouth.

Although Mr Parkes was a scientific man, he had a sneaking suspicion that the camera had somehow captured the dead woman's spirit leaving her body.

Parkes wrestled with his ethical principles for some time, then finally decided he would show the unsettling photographic plates to Mr Marwood.

Charles Marwood recoiled in terror when he saw the plates, and accused the photographer of faking the strange effects his camera had recorded. Mr Parkes pointed out that he had not even been present during the exposures; he had been standing outside the parlour as the camera recorded the strange images.

After Mr Parkes left in a huff, a niece of Mr Marwood came forward and said that something strange had happened when she had gone into the parlour to pay her last respects to her late auntie. The girl had been praying four feet away from the open coffin, when she heard a sound. She opened her eyes and saw that three of the roses from the enormous bouquet on Mrs Marwood's chest had just been hurled across the room and had landed on the keyboard lid of the piano. Then something even more startling happened – the niece swore that she saw her dead auntie open one eye for a moment then shut it again. The girl was so scared she immediately left the parlour.

What became of the weird photographic plates is unknown, but they were meticulously analyzed by the American Psychical Research Society although never explained. However, the neighbours of the Marwood family later claimed that the ghostly goings-on at the wake were due to the fact that Mr Marwood was having an affair with the very florist who had supplied him with the floral tributes for the funeral. It is said that, even today, the former home of the Marwoods in Nob Hill is still haunted by the forlorn-looking phantom of the betrayed Mrs Marwood.

Cannibal Captain

The following salty spine-tingler was reported in an old nineteenth-century newspaper called the *Liverpool Albion* . . .

In July 1884 a cargo-carrying brigantine called the *Pierrot* set sail from Montevideo for a return journey back to the port of Liverpool. The *Pierrot* was a large vessel, some 110 feet long and 30 feet across the beam. She weighed 282 tons.

The ship was under the command of a seasoned old Liverpool captain, Edward Grace, a man who was renowned in Liverpool's maritime community as a sinister eccentric. Grace was known to be a member of a bizarre club in London called the Society for the Acclimatization of Animals in the United Kingdom. This was an organization devoted to increasing the nation's food supplies by breeding anything from kangaroos to bison in the fields of England. The founder of this fellowship of crackpots was a friend of Captain Grace named Francis Buckland, a wealthy surgeon and eminent naturalist. Buckland was notorious for eating boiled elephant trunk, mice on toast, and stewed mole with bluebottles. On one occasion, Buckland and Grace allegedly ate the preserved relic of a monarch, just to prove that it was edible. The organ they dined upon was the heart of Louis XIV, which had been plundered from the royal tomb during the French Revolution. Buckland and Grace did not even suffer from the slightest effects of indigestion, and both agreed that the heart tasted better with gravy made from the blood of a marmoset monkey.

Only two members of the *Pierrot*'s crew of nine knew about the captain's perverted appetite. They were First Mate Jack Burbage and Second Mate Albert Gribbin, and they found Grace a repulsive and domineering man. Both men vowed that they would never serve under his command again after this voyage was completed.

However, in the middle of the Atlantic the *Pierrot* ran into a violent storm which blew the vessel into an unchartered rock. The rock created a 30-foot gash in the brigantine's hull, and the ship's hold started to fill with water. Suddenly, an enormous wave swamped the stricken vessel and swept five crewmen overboard. Captain Grace and the four surviving crew-members managed to launch the lifeboat and tried to row away from the rapidly sinking ship before the suction could drag them all down with it. As the survivors rowed furiously, they heard a voice shouting to them. The old cook stopped rowing and pointed to a head, bobbing up and down next to the lifeboat. The cook said, "It's the purser – Mr King!"

Captain Grace uttered a stream of profanities and said, "He's damned! Leave him and save yourself."

"We can't leave him, sir," said the 16-year-old cabin boy Richard Tomlin, who also stopped rowing.

The other two rowers in the boat, the first and second mates, were also regarding the drowning purser with sympathy.

The old cook let go of his oar and leaned over the side of the boat. He reached out towards the purser and said, "Give me your hand, lad."

Captain Grace shouted, "You old fool! He'll capsize us!'

The cook took no heed of Grace's warning, so the captain picked up the elderly man's oar and lifted it high above him. The three other survivors were speechless with shock. Grace brought down the heavy oar on the cook's head and smashed his skull like an eggshell. The sickening impact sent blood spraying out of his ears, and the old man fell into the sea. The purser swore at the captain and grabbed hold of the corpse in a vain attempt to stay afloat. Grace then turned to the other survivors, wielding the oar in a threatening manner. In a grim low voice he said, "You row this boat from here now or you'll follow him!"

The cabin boy Tomlin and the two other men did as he said, and by some miracle, the boat survived the storm. Then the real hardship began.

The lifeboat drifted in the vast expanses of the Atlantic, under a bleaching, blistering sun all day, and through the freezing, biting cold of the night. The survivors became thirsty, but they had no fresh water to quench their parched, burning throats. They tried gargling with the seawater, but always had the strong urge to swallow the cold saltwater, which made them vomit. The captain and his surviving crew were soon suffering from heat stroke, dehydration and starvation. Day after day they scanned the horizon for ships or the welcoming sight of a coast, but saw nothing but waves for as far as their tired eyes could see. By the fifth day, the survivors were too weak to row for more than a few minutes. Now it was only a matter of time before they died of thirst and starvation.

But Captain Grace had a suggestion which sent a shiver down the spines of the two officers and the cabin boy. The captain coughed to clear his dried-up throat and, in a gruff voice, he said: "There's only one alternative left. We draw lots, and the unlucky one gets eaten."

The first mate flinched in horrified disbelief and shook his head.

Captain Grace opened the lifeboat's small medicine box. All it contained was a roll of bandage, iodine, and a needle and thread of suture. He suggested cutting four lengths of bandage. The one who chose the short length had to be killed to feed the other three.

The second mate said, "No, captain. Someone will pick us up soon. It won't be long now. A ship's bound to pass us soon."

Grace took out his clasp knife and said, "It's the only way we can survive. We eat animals, don't we? Well, man is just an animal too. They do it in the Polynesian Islands."

"It's three against one, sir," said the first mate, and he picked up the oar, ready to hit the captain with it.

Grace smiled, then put the knife away and said, "You're right. I'm outnumbered." And he closed his eyes and started to doze off.

In the golden rays of sunrise on the following morning, the first and second mate awoke to a nightmare. The captain's mouth was dripping with blood. He was eating the cabin boy Richard Tomlin. He had evidently slit the boy's throat, probably while he was sleeping, and was now carving the flesh from the boy's forearm with the clasp knife. The hungry captain made vile slurping noises, and seemed unaware that he was being watched. Fearing for his own life, First Mate Jack Burbage picked up the oar and struck the cannibalistic captain with it. The blow sent Grace across the boat, and he lay on his back, out cold. The two officers stared in horror at the slaughtered teenager, then Burbage picked up the captain's clasp knife and kneeled down, ready to slit Grace's throat. The second mate persuaded his colleague not to commit murder, or it would look as if he had killed the captain and the cabin boy.

When Grace regained consciousness, he saw the first mate standing over him with the knife. Grace said, "I only did it so we could survive. I didn't want to kill the boy."

Over the next two days, the first and second mate had to take turns to sleep, because they obviously couldn't trust the demented Captain Grace.

But through the effects of starvation and thirst, the officers became weak, and in the end they both collapsed. Grace didn't harm them; instead, he attempted to nurse them back to health by force-feeding them with the flesh of the cabin boy. To stop the skinned corpse from perishing in the noonday heat, the captain dipped the roll of bandage from the medicine box in the seawater, then wrapped it around the remains of Tomlin.

Several days later, when all three men were close to death, a British naval vessel sighted their boat and came to the rescue. The sailors from the navy ship felt nauseous when they saw the bandaged corpse of the boy. And when the sailors saw the streaks and smears of blood around the mouths of the semiconscious survivors, they put two and two together.

Captain Grace and his officers were taken to Portsmouth and charged with murder, but the Home Secretary thought the men had been through enough already, so he commuted their sentences to six months hard labour at Dartmoor prison.

When Grace had served his time, he changed his name and grew a beard before returning to Liverpool to look for work. He was employed as a stevedore but, as soon as he was paid, he would squander his entire wages in the saloons of the Dock Road. Around this time, the hallucinations began. One night he saw the decomposing face of the cabin boy he had murdered, peering at him through the windows of a pub called the Crow's Nest. On another occasion, as Grace was staggering down a waterfront street in a swirling fog, he was confronted with the bandaged and bloodstained corpse of

Richard Tomlin. The cabin boy, almost devoid of any skin and flesh, held his arms out to the terrified ex-captain and chased him.

These grotesque and distressing hallucinations became steadily worse, and wherever Edward Grace went in the city, the thing in bandages followed him.

In the end, Grace went to the police in a frantic state and ranted on about the awful revenge Tomlin's ghost was exacting on him. The police surmised that the only spirits troubling the hysterical old man were those of the alcoholic kind, and they decided it would be in the public interest to throw him in a cell for the night. Grace was locked up at the police station, but on the following morning, he was found dead in his cell. The mariner's body was lying under the bed, and his eyes were wide open with a look of sheer terror. In Edward Grace's right hand, he was clutching a strip of torn bandage.

The Coffins are Restless Tonight

Situated in the icy expanses of the Baltic Sea, the bleak rocky island of Oesel is better known for the whisky it exports to the world, but in the nineteenth century the island became the talk of Europe for much less mundane reasons: the sinister "unquiet graves" saga.

Upon the island of Oesel on 22 June 1844 Mrs Dalmann, the wife of a local tailor, rode a cart carrying her two children up the long lonely lane which ran parallel to the town cemetery. Mrs Dalmann was going to visit her mother's grave as she did every month. The cart trundled past the many chapels adjoining the cemetery which had been built by the island's wealthier families and finally came to a halt in front of the Buxhoewden family chapel, where Mrs Dalmann hitched the horse to a post. She then went into the cemetery with her two children, clutching a bouquet of flowers, ready to pay her quiet respects to her much missed mother at the graveside.

A quarter of an hour later, Mrs Dalmann and her children returned to the cart and found the horse acting hysterically. It was lathered in perspiration and had almost uprooted the post to which it had been tethered. Mrs Dalmann tried her utmost to calm the horse down, but the animal reared up on its hind legs and seemed terrorized by something. Mrs Dalmann called out a veterinarian to treat her animal, and he bled the horse – which was a common practice to remedy almost anything in those days. The horse finally settled down, and the vet suggested that the animal had perhaps been stung by a bee.

On the following Sunday the same phenomenon happened again, this time to three horses simultaneously. All the horses that had been tied to posts outside the Buxhoewden chapel were found quivering and acting strangely when their owners came out to mount them. The same explanation was offered by the vet who had treated Mrs Dalmann's horse: bee stings.

However, on the very spot where the four horses had been terrified by something, a number of villagers heard heavy rumbling sounds emanating from the Buxhoewden family vault beneath the chapel. Over the next few days, the strange subterranean disturbances continued to be heard, and eerie rumours about the unquiet graves of Buxhoewden chapel began to circulate through the town. The strange gossip finally reached the ears of the Buxhoewden household via the servants, but the weird tale was dismissed as the slanderous invention of some enemy of the family. The tittle-tattle about the supernatural goings-on in the vault refused to die down, so the Buxhoewdens informed the authorities and arranged for them to witness the reopening of the vault in an effort to end the silly rumours. When the Buxhoewden family vault was opened, the investigators found a chilling surprise awaiting them. All of the coffins were piled on top of one another in the centre of the vault. Three members of the Buxhoewden family and the party of official investigators took half an hour carrying the heavy coffins back to their iron racks which were mounted around the walls of the vault. No one spoke so much as a word within the vault during this time because the air seemed charged with a terrible presence of dread. When all of the living had left the underground chamber of the dead, the vault was locked and molten lead was poured over the broken seals of the door as a precaution against any future tampering. The Buxhoewdens and the group who had accompanied them into the vault racked their brains trying to think of a natural explanation which could account for the stacked coffins, but no such explanation was forthcoming. It was therefore agreed that the incident should be kept secret from the people of Oesel.

On the third Sunday of that July 11 horses tethered to posts outside the Buxhoewden chapel became hysterical during evening Mass. Half of the unfortunate creatures fell down and resisted all attempts by their owners to make them stand. Three of the horses died where they fell, while others became so frenzied they snapped their reins and galloped off in blind panic. Throughout all this commotion, the chapel-goers felt strange throbbing vibrations pounding the ground beneath them. The localized tremors were evidently coming from the exact spot where the Buxhoewden family vault was located.

The mystery of the restless dead beneath the chapel could no longer be kept secret, and the people who had lost their horses, together with a mob of the town's superstitious inhabitants, joined forces and sent a petition to the Consistory – the supreme governing church body which periodically held official hearings regarding religious visions and supernatural incidents. While the tardy white-haired elders of the Consistory considered what actions to take over the rumbling vaults, one of the Buxhoewdens died. After the funeral, several members of the wealthy family melted the seals of the now infamous vault and unlocked its heavy six-inch reinforced doors. Once more, they found the coffins in a stack in the centre of the vault, and this time there were strange marks on one of the larger coffins, as if it had been battered and chipped by something. The Buxhoewdens and several brave volunteers positioned the coffins back onto their iron wall racks and quickly retreated from the vault. The locks were changed this time and fresh lead was poured onto the seals around them. Word got out about this second bizarre incident, adding more fuel to the creepy rumours of the jumping coffins in the Buxhoewden vault. Now the people of Oesel feared something evil was at large on their island and they made further demands to the sluggish Consistory to take immediate action. The church court decided to act under this growing pressure, and they opted for a thorough investigation of the haunted vault. The president of the Consistory, Baron De Guldenstubbe, went along to the vault with two members of the Buxhoewden family. He noted that the doors were locked and their lead seals had not been broken or tampered with in any way. Another witness was summoned and he observed the baron and the two Buxhoewdens break the seals, unlock the door, then enter the vault with lanterns. This witness was given permission to enter the vault, and when he did, he came upon a most distressing scene. This time, the coffins were scattered everywhere in disarray, and some of them had been smashed open, partially revealing the decomposed corpses they contained. There was no way grave-robbers could have tunnelled into that vault, which was lined with thick slabs of granite. The slabs were intact, and there was no evidence of any secret openings to the vault. Furthermore, had grave-robbers been responsible for the gross acts of desecration, they would certainly have taken the diamond rings and other items of jewellery from the bodies.

New coffins were brought into the vault and the bodies were put into them. Someone suggested sprinkling fine wood ashes on the floor of the crypt so that the ghouls responsible for the grim deeds would leave their footprints behind. This ingenious suggestion was taken up, and a fine layer of ash was duly sprinkled on the vault floor. The Buxhoewden vault was then locked and sealed once again, but Baron De Guldenstubbe still suspected foul play by persons unknown who were perhaps tunnelling into the chamber, so he employed workmen to dig a six-foot-deep trench around the vault and posted armed guards at the crypt's entrance.

After 72 hours, the baron turned up unannounced with two of the Buxhoewdens and stormed the troubled vault. Inside, they found all the coffins off their wall racks, each of them standing on end against the wall. On the floor, there were no footprints in the layer of ash. This left the baron and the Buxhoewdens completely baffled – and somewhat afraid of the dark forces which were apparently at work in the crypt.

Baron De Guldenstubbe filed his report to the Consistory, and the only suggestion they had regarding the unexplained disturbances was to bury the Buxhoewden coffins elsewhere. This was subsequently done, and the old family vault was sealed up for good.

More Mobile Coffins

The mysterious movements of the coffins in the Buxhoewden vault are paralleled in similar accounts of mobile burial caskets that have been reported in various countries. According to church records at Stanton, in Suffolk, England, a vault belonging to a French family became the source of loud thudding sounds one evening in the mid-eighteenth century. When the vault was opened for an additional interment in 1755, the large lead-covered burial caskets were found scattered about the place. One of the coffins was resting on the fourth step on the stairway leading out of the crypt, and was so heavy that it took eight men to reposition it on its wooden bier. Grave-robbers were initially blamed, but the locks on the vault hadn't been tampered with, and nor had the seals.

A similar mystery was investigated on the island of Barbados in the nineteenth century. This was the so-called mystery of the "creeping coffins". The chilling story dates back to 1724, when the Walronds, a rich family of planters, constructed a magnificent blue Devon marble tomb at Christ Church, Barbados. The locals thought the ostentatious tomb was more of a fortress than a resting place of the dead. The floor space measured 12 feet in length, almost 7 feet in width, and was sunk into the ground. For some inexplicable reason, none of the Walronds were inhumed in their tomb. The first body that was interred there was that of Mrs Thomasina Goddard on 31 July 1807. In the following year the vault came into the possession of the wealthy slave-owning family of Thomas Chase, who purchased it to entomb two daughters in 1808 and early 1812. When the Chase tomb was reopened in July 1812 to lay Dorcas Chase to rest, the coffins containing the Chase daughters were seen to be standing on their heads. Thomas Chase, the head of the family, never recovered from the shock of seeing the inverted coffins and he became so

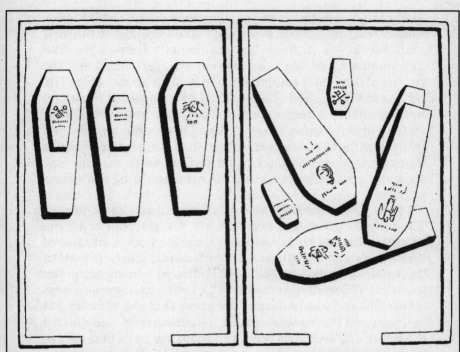

The coffins as they were placed   The coffins as they were found

Plan of the coffins in a Barbados vault, showing how they were placed and how they were found disturbed on the last occasion in 1820

mentally disturbed he committed suicide a month later. On 9 August his heavy lead-lined coffin was also placed in the vault by eight pallbearers. On 25 September 1816 the Chase vault was reopened to receive the coffin of Samuel Brewster Ames, a little boy who was distantly related to the Chase family. Once again the coffins in the vault were found disarranged. Only the burial casket of Mrs Goddard was still in its original place. The other coffins looked as if something had scattered them across the vault. There was little the enraged mourners could do but return the coffins to their rightful places. Later that year, on 17 November the vault was opened once more for the interment of Samuel Brewster, whose coffin was being transferred from its original grave in a St Philip churchyard.

The sinister reputation of the vault was now so well known that crowds of curious people gathered around it in eager anticipation of further developments. They were not disappointed, because once more it was discovered that the coffins of the Chase tomb had been thrown about again. The coffin containing Mrs Goddard had been battered open and her remains had been exposed. The desecration was linked with an abortive slave rising that had been severely subdued by the authorities with much bloodshed earlier that year, but that connection was later ruled out, as there was no way anybody could have entered the stronghold of the Chase tomb.

On 17 July 1819 the vault was opened and the coffin of Thomasina Clarke was taken inside. Outside the crypt the Viscount Combermere, the governor of Barbados, and two of his officials waited with bated breath, along with hundreds of hushed spectators. Yet again, the coffins were lying about the tomb in different directions. Viscount Combermere was allowed in and was baffled by the scene that met his eyes. He had watched the masons cutting free the marble slab door of the tomb, and had seen the exertion on the faces of the slave gang who had dragged that slab aside. He wondered what force or entity could have invaded such an impenetrable crypt to throw the coffins about. After the coffins were lugged back to their original positions, a fine sand was sprinkled over the entire floor. This would surely reveal the traces of the mysterious desecrator, the viscount reasoned. This time when the vault slab was closed, the viscount left the impression of his seal in the cement.

By April of the following year burning curiosity had got the better of everybody on the island, and they begged the Viscount Combermere to reopen the Chase tomb to see if anything had happened. After a protracted debate on the requests of the islanders, the governor of Barbados bent to public pressure, and he authorized the reopening of the notorious vault. The seals on the cement were intact, yet when the interior of the crypt was inspected, the coffins were again found strewn across the vault. Whatever had moved the coffins had done it with such violence that there were large dents in the walls of the chamber made by the impact of the lead coffins, and yet there were no marks in the sand on the floor of the vault. Viscount Combermere – a fearless man who had been one of the Duke of Wellington's finest cavalry commanders – later admitted that his blood had run cold when he saw the state of the vault and the positions of the coffins that day. In the end, the viscount had the coffins removed from the accursed tomb and had them buried elsewhere. The Chase tomb was put on the market, but because of its eerie reputation it was never purchased and still lies empty. Even today people on the island will not venture near the black mouth of the open tomb's entrance after dusk.

In September 1976 there was a well-documented report of a coffin jumping off its stand during a wake at a house in Compton, Los Angeles. An Irish-born man named Danny Donovan who had died from a heart attack was laid in an open coffin for a few days at his home. During this period the dead man's three friends and his widowed wife lit a candle in the parlour and talked about old times as they drank wine. At one point in the reminiscences, someone said Danny had often dabbled with the ouija board, and his wife went upstairs and brought one down which belonged to her daughter. The four intoxicated mourners put their fingers on the top of the upturned glass and Mrs Donovan attempted to summon up the spirit of her recently deceased husband. Seconds later the candle flickered, and Mrs Donovan let out a scream. The coffin containing her dead husband started to shake, then slid off its stand and stood up. The white-shrouded body of Mr Donovan was then thrown towards the ouija dabblers, and fell against a man named Edwards, who had been a work-mate of the dead man. Edwards yelled out and pushed away the body. Then the candle went out even though there were no draughts in the room.

Edwards later suffered a nervous breakdown and admitted that he had been having a three-year affair with Mrs Donovan behind her husband's back.

PART SIX

Phantom Encounters
● ●

The Evil Assailant

The following chilling story is from the annals of the now-defunct Lancashire Spiritualists Society, which was based in Liverpool, England, until 1939.

There stands a Victorian house in Bidston on the Wirral in north-west England that was once the scene of a disturbing supernatural incident that allegedly occurred in 1920. The house was bought by two sisters who had been left a substantial legacy in 1919, and their names were Victoria and Margaret Webster. Margaret was 19 and Victoria was 24, and they originally came from Neston, but heard about the beautiful terraced house in Bidston after the death of their father, a wealthy shipping magnate who left his daughters thousands of pounds. Mrs Webster had died after giving birth to Margaret in 1901.

The Webster sisters soon settled into their new home, and found the neighbours agreeable enough. Both sisters were said to be very good-looking, and naturally attracted the attention of the males in their new neighbourhood.

One night early in December 1920 Victoria, the older sister, went out on the town with a local government clerk named William. She'd been seeing him for three months, and he really loved her already. Victoria's teenage sister Margaret stayed at home and read a book. Around midnight, Victoria still hadn't returned, so Margaret went to bed, where she continued to read her book by the light of a candle. She was starting to doze off, when she thought she heard a noise downstairs. Margaret got up and went to the landing, then shouted down the stairs, "Is that you. Victoria?"

No reply came, but Margaret saw the shadow of a figure flit across the bottom flight of steps and heard a faint chuckle. Margaret thought it was William, Victoria's fiancé, messing about with her sister. Margaret liked William. He made her laugh the way he fooled about, so she went downstairs, carrying the candle, expecting to see William staging some prank. Margaret reached the bottom flight of steps and saw the flickering flames of the coal fire, still burning in the grate. Margaret had forgotten to put the safety guard around the fire, and as she walked to the parlour, she noticed a figure standing in the shadows of the hall to her left. She turned, and saw a strange-looking man standing there. He wore a long curly white wig like the one worn by a judge, and a long embroidered satin coat with large turned-up sleeves, just like the coats worn in the eighteenth century. Beneath this the stranger wore a silvery waistcoat and, instead of trousers, he had on outdated breeches to his knees. On the lower parts of his legs, the man wore white stockings and on his feet he sported square-toed shoes with shiny brass buckles on them. What really gave young Margaret the creeps was the intruder's face, which was plastered in white make-up. He looked at the terrified girl with an evil expression, then rushed towards her.

Margaret dropped the candlestick and ran into the parlour. She closed the door behind her and leaned against it with her heart pounding. The intruder started to steadily force the door open, then backed up and charged at it, throwing Margaret across the room with the impact. The outdated-looking stranger then started to chase the terrified teenager around the table, and she was so traumatized that she found herself unable to scream. Her throat seemed weak with terror. The eerie man suddenly stopped chasing, and in a weird accent, he said, "Now, my pretty one, stay still, for I must have you." And he jumped onto the table with amazing agility, then leapt onto the girl. She fell to the floor by the fire, and he started to molest her. He tore at her dress and violently kissed and bit at her neck and breasts. The girl felt powerless, then suddenly saw the hot poker in the grate. She grabbed it with her left hand, and pushed it into the attacker's face. He let out a scream, then clawed Margaret's face. The girl retaliated by clubbing him on the head with the poker. What's more, Margaret suddenly regained the power to shout out, and she let out a scream that sent her weird attacker running from the room.

Margaret got to her feet and heard the attacker's footsteps running down the stairs to the cellar. The girl ran into the street in a dreadful state, and Victoria and William came running to her aid. Several neighbours also came out to see what all the screams were about. Margaret screamed that the assailant had run into the cellar, but when William went down to look he found the cellar empty. William and Victoria thought the tale of the eighteenth-century attacker was a bit far-fetched, and virtually accused Margaret of having an over-active imagination. Because she was unable to explain the "love-bites" on Margaret's neck and chest and the scratch-marks on her face, Victoria theorized that Margaret had been canoodling with some local boy who had fled upon hearing that the older sister would soon be home. But Margaret stuck by her story, and weeks later Victoria and William also saw the outdated man in the powdered wig peering out of the parlour window one Sunday morning when the couple were returning from church. Around this time, the Webster girls learnt from their neighbours that the previous occupiers who had lived in their home had left after saying the house was haunted. The family who had lived in the Websters' house had said that in the wee small hours the sinister apparition of a old-fashioned-looking man often appeared in the bedroom of their daughter with a lecherous look.

In the winter of 1922 a water pipe burst in the Webster sisters' house, and workmen were called in. While these workmen were digging to get to the pipe – which ran under the cellar – they unearthed an unmarked red mahogany coffin. When this coffin was opened by the authorities, it revealed the skeleton of a man wearing a long white curly wig, and tattered early eighteenth-century clothes. These clothes and the wig matched the wig and clothes worn by the sinister intruder who had recently attacked Margaret Webster. Local historians later deduced that the skeleton was that of Richard Tilly, a notorious, but wealthy eighteenth-century rake and

Devil worshipper. Tilly was charged with sorcery, sacrilege, blackmail, rape, and even a ritual murder, but he had bribed the magistrate and escaped sentencing by promising to live in obscurity. It was thought that he had been secretly buried on the site of the Webster sisters' house around the year 1730. In Tilly's coffin there was a crumbling book entitled *Lucifer's Bible*, and on the front page there was the sign of an upside-down pentagram – the symbol of a satanist. The text on the pages was too faded to read, but probably contained references to satanism and black magic practices.

Understandably, the Webster sisters soon left the house and moved to North Wales. Tilly's coffin was not allowed to be buried in a Christian churchyard, and is thought to have been reburied near Bidston Hill.

The Witch of Endor

One of the earliest spooky tales about witchcraft is recorded in the Bible's Old Testament in the Book of Samuel. The Bible condemns dabblers in the so-called "black arts", but the Holy Book apparently doesn't condemn dabblers to death; the most famous anti-witch text in the Old Testament, "Thou shalt not suffer a witch to live", properly translates as "Thou shalt not suffer poisoners to live." By the time this translational error had been uncovered, the medieval inquisitors had put to death a staggering 9 million people who had been suspected of being witches and warlocks.

Around 800 BC, Saul, the first king of Israel, was, to put it mildly, having a hard time. The invading Philistines were on the warpath again, and Saul's henchman (and son-in-law) David was daily receiving more adulation than the king himself. Saul's insane jealousy of his former military commander had forced David to flee from the court into the wilderness of Negev, where he attracted a band of 600 outlaws, and subsequently became a vassal of the Philistine king of Gath.

The First Book of Samuel tells us:

And the Philistines gathered themselves together, and

The Witch of Endor

came and pitched in Shunem . . . and when Saul saw the host of the Philistines, he was afraid, and his heart greatly trembled. And when Saul enquired of the Lord, the Lord answered him not, neither by dreams, nor by Urim, nor by prophets. Then said Saul unto his servants, "Seek me a woman that hath a familiar spirit, that I may go to her, and enquire of her."

And his servants said to him, "Behold, there is a woman that hath a familiar spirit at En-dor."

That night Saul dressed in anonymous-looking garments and set out for the woman's house with two burly bodyguards. Upon reaching the woman's abode, Saul said, "I pray thee, divine unto me by the familiar spirit, and bring me him up, whom I shall name unto thee."

A sinister female came out and replied that Saul had driven all the wizards and witches away. Suspecting that the stranger's request was a trap, she went on, "Behold, thou knowest what Saul hath done, how he hath cut off those that have familiar spirits, and the wizards, out of the land, wherefore then layest thou a snare for my life, to cause me to die?"

Saul swore that no harm would come against the sorceress, and he beseeched her to summon up the spirit of the man who had anointed him as king – Samuel.

The biblical tract then tells us:

And when the woman saw Samuel, she cried with a loud voice; and the woman spake to Saul, saying, Why hast thou deceived me? for thou art Saul. And the king said unto her, Be not afraid for what sawest thou? And the woman said unto Saul, I saw gods ascending out of the earth. And the king said unto her, What form is he of? And she said, An old man cometh up, and he is covered with a mantle. And Saul perceived it was Samuel, and he stooped with his face to the ground and bowed himself.

And Samuel said to Saul, Why hast thou disquieted me, to bring me up? And Saul answered, I am sore distressed; for the Philistines make war against me, and God is departed from me, and answereth me no more . . . therefore I have called thee, that thou mayest make known unto me what I shall do.

Samuel answered: "The Lord hath rent the kingdom out of thine hand, and given it to thy neighbour, to David, because thou obeyeth not the voice of the Lord . . . Moreover the Lord will also deliver Israel with thee into the hand of the Philistines; and tomorrow shallt thou and thy sons be with me . . ."

Then Saul fell straightaway all along the earth, and was sore afraid . . . and there was no more strength in him, for he had eaten no bread at all the night.

The woman said to Saul: "Now therefore, I pray thee, hearken thou also unto the voice of thine handmaid, and let me set a morsel of bread before thee; and eat, that thou mayest have strength, when thou goes on thy way."

But he refused, and said, I will not eat. But his servants, together with the woman, compelled him, and he hearkened unto their voice, and sat upon the bed. And the woman had a fat calf in the house, and she hasted, and killed it, and took flour, and kneaded it, and did bake unleavened bread thereof; and she brought it before Saul, and before his servants; and they did eat. Then they rose up, and went away that night.

The rest, as they say, is history. Shortly after the ghostly communication at Endor came Saul's final battle against the Philistines at the foot of Mount Gilboa. It was an act of desperation. The level ground gave the Philistines' chariots a distinct advantage. Saul was mortally wounded in the battle and took his own life. His three sons were also slaughtered. The ghost's prophecy was fulfilled.

The witch of Endor's method of prophesying by calling up the dead is an example of "necromancy"; from the Greek words *nekros* (death) and *manteia* (prophecy).

The Night Terror

This is a bizarre story to keep you awake at nights, and it took place at Moreton on the Wirral peninsula, England, in July 1863.

Stewart Parker, a retired hangman, was sitting in bed next to his wife, reading a book, when he nodded off. The time was just after 1 a.m.

At 2 a.m. Mrs Parker woke up and turned in the bed to see her husband fighting for his breath. He was drenched in sweat and was making choking noises. She shouted his name repeatedly, but Mr Parker wouldn't wake up. This naturally worried Mrs Parker; her husband had a weak heart, and seemed so afraid of the nightmare he was having that he looked as if he'd kill himself with fear.

Mrs Parker slapped her husband across the face, to no avail. As a last resort she poured a glass of water over his face and shook him violently.

Mr Parker's eyes flew open, and he seemed to be paralyzed for a few moments. Then he grabbed at his throat and in a raspy dry voice said, "Thank God – it was just a dream."

Mrs Parker said she thought he was a goner for a moment, and asked him what he'd been dreaming about. Mr Parker said, "I dreamt this man in a black hood came forward. I asked him who he was and he said he was Peter Woods."

"Who was he?" asked Mrs Parker.

Her husband looked worried, and said, "An old house-breaker who was hanged for the murder of a widow in Ashton town. After he was hanged, the real murderer was caught and confessed. Peter Woods said he'd return to haunt me, the jury and the judge. He said he had gypsy blood in him."

"Oh, it was just a nightmare," said Mrs Parker, and she shook her head when she saw the wet patch she'd caused when spilling the glass of water.

"But it was a horrible dream, dear," said Mr Parker, and he told her the rest of the nightmare. "Woods tied my hands behind me and put a strap round my ankles. He then pushed me so I was standing on the trapdoor of a gallows. Just as he put the noose over my head you woke me up. I'm not that keen to go back to sleep now."

"Oh, don't be so silly. You ate toasted cheese before you went to bed didn't you?" said Mrs Parker.

"Yes, but I've never had a nightmare so vivid and so real before," replied Mr Parker.

"Cheese does that," said his wife. "It's well known that cheese upsets the brain when you sleep."

Half an hour later, Mr Parker fell asleep, and around 3.30 a.m. his wife woke to hear a strange snoring sound. It was Mr Parker having another turn in his sleep. This time she had to push him out the bed and roll him across the floor to awaken him. Mr Parker got up and gasped for air. He threw open the window and inhaled the fresh air.

"Are you alright? Shall I call a doctor?" said the concerned Mrs Parker.

"No. It was Woods again," gasped Mr Parker. "He tried to hang me again. This time the trapdoor opened. I fell through the trapdoor and was hanging, but you awakened me in time. Am I going insane?"

By 4.40 a.m. the couple were drowsy, and were already laughing at the ordeal, but now Mr Parker really did seem ready for a good night's sleep. He turned to kiss his wife, then rolled over and went straight to sleep, and on the next morning, at 8 a.m., his wife woke up to find him dead. His face was purple, and the veins in his face stuck out. His eyes were open, and seemed to be bulging out of their sockets. Mrs Parker let out a scream and ran to her sister in the next street, and her sister summoned a doctor. The doctor believed Mr Parker had died of a heart attack brought on by what is known as "night terror" – a very traumatic nightmare in which the dreamer is unable to wake up. Night terror is rare, but there are around 100 cases in England each year.

The pathologist who performed the post mortem on the old hangman's body was baffled by a reddish band around Mr Parker's neck. Such a mark was often made on the necks of condemned criminals who had been hanged. It was caused by rope-burn from the noose. The coroner could not explain the mark, and surmised it was produced by haemorrhaging of the blood vessels in the neck caused by the coronary – but when Mrs Parker saw the strange mark on her husband's neck, she knew that Peter Woods had somehow exacted his revenge.

The Girl who Married in Haste

This has got to be one of the strangest ghost stories on record. The following incident has been investigated by writers and researchers since the 1930s, but to date no one has ever been able to provide a rational explanation.

In 1930 a 25-year-old woman from Chester, England, named

Eleanor May was staying with her sister's family in Warwickshire at a little house that was situated on the periphery of Stratford-upon-Avon. One evening Eleanor accompanied her sister Emily to a dance that was held in the hall of a local church. The two sisters danced all night, and by midnight Emily had gone home to her husband, leaving her sister in the arms of a man who said his name was Freddie Barclay. Freddie had receding blond hair, a distinguished aquiline nose, and was quite tall and handsome, but he said very little, and seemed a bit shy. He said he was 40, and that he worked for a local printer.

Anyway, Eleanor found herself falling head over heels in love with Freddie, and asked him to meet her at an old country pub called the Magpie and Crown on the following Thursday at eight. Freddie walked her home and promised he'd be at the pub next week. He kissed her gently and walked away.

The Magpie and Crown was a cosy pub with a thatched roof and a large blazing fire. It was rumoured that Shakespeare himself had once drank at an old tavern that had stood on the site of the pub in the sixteenth century. At 8 o'clock on the Thursday night, Freddie turned up and soon afterwards Eleanor walked in. The couple were soon sitting in the corner, gazing deeply into each other's eyes and holding hands. Freddie and Eleanor met at this pub for about a month, and one evening Freddie shocked Eleanor – and all the drinkers at the pub – by going down on his bended knee and proposing. Eleanor wasn't sure, but said she would marry him. The couple didn't have much money, but arranged to marry at the local Church of the Holy Trinity.

Emily was very suspicious about her sister's future husband. He never talked about his home life and only said that he lived with his domineering, old-fashioned mother. Furthermore, he just mentioned the general area where he lived without specifying what his address was. Emily thought Freddie's reluctance to say where he lived was suspicious, to say the least, and she warned Eleanor to be wary of the printer, but Eleanor seemed blinded by her affection for Freddie and said she trusted him. Emily said, "For all you know he could have a wife and children. Bigamy is a serious crime, you know."

But Eleanor told her sister she was just being jealous because her own marriage was a flop, and the outraged Emily told her sister she would certainly not be going to the wedding.

The marriage ceremony finally took place a month later, and it was a very low-key affair indeed. Only Freddie, Eleanor, the barman from the Magpie and Crown, and a few of the drinkers from the pub were present. Freddie said his mother had been too ill to attend.

After the wedding the barman and the drinkers showered the newly-weds with rice and confetti, then there was a party back at the Magpie and Crown. And this is where events took a sinister turn. During the merrymaking and singing, Eleanor noticed that Freddie was absent. She asked the barman where he was, and he said he'd probably gone to the toilet. But it turned out that Freddie was not in the toilet. In fact, Freddie was nowhere to be seen. Days went by, and Eleanor refused to take off her wedding dress. She went to her sister and told her what had happened, and Emily said, "I told you there was something fishy about him and you attacked me. I've seen all these whirlwind romances before."

Eleanor went to the village police station to report the strange disappearance. The old sergeant who listened seemed intrigued by Eleanor's account. "You'd better come through," he said, and escorted the young lady into his office, where he sat her down and offered her a cup of tea.

The sergeant said to her, "Look Miss. We've heard of this Freddie Barclay before. About ten years back. He did the same thing then. Promised a young lady like yourself that he'd marry her, then vanished."

"I don't understand," said Eleanor.

"Call me superstitious, and let it go no further than these four walls, but I reckon this Mr Barclay is a ghost," said the sergeant, solemnly.

"A ghost?" Eleanor recoiled, and smiled disbelievingly.

But the sergeant remained sombre-faced, and said: "I took the liberty on the last occasion of checking up on Freddie Barclay. I discovered that a man of that name and of the description you gave once worked at a printer's works called Maggs Brothers about a mile away. He was about to marry a girl in the village who was a dead ringer for you, but she jilted him, and Freddie took arsenic and died. His old widowed mother was devastated and she died herself afterwards from pneumonia brought on by the shock."

"But he was no ghost. He was real. I kissed him," Eleanor told the old policeman.

The sergeant sighed and said, "That's what the last girl told me. I can't say for certain he was a ghost. But the last girl who was stood up by Freddie Barclay never saw him again. But I showed her his grave in the cemetery outside of the Holy Trinity Church – where you were married."

Eleanor never could accept what the sergeant told her, and she never married again, and she never heard from the sinister Freddie Barclay again. Weeks after her husband's mysterious disappearance, Eleanor awoke one morning to find her wedding ring was missing. It was never seen again either.

George Washington's Vision of the Future

There are around 900 angels mentioned in the Bible, and none of them are actually described as having wings. The medieval artists added the wings and the halos and the harps, but the Bible just says that angels are superior to human beings, and act as messengers. They are usually described as human-like, clad in radiant clothes, and are often described as being very tall.

Throughout history a number of prominent people have claimed to have met angels. One of these people was George Washington. Washington was a very religious man, who often drew jibes because he used to go into the bushes to pray.

During the dark days of the American War of Independence (1775–83), Washington emerged from his house looking very pale. When Anthony Sherman, one of his staff, asked him if he was feeling okay, Washington told him he had just had an encounter with an angel. Washington made Sherman swear he would not tell anyone about the matter until the president died.

Washington gave an account of how he had been sitting in ☞

his study, browsing through his collection of books, when a light shone brilliantly through the room.

He turned around, and there was an extremely beautiful woman standing there in a one-piece silvery blue garment. "Who let you in? I gave strict orders that I am not to be disturbed," Washington told the woman, thinking she was an important person.

According to Washington, the woman said, "Son of the Republic, look and learn!" and she pointed to a ball of mist that appeared in front of her.

In this mist, Washington saw terrifying scenes of warfare, and a strange flag with an unchristian cross of stars, and the faces of black people crying. This has been interpreted as the American Civil War, which erupted about a century later. Then the mist cleared and Washington saw a futuristic age when North and South America and the entire free world would be united under a blue and white banner depicting the entire Earth. Then the angel faded away. This story is actually mentioned in Sherman's biography, although a lot of historians dismiss Washington's tale as an example of religious mania.

Haunted Roads

If the following collection of spooky tales are to be believed, even the highways and byways have their ghosts. In all of the thought-provoking accounts I am about to relate, there is one common denominator: the apparent solidity of the apparitions, which are often seen by more than one witness.

One sultry summer night in July 1983 a 42-year-old hairdresser named Gareth set out from Northwich on his 250cc Honda motorcycle and headed for his girlfriend's home in Frodsham. Gareth was travelling along the B5153 route, which he knew quite well, as he had been making the journey three or four times a week for a couple of months. On this particular night, the full moon hung in a cloudless sky, illuminating the fields and lighting up the long winding road ahead for miles.

As Gareth sped past the village of Crowton, he happened to glance at the luminous dial of his analogue wristwatch and saw that it was midnight. He then looked up, and by the bright light from the lunar disc he saw the silhouette of a person standing at the side of the road up ahead, about half a mile away. Gareth slowed down slightly and regarded the shadowy figure with caution, wondering if it was a decoy for a roadside mugging. But as he neared the shadowy figure, he saw that it was a woman, and she was waving and gesticulating for the biker to stop.

Gareth decided to pull over, and he looked about suspiciously in case the woman had associates lying in wait. But the girl was alone, and she ran over to the hairdresser with a broad smile on her face. She had long straight black hair and quite a pale, round but attractive face. She was unusually tall – Gareth estimated her height to be just over 6 feet – and although it was a sweltering summer night, the girl wore a long dark overcoat.

"Thanks for stopping," the girl said, standing in front of the motorbike. She didn't speak with a local accent at all, but in a cultivated, urbane sort of voice; almost aristocratic in fact. The stranger then asked Gareth if he was going to Helsby.

Gareth said he wasn't but offered to give the girl a lift as far as the fork in the road beyond Kingsley.

The girl nodded and with a grateful expression clasped her hands together as if in prayer and closed her eyes.

"What are you doing out here on your own, anyway?" Gareth asked, and offered her the spare crash helmet he'd unfastened from the rear seat.

The girl pushed the helmet down on her head and replied, "Oh I lost my way." And she didn't elaborate on what she meant by that. She mounted the pillion seat and threw her arms around Gareth's waist.

The hairdresser rode off on a short journey of around four miles to the fork in the road just beyond Kingsley – when something eerie happened. Gareth suddenly noticed that the girl's arms were no longer holding on to his waist. The hairdresser stopped the motorcycle and twisted in his seat. The pillion seat was unoccupied, and the helmet was attached to its usual space there. Gareth was understandably baffled, and a little scared by the hitch-hiker's sudden disappearance. As he tried to get his head around the bizarre incident, he noticed a light in his wing mirror coming down the road behind. It turned out to be a police car. A policeman wound down the window and politely asked Gareth if everything was well.

Gareth didn't know what to say because he doubted that the police, or anyone for that matter, would believe his strange tale.

After an uncomfortable pause, Gareth finally said, "I gave a girl a lift, and the next minute she's not there."

The two policemen looked at each other with a knowing, grave expression, then the driver said, "Did you pick her up near Crowton, by any chance?"

"Yeah, why?" Gareth inquired, a bit surprised.

"We've had a few reports of a phantom hitch-hiker along here over the years," the policeman replied, and he turned to his colleague and said, "You saw her once didn't you?"

The other policeman nodded and said to Gareth, "Did she ask to be dropped off at Helsby?"

"Yeah, she did. What do you mean, phantom hitch-hiker?" said Gareth, getting goose bumps at the thought.

"Ah, let's leave it at that. More things in heaven and earth and all that," was the policeman's enigmatic reply, and he wound up the passenger window, diverting his gaze to the road ahead.

"What do you mean? Who is she?" Gareth asked, but the police driver merely flashed the headlights of the patrol car before continuing down the moonlit road.

Gareth didn't hang around, and he sped off to his girlfriend's house. The hairdresser later heard from several people in Frodsham that the ghostly hitch-hiking girl is often seen standing at the side of the road near Crowton on nights when the moon is full. No one seems to know who the girl is – or was – which adds an extra dimension of mystery to the solid-looking apparition.

Not all phantoms of the road are as innocuous as the Crowton hitch-hiker; some night-time apparitions which roam the macadam are nothing short of terrifying. In the early hours of 15 October 1987 Angela Smith and Helen

Messenger, two barmaids from Winsford, northern England, were travelling to Crewe to visit friends. The time was precisely 1.15 a.m., and the barmaids were travelling down the A530 in Helen's mini, when they saw a woman in black standing on the hard shoulder, next to a Volkswagen Beetle car, which seemed to have broken down.

As Helen drew nearer to the stranger she could see that the woman was a nun, so she pulled over. Angela wound down the nearside passenger window and asked the nun what was wrong.

"It just packed up," the nun told her, and smiled. She looked elderly, about 75 or older.

"Have you called anyone out?" Angela asked.

"No, my friend only lives a mile down the road. I'll walk," said the nun, and she started to walk off down the edge of the road.

"No, wait. We'll give you a lift," Angela told the nun, and the barmaid opened the door. Helen pushed forward Angela's seat and moved some luggage to allow the nun to get into the back of the little car.

"Oh, thank you. You're so kind," said the nun, and she went over to the mini and got into the vehicle. Helen asked her where she wanted to be dropped off, and the nun said, "It's just a little slip road before Willaston. You'll miss it if you blink. I'll point it out to you."

Helen told the nun that she and Angela had two days off work and were going to spend them with their friends in Crewe. The nun replied, "Good for you," then became silent for a while.

The stillness in the claustrophobic mini became tense, so Angela asked the nun what convent she was from, but received no reply. The nun just stared at the road ahead. Helen became a bag of nerves and started wondering if the woman in the back seat really was a nun; she started to suspect that she was some psychotic impostor, who had perhaps donned the disguise to gain the girls' confidence. The possibility of the passenger having a knife also crossed Helen's mind.

After a few minutes of deadly quietude, the nun suddenly said, "There's a terrible storm on the way. It's going to kill people and do a lot of damage."

"Really?" Angela asked, immensely relieved that the passenger was talking at last.

Helen had heard the national and local weather forecast before setting out, and there hadn't been a mention of a storm, so she thought the nun's comments were unfounded.

Then the nun became quiet again. A road sign notified the passengers that Willaston was just a few miles ahead. Helen said, "Are we near the turnoff yet?"

Angela let out a scream.

"What's wrong?" Helen asked, and instinctively slowed the mini.

"She's gone," Angela replied in a trembling voice.

Helen pulled over and saw that her friend was right. The back seat was empty. The nun had inexplicably vanished. The girls then noticed the faint smell of something in the vehicle. It was an aroma of church incense.

When the petrified young women reached their friends' house in Crewe they told them of the terrifying encounter with the phantom nun. The barmaids sat up for the remainder of that morning drinking coffee, and going through all the details of the creepy encounter. They told their friends about the nun's curious warning about a terrible storm and the ensuing loss of life. Helen and Angela's girlfriends were a bit sceptical at first, but could see that something had made the barmaids very anxious and jumpy. Later that morning, Angela telephoned the police and told them about the chilling encounter. The police were naturally amused, but Angela asked them to find out if an abandoned Volkswagen Beetle car was on the hard shoulder of the A530. The police promised they'd investigate and, true to their word, they phoned her back a few hours later and said there was no Beetle car broken down on the motorway and the AA and RAC had not been called out to repair or tow away such a vehicle.

Of course, later that day, weather forecasters failed right up to the last moment to predict the arrival of Britain's worst storm in two centuries. A hurricane swept across Britain, uprooting 19 million trees, killing 19 people, and causing £1.5 billion worth of damage. Strangely enough, there was another uncanny warning about the approaching hurricane which went unheeded. BBC weatherman Michael Fish calmly told millions of TV viewers that he had just received a frantic telephone call from an anonymous woman saying that a hurricane was approaching the UK. Fish ignored the woman's claim and asserted that no such storm was posing a threat.

Who was the nun who prophesied the storm? My own research has drawn a blank but, curiously enough, in April 1980 scores of motorists in the north-western American states of Washington and Oregon reported picking up a nun stranded on the highway who subsequently warned them of a volcano that was going to erupt in the USA. On 18 May a volcano did erupt on Mount St Helens in south-west Washington, causing widespread destruction in which more than 50 people died.

The following phantom hitch-hiker story was reported in the British press in the late 1950s but, unlike the ghostly nun of Cheshire, this apparition had no warnings to impart; it merely became obsessively interested in riding on a long-distance lorry and shattering the nerves of its driver.

During the early hours of a rainy autumnal morning in 1958 a long-distance HGV driver named Harry Unsworth was driving his vehicle along the A38 towards a depot in Cullompton in Devonshire, when he noticed the silhouette of a man about 300 yards in front of him, standing in the middle of the road.

Unsworth decelerated his vehicle and stared beyond his busy windscreen wipers at the figure ahead. The stranger was middle-aged, with a mop of curly grey hair, and he wore a saturated grey raincoat. The man produced a torch from his pocket and flashed it at Unsworth, who responded by pulling his lorry up. Unsworth wound his side window down to get a better look at the hitch-hiker.

The man stood there on the macadam, looking up at the driver with a dripping, expressionless face.

"Come on, then!" Unsworth shouted, impatiently.

The man climbed into the driver's cab, and in a well-spoken voice he asked Unsworth to drop him off four miles down the motorway at the old bridge at Holcombe. The lorry drove on into the night down the deserted motorway, and the hitch-hiker suddenly started to chuckle. Unsworth glanced at him while he laughed, but the stranger turned his face away and looked out the passenger window, sniggering to himself for no reason.

Unsworth asked him what was funny, and the man suddenly turned to face him. His face was contorted with an eerie smile.

"Did you know there was a real tragic pile-up here a few years ago? Arms and legs everywhere," said the hitch-hiker. And he continued to recount grisly stories about all the traffic accidents that he'd witnessed on the stretch of motorway. Unsworth had seen a few disturbing automobile crashes in his time, but the gruesome blow-by-blow accounts of the fatalities told to him by the hitch-hiker really turned his stomach. Unsworth told the man to shut up, and was only too glad to be rid of his morbid passenger when the lorry reached the drop-off point at the old bridge.

Three days later Mr Unsworth was driving his lorry through the dead of night along the same section of the A38, when he came across the same hitch-hiker again. As before, he stood in the middle of the motorway flashing a torch and waving his arm.

With an impending sense of *déjà vu,* Unsworth pulled up beside the man, and again, the hitch-hiker asked to be dropped off at the old bridge at Holcombe. This time the man said nothing throughout the journey, but kept smiling and looking at Unsworth out of the corner of his eye. This behaviour made the lorry driver's flesh creep. When the man got out at the bridge, he didn't offer a word of thanks. He walked away into the darkness.

A month after that, Unsworth was again heading along the A38 to the lorry depot – when he saw the dreaded hitch-hiker again, standing in the road on the same stretch of motorway as before. The weather was even the same as it had been on the two previous occasions: torrential rain. And the hitch-hiker's request? To be dropped off four miles down the road at the old bridge.

Understandably, Mr Unsworth was rather reluctant to give the man a lift, but decided to take him to the confounded bridge for the last time. Once more, the hitch-hiker remained silent during the journey, but occasionally burst out laughing.

On the following night, Harry Unsworth was on the same route to the depot. As his vehicle neared the section of the A38 where the oddball had a habit of appearing, he anxiously scanned the road ahead. But on this occasion the hitch-hiker was nowhere to be seen.

Three months later Unsworth was whistling in his cab as he drove along the stretch of the A38 where he had first set eyes upon the hitch-hiker. He remembers smiling as he thought about the crazy man with the torch, and he also remembers the sight that wiped the smile off his face. Standing in the pouring rain in the middle lane of the motorway was the grey-haired man waving his torch frantically.

Unsworth braked by the lunatic, and was astonished to hear the same hackneyed request from him. But Unsworth was more intrigued than scared, and he dropped off the man at the bridge again – but this time the hitch-hiker broke the repetitive pattern by asking Mr Unsworth to wait for him whilst he went to "collect some suitcases", because he wanted to go to a destination further down the road this time.

But the man didn't return to the lorry after 20 minutes had elapsed, and Unsworth was running to a tight schedule and couldn't afford to wait. So he started the vehicle up and drove on.

Three miles down the road, the lorry driver's heart jumped when he saw the hitch-hiker waving his torch in the middle of the motorway. Unsworth was baffled as to how the man could have travelled such a distance in so short a time. The man obviously hadn't hitched a lift, for no vehicles had passed along the deserted motorway, and this fact gave Unsworth the creeps. He tried to drive around the sinister man, but the hitch-hiker dived headfirst into the path of the heavy-goods vehicle!

Unsworth slammed on the brakes and almost jack-knifed his vehicle. He leaped out of his cab and looked for the body of the madman in the road. He expected to find a flattened corpse, but there was none. Forty feet away stood the hitch-hiker, swearing at the lorry-driver. He started to jump up and down with derision and waved his fist at Unsworth. And then he simply vanished.

Unsworth ran back to his vehicle and drove off at high speed. He never encountered the A38 apparition again. But others are still seeing the solid-looking ghost. In December 1991 a woman driving to Taunton via a stretch of the A38 was rounding a bend near the village of Rumwell when she saw a man in a grey raincoat flashing a torch at her in the middle of the road. The woman couldn't brake in time, so she was forced to swerve her vehicle into a ditch. She left her Vauxhall Astra fuming, ready to give the suicidal jaywalker a piece of her mind, but she was amazed to see that the road was completely deserted in both directions. The man with the torch had mysteriously disappeared.

Psychical researchers who have investigated the case say that the A38 hitch-hiker is probably the earthbound spirit of one of the numerous people who have perished on the stretch of motorway in car accidents over the years.

On 10 November 1992 the front-page headline of the *Kent Today* newspaper read: "Ghost Girl Seen Again". The story beneath the sensational headline told how the phantom of a girl who had died in a car crash (along with two others) in 1965 had reappeared. At precisely midnight on the previous Sunday motorist Ian Sharpe had allegedly passed the Aylesford turn-off on the Maidstone-bound carriageway of the A229 at Blue Bell Hill, one of the highest points of the North Downs in Kent, when the figure of a girl suddenly appeared in the path of the vehicle. Before Mr Sharpe could take evasive action and swerve, the girl actually ran towards the car and, as the vehicle struck her, she fell and went under it. Mr Sharpe braked, and in a trembling state of dread he got out of his car and looked under it. There was nothing there. Thinking that perhaps the jaywalker had been knocked a short distance by the force of the impact, Mr Sharpe began to search the bushes of the wide verge, but he could find no body. Sharpe called in at Maidstone police station and told an officer that he had just run down a woman at Blue Bell Hill but could not find the body.

The policeman looked at a colleague and, after a short pause, he told the distressed motorist that he had probably not hit anyone at all – just a well-reported ghostly jaywalker. Nevertheless, the police accompanied Mr Sharpe to the scene of the alleged accident at Blue Bell Hill and they could find no sign of a girl's body either. Another search commenced on the following day and Mr Sharpe expected the police to tell him that they had found the girl's body, but no corpse was found. Furthermore, Mr Sharpe's car had no signs of damage, reinforcing the astounding police claim that the vehicle had not hit a real person at all. In fact, Mr Sharpe is just one of many motorists who have encountered the spectral jaywalking girl. In July 1974 a bricklayer named Maurice Goodenough also told police one night that he had knocked down a girl at Blue Bell Hill and had wrapped her in a blanket at the accident scene. The police accompanied the bricklayer to the site of the apparent traffic accident, only to find no trace of an accident victim – just a discarded blanket. Mr Goodenough was adamant that he had knocked down a girl who looked about ten years of age, and could even vividly recall what she had worn: a lacy white blouse, a skirt and white ankle socks. The girl was dazed by the impact and had sustained cuts to her forehead and knees. Mr Goodenough said he had wrapped her in a blanket and left her at the roadside before running to the police station. The bricklayer's car was inspected, and seeing there wasn't even a mark on it, the police suspected the real "victim" was the spectre of a girl who had been seen dozens of times on Blue Bell Hill. The police had to follow the orthodox lines of inquiry, but no one answering the girl's description was ever traced.

The ghostly jaywalker which is still allegedly haunting Blue Bell Hill today is thought to be the earthbound spirit of 22-year-old Judith Lingham of Rochester, who died the day before she was to be a bridesmaid at a friend's wedding. On the evening of Friday 19 November 1965, Judith and three friends set out in their Ford Cortina to meet the bride's fiancé at a local pub. As the car neared the top of Blue Bell Hill, the Ford Cortina hit an oncoming Jaguar. Susan Browne, aged 23, died several days after the smash, while Judith Lingham passed away from her terrible injuries on the following day. Another passenger, 23-year-old Patricia Ferguson, was killed outright in the crash, while the other driver, Gillian Burchett, made a full recovery after spending months in hospital.

However, several ghost researchers who have looked into the Blue Bell Hill hauntings think more than one ghost is haunting the spot; that of a girl in her early twenties, and the shade of a girl of around ten years of age. The latter may be the tactile apparition that Maurice Goodenough picked up and wrapped in a blanket in 1974.

If you're on the road tonight, have a safe and spook-free journey.

The Wail of the Banshee

From the many years I have put in researching paranormal incidents, I have come to accept that besides the known dimensions of space and time, there are other realms in our universe of which we are entirely ignorant. Furthermore, I would hazard a guess and say that these undiscovered domains next door to our dimension are inhabited by various strange species of life-forms, ranging from the amorphous to the humanoid. These "extra-dimensionals" or "ultra-terrestrials" may be responsible for the ancient worldwide myths of elves, fairies and many other legendary creatures now forgotten and filed away under "folklore".

Those who think that the notion of unknown exotic and alien beings living in close proximity to us is nonsense only have to reflect on the peculiar life-forms inhabiting our world. Imagine what Captain Cook would have made of the surreal-looking kangaroo during his exploration of Australia. The existence of such an animal, carrying its young in a pocket-like pouch, was entirely unexpected. Another comical-looking animal which eluded zoologists until 1937 was the giant panda of northern China. In 1912 another unusual creature was discovered when a pilot was forced to make an emergency landing on an island off Malaya. He was confronted with a living dinosaur; a huge 10-foot-long monitor lizard now known as the Komodo dragon. This fearsome 135-kilogram animal has a long tail and enormous jaws which can kill a man.

Nearer to home, on your clothes and in your bed, there are hordes of grotesque microscopic monsters known as dust mites, prowling all over you as they munch avariciously on the tiny detached flakes of your skin. These minute creatures look like some nightmarish bug-eyed monsters from an Hieronymous Bosch painting under the electron microscope, but thankfully, because they live on another scale of reality, we are never aware of them crawling about in the carpet and in our beds.

Similarly, could there be undiscovered species of weird but intelligent creatures living alongside us in a parallel dimension, perhaps secretly observing us and occasionally meddling in human affairs? Would this hypothesis explain poltergeists, the mysterious "greys" allegedly responsible for global abductions, angels, and perhaps even some UFO sightings? In recent years many respected researchers into the paranormal, including ufologists such as Jaques Vallee and John Keel, have presented convincing conjectures suggesting that some unknown agency outside space and time has been preying on the collective subconscious of mankind for many millennia, manifesting itself as angels, demons, visions, fairies, spirits, will-o'-the-wisp and various other supernatural guises. In this section we will take a look at one of these sinister entities: the banshee.

The banshee is one of the most well-known figures of Irish folklore. The name is derived from the Irish Gaelic "bean sidhe", meaning "woman of the fairies". According to tradition, the banshee's mournful cry is said to foretell death. The banshee is described as having long straight white or red hair which covers her face, and she combs her hair as she wails outside the family home of the person who is about to die. The person who is about to pass away never hears or sees the banshee, and once the death takes place, the crying ceases and the eerie apparition immediately vanishes. Although we're living in the modernistic hi-tech age of computers, genetic engineering and space travel, it seems from the following cases that the chilling Celtic mourner is still doing her rounds, and not only in Ireland; she is evidently active all over the world.

Banshee

In Ellesmere Port, England, in the autumn of 1997, a 50-year-old housewife named Sarah Wayne was sitting up late one Saturday night, waiting for her 18-year-old daughter Cheryl to return from a nightclub. Sarah hadn't been keen on her teenage daughter going out to the club, but Cheryl had argued that she was old enough to look after herself and added that Liam, the boy she was after, went to the club on a Saturday night.

Sarah's husband Derek was in Nottingham driving a heavy-goods vehicle to a depot. Derek was very protective towards his only daughter, and certainly would have done his utmost to prevent Cheryl from going to the nightclub.

The time was 2.30 a.m. and still there was no sign of Cheryl, so her mother dimmed the lights in the parlour and peeped through the net curtains at the deserted street outside. A wind was starting to stir, and a clutter of dried leaves scraped by on the pavement. Sarah scanned both ends of the road for 20 minutes, but Cheryl was nowhere to be seen. Around 3 a.m.

Mrs Wayne sat sipping a cup of tea in the living room, watching the BBC News 24 service on the muted TV. At around 3.30 a.m., she fell into a light sleep, but a sound woke her up minutes later. Sarah opened her eyes, startled, and saw Cheryl walk past the living room in the hall outside. The girl was sobbing, and her platinum blonde hair was a mess. It hung down in front of her face.

"Cheryl! What's wrong, love? Where have you been?" Mrs Wayne bolted from the armchair and followed Cheryl, who had headed straight to the kitchen. Sarah assumed that her distraught daughter had been rejected by Liam at the club, but when she walked into the kitchen, the woman got the shock of her life. The kitchen was empty; Cheryl was nowhere to be seen.

Then came the sounds of a Yale key rattling in the front door. Cheryl came in with her friend Jacqueline, laughing and talking about boys they'd danced with.

Cheryl had her long blonde hair piled up in a bun on her head and wore a bright red mini skirt and a white sleeveless top. The figure her mother had pursued to the kitchen had its hair draped over its face and seemed to be wearing black clothes. Sarah Wayne suddenly realized that she had mistaken a weeping ghost for her daughter, and her heart somersaulted. She told Cheryl and her friend about the weird apparition, and the girls and Mrs Wayne became so scared that they all refused to go into the kitchen until it was dawn.

Later that morning, at 8.30 a.m., a policeman and policewoman called at Sarah Wayne's house to inform her of her husband's death in Nottingham. He had left the cab of his lorry at 3.30 a.m. that morning and suffered a fatal heart attack. The death happened at the precise time when the crying ghost walked through the Waynes' home. Was the apparition just a so-called "open-eye" dream of Mrs Wayne, who had just woken up, or was it a banshee? Mrs Wayne believes it was a banshee, and was so unnerved by the experience that she later moved from the house and now lives in Bebington, Merseyside.

The second report of a banshee comes from three witnesses. It all began in the early hours of a Wednesday morning in

August 1998 when Freda Piers, a 44-year-old housewife of Saltney, Chester, had difficulty sleeping. Freda usually had no trouble getting to sleep, but on this balmy morning at 2 a.m. she became restless, and insomnia began to steadily set in. Freda therefore left her snoring husband and went down to the kitchen to make a coffee. She turned on the radio and for about a minute she listened to Magic 1548, a Liverpool-based station. She was just about to tune into the MFM radio station, when the disc-jockey Jon Jessop urged listeners to go and look out their window to see if there was any sign of a lost snow-white terrier named Brandy, because its owner was frantic. Freda dimmed the lights, opened the window blinds, and gazed out at the moonlit close. She then heard a low howling sound which sent a shiver down her spine. The DJ then said that the terrier had been lost in northern Liverpool, so Freda realized that there was no hope of the dog being outside her house in Saltney. She took a quick look through the gaps in the blinds – and saw a hooded figure in black standing across the road. The figure looked like a monk wearing a black habit and cowl. What's more, the figure seemed to be the source of the uncanny weeping, and it was looking up at the bedroom window of the house opposite. Red curtains were drawn in this window and a faint bulb burned behind them.

Freda telephoned her best friend Eunice, who lived next door to the house where the strange figure was lurking. After some 20 or so rings, a bleary-eyed and grumpy Eunice answered her phone, and Freda told her about the figure in black standing in the neighbouring garden on the lawn. Eunice took her cordless phone to the window and peeped out. She told Freda that an old white-haired woman was looking up at next-door's window with a sorrowful but demented look, and she appeared to be crying. Eunice was so frightened at the sight of the deranged old woman that she hung up on Freda, dialled the police and shook her husband awake. Eunice's husband Kevin reluctantly hauled himself out of bed and took a look out the window. He too saw the eccentric old woman in black. He opened the bedroom window, despite his frightened wife's pleas not to, and he shouted down to her, "What's wrong, love?" The creepy-looking woman failed to reply, and continued to stare up at next door's window and started to make a bloodcurdling howling noise.

Freda, meanwhile, was attempting to awaken her husband Sam from his slumbers to tell him about the crazy old woman on the other side of the close.

A police car zoomed to the scene with its roof-light flashing. Eunice and Kevin were distracted from looking at the old woman by the blue flash of light from the police car, and when they glanced back at the lawn, the nocturnal visitor had inexplicably vanished, in what must have literally been the blinking of an eyelid. Two policemen rushed from the squad car with high-powered torches and flashed their beams across the garden where the mysterious figure had stood. Eunice felt so stupid and confused at the woman's vanishing act that she withdrew from the window and pulled her husband back too. Seconds later, out of burning curiosity, she chanced a peep through the net curtains and the blinding beam of a police torch singled her face out at the window. Eunice had no option but to lean out the window and admit that she had rung the police because of the strange prowling woman.

The police listened, then knocked on the front door of Eunice's neighbour. A middle-aged man came to the door not long afterwards and invited the police in. About 15 minutes later an ambulance roared into the close. The ambulance men hurried to the house next door and were admitted by the policemen. By now, Freda, Eunice and their husbands were standing on the pavement near the house that was the focus of all the activity. Eunice and her husband recalled that an Irish couple named O'Brien had recently moved into the house.

About 15 minutes later, the covered body of Mrs O'Brien was taken to the ambulance on a stretcher. Later that morning, Freda and Eunice heard from neighbours that Mrs O'Brien had died in her sleep. Her husband Pat had awoken at 2 a.m. to the sounds of someone crying outside in the distance. He had tried to wake up his wife Philomena to tell her about the strange sobbing sound, but Mrs O'Brien failed to respond, and wouldn't wake up. Mr O'Brien panicked when he felt her neck and got no carotid pulse. She felt cold, and Mr O'Brien realized his wife was dead.

Mr O'Brien claims that his own mother's death 25 years earlier was foreshadowed by the wailing of a banshee, and has no difficulty accepting that a banshee cried for his late wife in the early hours of that warm August morning.

The aforementioned banshee reports are just a couple of examples of the many cases I've looked into, and a majority of the accounts are difficult to rationalize as hallucinations or outright lies, given the calibre of the witnesses. In many instances, the ghostly mourner was seen by several unrelated observers simultaneously, which surely rules out some sort of subjective mirage in the minds of the witnesses. A classic case in point is the doomed Piper Alpha oil platform disaster in 1988. Derek Ellington, a rig fitter, and many of his workmates on the oil platform heard an eerie screeching noise which sounded like a woman crying hysterically. Less than a minute later, an enormous fireball engulfed the Piper Alpha rig and 160 workers perished. Derek Ellington was one of the lucky survivors who was later plucked from the icy waters of the North Sea. He was later asked to describe the strange sound which seemed to be some portent of the disaster, and he recalled it was "like the wailing of a banshee".